THE COUNTERVOYAGE OF RABELAIS AND ARIOSTO

To My Mother and the Memory of My Father

THE COUNTERVOYAGE OF RABELAIS AND ARIOSTO

A COMPARATIVE READING OF TWO RENAISSANCE MOCK EPICS

Elizabeth A. Chesney

DUKE UNIVERSITY PRESS   DURHAM, N.C.   1982

Library of Congress Cataloging in Publication Data

Chesney, Elizabeth A., 1949–
  The countervoyage of Rabelais and Ariosto.

  Originally presented as author's thesis (doctoral—
Duke University)
  Bibliography: p. 215.
  1. Rabelais, François, 1490–1553? Gargantua et
Pantagruel. 2. Ariosto, Lodovico, 1474–1533. Orlando
furioso. 3. Roland—Romances—History and criticism.
I. Title.
PQ1694.C53 1982   843'.3   81–5410
ISBN 0–8223–0456–2   AACR2

CONTENTS

ACKNOWLEDGMENTS

To Professor Marcel Tetel, who first introduced me to the *tonneau inexpuisible* of Rabelais and Ariosto, I am greatly indebted. It was he who suggested the need for a study such as this and who directed it in its original form as a dissertation at Duke University. Without his continued assistance, criticism, and encouragement throughout a tedious and often discouraging revision process, the comparison would never have reached its present, albeit imperfect, degree of completion. That it falls short of our original expectations, as realized projects often will, is my responsibility alone.

Acknowledgment is also due to the late Professor Franco Simone and his colleagues at the University of Torino, for their assistance during my initial research efforts; to the Graduate School of Duke University, for its generous financial support during the writing of the thesis; to those members of the Department of Romance Languages at Duke University who sat on my dissertation committee, for their helpful comments and criticisms; and to those readers and editors of the Duke University Press who scrutinized the manuscript, for their invaluable suggestions and corrections.

Special thanks must finally be extended to my family—to my father, who never finished his book, and to my mother, who has always dreamed of writing one. For their unselfish contributions, tangible as well as intangible, to my own work, I am most grateful.

THE COUNTERVOYAGE OF RABELAIS AND ARIOSTO

"Siècle de vitesse! qu'ils disent. Où ça? Grands changements! qu'ils racontent. Comment ça? Rien n'est changé en vérité. Ils continuent à s'admirer et c'est tout. Et ça n'est pas nouveau non plus."

—Louis-Ferdinand Céline, *Voyage au bout de la nuit*.[1]

1. In *Romans* (Paris: Bibliothèque de la Pléiade, 1962), 1: 11.

INTRODUCTION

Rabelais's and Ariosto's own claims to novelty and uniqueness scarcely support a comparative reading of their masterpieces. The one insists that his work is "sans pair, incomparable et sans parragon" (P.prol.168), while the other claims to recount "cosa non detta in prosa mai né in rima" (I.2.).[2] Even more pointedly, Rabelais specifies the *Orlando furioso* as one of several works which, despite their "haulte fustaye" and "propriétés occultes," are not "comparables" (P.prol. 168–69) to his own *Pantagruel*. Yet scholars, apparently taking the Gallic monk's denial of plagiarism as a challenge, have long coupled together the two great Renaissance mock epics. Turn-of-the century critics unconvincingly sought to prove that the Abbaye de Thélème and Pantagruel's proposed journey to the moon were inspired by Alcina's realm and Astolfo's voyage, respectively, while Victor Hugo attributed their kinship to a more general "grotesque."[3] In view of Rabelais's warning against such comparisons, however, and the failure of source studies to establish any direct borrowings, one might well

2. Quotations of Rabelais are from *Œuvres complètes*, ed. Jacques Boulenger and Lucien Scheler (Paris: Bibliothèque de la Pléiade, 1955). Henceforth the abbreviations G (*Gargantua*), P (*Pantagruel*), TL (*Tiers Livre*), and QL (*Quart Livre*) will designate the book; roman numerals, the chapter; and arabic numerals, the page. Because of problems of authentication, the *Cinquième Livre* (CL) has been excluded from the main body of our discussion, and references from that source will be cited only in footnote form. All citations of Ariosto are taken from *Opere*, ed. Giuliano Innamorati (Bologna: Zanichelli, 1968).

3. In his preface to *Cromwell* (Paris: Flammarion, 1932) Hugo says that the grotesque "jette du premier coup sur le seuil de la poésie moderne trois Homères bouffons: Arioste, en Italie; Cervantes, en Espagne; Rabelais, en France" (p. 14). For discussion of Rabelais's possible debts to Ariosto, see Francesco Biondolillo, *Poeti e critici* (Palermo: Trimarchi, 1910), p. 98; and Bonaventura Zumbini, "La Badia di Thélème del Rabelais," *Studi di letteratura straniera*, 2d ed. (Florence: Le Monnier, 1907), pp. 338–39.

question the need for renewed research on the subject. Why beat a dead horse or, like mad Roland, attempt to pawn it off upon an unwilling customer?

The only justifiable answer, to borrow again from the poets, is that there is something new and incomparable to say about these works, "cosa non detta in prosa mai né in rima." It is no longer, first of all, a question of determining whether Rabelais plagiarized Ariosto. The problem, barring new documentation, is virtually unsolvable, and, even if such evidence were discovered, it would shed little light on the works' "sustantificque mouelle." For the latter, one must instead return to the concepts of "newness" and "incomparability" themselves. Both are not only attributes of the text but also themes that reflect on the period of rebirth itself. According to the arists, it is a time of "nouvi Argonauti e nuovi Tifi" (XV.21) who discover "nouveaultéz" (QL.IV. 550); of modern studies which brighten gothic darkness; of enlightened princes who govern utopian kingdoms and foster humanistic advances; of inspired artists such as "Michel, piú che mortale, Angel divino" (XXXIII.2) who modernize painting and sculpture; and of inventions which harness nature for human exploitation.

All this, so far, is a typical Renaissance scenario, filled with encomiastic clichés about newness and incomparability. As such it does little to distinguish Rabelais and Ariosto from other contemporary panegyrists and, in itself, is insufficient to justify a bitextual comparison of the *Orlando furioso* and Pantagrueline tales. Yet it stands to reason that what is new and unique must be different as well, contrasting rather than comparable. And certainly the *Orlando furioso* and Pantagrueline tales do not lack for contrasts, since the positive panegyrics are coupled with their negative "other," the true "uniqueness" of Rabelais and Ariosto. In the *Furioso*'s African invasion, one sees the "naval conflitto" (XL.1) between Ferrara and Venice on the Po, which found its "onde . . . di sangue umano infette" (XL.2); in Panurge's "faulte d'argent," both Rabelais's own hardships as a struggling physician and a reflection of the lower classes' abject poverty; in the "fame" of Senapo's Ethiopia, an insight into the "povertà" and "affanni" (XXXIV.2) of northern Italy during foreign invasions and internal wars; in Picrochole and the allegorical Avarizia, a reflection of the greed upon which Renaissance ambition is based; and in Bridoye's and Scotland's arbitrary legislation, a critique of abuses and inequities in the judiciary system. Gone, in this picture of *l'envers du siècle*, is the creative newness so eulogized by Renaissance poetry and in its place remains a difference which is not different at all but which is, in fact, as old as man himself.

The similarity between Rabelais and Ariosto lies, then, in this difference itself, in their propensity for exploring the opposite of every truth and the other side of every argument. At first glance, of course, it may appear that some positive topics can have no other side. What element of negativity can one find, for example, in the literal and physical voyages of discovery, which for Rabelais and Ariosto become the metaphor for all humanistic advances? For an answer one need only consult the texts and reflect on the period itself, reinterpreting the epic journey in light of recent events. While the protagonists' journeys beyond the geographical and conceptual Gates of Hercules may resemble a conquest of sorts, they are in truth the mere breaking of a dam, a transgression of medieval society's secure closure. While there are new lands to conquer outside these gates, the Renaissance explorer must first navigate a vast and chaotic sea of phenomena that threatens to inundate him. Thus the epic tempest takes on a new meaning to coincide with the Renaissance's unstable world. Granted, the voyage opens up a new and marvelous universe; but it is also filled with monsters, which are definitionally "different" and, as such, sources of both fear and conflict. So great is Panurge's terror at the *Quart Livre* isle of Ganabin, for instance, that he "se conchie . . . de male raige et de paour" (LXVI.724).

Trauma results not only from fear of the newness itself but also from an instinctive sense of betraying the "old." Any move from homogeneity to heterogeneity, from a synthetic world to an antithetical one, after all, can scarcely be devoid of stress. It produces doubt concerning not only the old but the new as well. For the former, still present in the latter, reminds Renaissance man that God punishes those who aspire to "saper troppo" (*Satira* VI.45) or to "voler" (QL.XXIV. 608) like birds. Odysseus, after all, was condemned to hell by Dante for attempting to "divenir del mondo esperto."[4]

What occurs is a countervoyage, a critical reflection upon each conceptual pole by its other. The purpose of this study will be to show that this dialectic is a global structure in Rabelais and Ariosto, which first takes account of textual ambiguities, as the word *counter* suggests; sets them, secondly, in the context of the humanistic voyages of dis-

---

4. *Inferno* (XXVI.98–99), in *Opere*, ed. Fredi Chiappelli (Milan: Mursia, 1965), p. 538.

covery, as part of a cognitive odyssey; and relates them, thirdly, in their negativity, to the period's antiprogressist, antirationalistic movement which Hiram Haydn calls the "Counter-Renaissance."[5]

This burgeoning of antitheses may be explained, historically and psychologically, by the Hegelian theory of negativity.[6] According to this theory, the passing of the self-consciousness or of civilization from one stage to the next higher involves a "process of what might be called immanent self-criticism—a process whereby each stage comes to a self-consciousness regarding its own purposes and its own meaning."[7] With the decay of medieval culture and the growth of Renaissance individualism, it is natural that the self should become alienated from its own different constituent modes of consciousness. In this transitional culture there occurs a critical recapitulation or reevaluation of the mind's successsive stages—of both the old, which is still preserved in the subjectivity that ostensibly renounces it, and the new, which remains incomplete and untested. The result is a conflict or struggle between opposites, of which one sees evidence in Rabelais and Ariosto.

To root the countervoyage movement in the philosophy of history, of course, is to suggest that it is also present in other works of the period; and to some extent, this is true. For the entire Renaissance is filled with contradictions, from beginning to end. One need only cite Petrarch's anguished debate with Saint Augustine in the *Secretum* or his dialectic between the spirit and the flesh in the *Canzionere*. At times, moreover, the contradiction occurs not within single works of art but between them. The deformed, monstrous universe of Bosch is counterbalanced, for example, by the luminous humanistic masterpieces of Botticelli, while the antihumanistic philosophies of Agrippa of Nettesheim and Nicolaus Cusanus find their antipodes in the more positive theories of Marsilio Ficino and Pico della Mirandola.

This presence of the countervoyage elsewhere in the Renaissance at once substantiates the theory and poses another problem: why limit the comparison to Rabelais and Ariosto if the similarities they share are so commonplace? A plausible explanation is provided by Lucien Goldmann, who, in justifying his own choice of Pascal and Racine for

5. *The Counter-Renaissance* (New York: Harcourt, Brace, and World, 1950).
6. In his *Lectures on Modern Idealism* (New Haven, Conn.: Yale University Press, 1919), Josiah Royce explains the theory as follows: "The law of finite being is: Every finite thing in heaven and earth, when taken alone, contradicts itself, that is, illustrates what Hegel calls the principle of negativity" (p. 227).
7. Ibid., p. 218.

a study of the tragic vision, suggests that "la prise de conscience varie d'un homme à l'autre et n'atteint son maximum que chez certains individus exceptionnels."[8] And in the Renaissance context Rabelais and Ariosto are these exceptional individuals, who, more than any other writers, unite the different ambiguities and tensions of their period in structurally coherent works.

Even their common sources, in their heterogeneity, contribute to the countervoyage movement and antithetical configuration of the text. Both works, first of all, evolve from burlesque romance versions of the French *chanson de geste*: the Pantagrueline tales, from the parodical *Chronicques gargantuines*, and the *Furioso*, from ultra-Alpine versions of the romanesque epic. Obviously, this common heritage facilitates comparison, by providing a common set of data with which to work, and moreover helps explain the folkloric setting, knights errant, magic and fantasy, the grotesque, and even much of the sublime in purely literary terms. It will be the Renaissance's task to infuse its own meaning into these traditional figures. More importantly, these similar sources bring with them their own inherent tensions, which accord perfectly with the Ariostan and Rabelaisian world view. The genre is traditional, in contrast to Renaissance "newness"; sociologically, it is a mixture of the popular and the aristocratic; and it combines the epic's immanence with romance transcendence in an uneasy and potentially subversive synthesis.

Ariosto's use of this anachronistic and foreign genre, so culturally and temporally different from its sixteenth-century Italian setting, helps clarify idiosyncrasies in Ferrarese society that make it, in the High Renaissance, no less tension-filled than France in her first awakening. Although the Carolingian cycle finds its way to other parts of Italy during its decadence, nowhere does it constitute such a continued vogue, during the Renaissance, as in the Estense duchy. Library holdings as well as literary production—Boiardo's *Innamorato*, the Cieco's *Mambriano*, and Ariosto's *Furioso*—support this contention.[9] On the one hand, this literary vogue parallels a tradition of strong cultural and political ties with France, which begins with the appearance of the troubadours in the thirteenth century, includes the importation of

---

8. *Le Dieu caché* (Paris: Gallimard, 1959), p. 27.

9. Edmund G. Gardner, *Dukes and Poets in Ferrara* (1904; rpt. New York: Haskell House, 1968), pp. 85–86. Cf. also Giulio Bertoni, *La biblioteca estense* (Torino: Loescher, 1903).

French musicians at the court in the 1470s, and culminates in an alliance between Ercole I and Charles VIII against the Venetians in 1494. The years that follow see an even greater wave of Francophilia sweep over Ferrara, with Estense courtiers even dressing *alla francese*.[10] On the other hand, however, this Gallic influence is itself symptomatic of a generally archaicizing trend, which coexists alongside humanistic advances in Renaissance Ferrara. There classical scholarship flowers within a neofeudalistic political structure; and brilliant paintings eulogizing court life, and filled with classical allusions, are executed in "the form of a kind of late international Gothic proto-mannerism" reminiscent of both medieval illuminations and the northern masters.[11] No less than France, Ferrara is caught in a tension between the old and the new, the northern and southern, the foreign and the nationalistic.

If this archaicizing, Gallicizing tendency in Ferrara lessens the cultural difference between Ariosto and Rabelais, so does the latter's familiarity with peninsular humanism, in both its contemporary manifestations and its classical roots, further bridge the gap one might expect between Italian and French, late and early Renaissance. By borrowing from such modern writers as Petrarch and Folengo, and from such ancient sources as the *Iliad* and *Aeneid*, Rabelais bears witness to a northerly surge of Italian humanism after Charles VIII's invasion of the peninsula.[12] More importantly, this humanistic element's presence within the romance epic genre sustains tensions between the new and the old, the pagan and the Christian, the classical and the medieval, the intellectual and the popular, which together contribute to the countervoyage dialectic.

While both authors' borrowings from antiquity, along with references to resurrected gods and goddesses, place them in the mainstream

10. Werner L. Gundersheimer, *Ferrara: The Style of a Renaissance Despotism* (Princeton, N.J.: Princeton University Press, 1973), pp. 193, 225–27, 294.

11. Ibid., p. 234; also pp. 229–71.

12. The possible Italian sources of Rabelais's work are explored by Cordelia del Fiume, *De l'influence de quelques auteurs italiens sur Rabelais* (Florence: Ramella, 1918); Lazare Sainéan, "Les Sources modernes du roman de Rabelais," *Revue des études rabelaisiennes* 10 (1912): 375–420; Pietro Toldo, "L'Arte italiana nell'opera di Francesco Rabelais," *Archiv für das Studium der neuern Sprachen* 100 (1898): 103–48; and Victor Waille, "Les Voyages de Rabelais à Rome et l'influence que l'art italien de la Renaissance a pu exercer sur lui," *Atti del congresso internazionale di scienze storiche* 7 (1904): 327–33. For a discussion of Ariosto's influence in France, see Alexandre Cioranescu, *L'Arioste en France des origines à la fin du XVIIIᵉ siècle* (Paris: Éditions des Presses Modernes, 1939), 1: 11–21.

of humanistic culture, certain of their particular sources just as effectively set them apart from their peers, increasing their works' negativity. Allusions to the Vergilian and Homeric heroic voyages, for example, are counterbalanced by reminiscences of the satiric Lucianic voyage. It is in fact this last link which, though superficially less important than the romance epic frame shared by both works, provides the most telling clue among the sources to similarities between Rabelais and Ariosto. The latter's upside-down moon and hippogriff, like Rabelais's hell and pig-god, bespeak a familiarity and spiritual affinity with the post-Hellenic Greek writer, whose satire, also the product of a decadent civilization, was considered subversive by orthodox Christian humanists. "En France, au temps de Rabelais," says Augustin Renaudet, "tout lecteur de Lucien devait être soupçonné d'incliner vers l'athéisme; il ne pouvait guère en être différemment en Italie."[13] While this does not mean that Ariosto and Rabelais were atheists, parallels with Lucian and Erasmus signal a mocking, critical attitude toward all aspects of contemporary society and culture, which in itself helps distinguish Rabelais and Ariosto from many of their contemporaries.[14] For while criticism of society is not uncommon among the Renaissance intelligentsia, who like to distinguish themselves from the bourgeoisie and aristocracy, Rabelais and Ariosto launch a Menippean satire against all quarters of society—including humanistic, intellectual, and artistic pursuits themselves. Instead of attacking a limited number of specific targets from a fixed viewpoint, they practice pure negativity, which sharply differentiates them from most topical satirists of the day.

The tensions suggested by common sources are only a small clue, however, to extensive intratextual ambiguities, which permeate the superstructure and infrastructure of each work. For a key to these it is helpful to return to the Rabelaisian text which first posed the possibility of comparison:

> Bien vray est-il que l'on trouve en aulcuns livres de haulte fustaye
> certaines propriétés occultes, au nombre desquelz l'on tient *Fes-*
> *sepinte, Orlando furioso, Robert le Diable, Fierabras, Guillaume*

13. *Érasme et l'Italie*, Travaux d'Humanisme et Renaissance 15 (Geneva: Droz, 1954), p. 67.

14. For a discussion of the Erasmian link, see Pio Rajna, *Le fonti dell'Orlando furioso*, 2d ed. (Florence: Sansoni, 1900), p. 547; Louis Thuasne, "Rabelais et Érasme," *Études sur Rabelais* (1904; rpt. Paris: H. Champion, 1969), pp. 27–157; and Rocco Montano, *Follia e saggezza nel Furioso e nell'Elogio di Erasmo* (Naples: Humanitas, 1942).

> *sans paour, Huon de Bourdeaulx, Montevielle et Matabrune,* mais
> ilz ne sont comparables à celluy duquel parlons. Et le monde a bien
> congneu par expérience infallible le grand émolument et utilité
> qui venoit de ladicte *Chronicque Gargantuine*: car il en a esté plus
> vendu par les imprimeurs en deux moys qu'il ne sera acheté de
> Bibles en neuf ans.   (P.prol.168–69)

Here one finds the principal points of encounter with the Ariostan
opus, the first of which is generic. Rabelais is associating his *Pantagruel* squarely with the burlesque epic, of which *Fierabras* and *Huon
de Bourdeaulx* are the medieval forebears and the *Furioso*, the Italian
Renaissance realization. The second coincidence is stylistic or discursive. Rabelais's about-face regarding whether or not the works are
similar reflects an ambiguity which is characteristic of much Renaissance discourse, notably that of Ariosto.

The third parallel, structural and thematic, provides the outline for
this study. In the above list of works one finds a microcosm of some
important themes and forms shared by the two Renaissance mock
epics: the voyage, myth and fantasy, the narrator, time and art, and
folly. These structures are worth comparing for four reasons. They
are all of major qualitative and quantitative importance in the works;
are developed in ambivalent fashion, to support the countervoyage
theory; are of topical value in the Renaissance and thus related to cultural manifestations; and are epistemologically oriented, a function of
the cognitive voyage of discovery.

First of all, *Huon de Bourdeaulx* and the accounts of Mandeville
(*Montevielle*) both relate marvelous journeys, like the Pantagrueline
tales and *Orlando furioso*. Secondly, the juxtaposition of existent and
nonexistent (*Matabrune* and *Fessepinte*) works within an already fictitious context foreshadows the dialectics between fact and fantasy
which persist throughout both the Ariostan and Rabelaisian opus. The
Gallic monk's reference to the works' "propriétéz occultes" and "haulte
fustaye," along with his comparison of the *Chronicque Gargantuine*
to the Bible, moreover reveals a rudimentary attempt to mythify his
creation through comparison, a process which, in both burlesque epics,
frequently involves allusion to classical mythological figures as well.
In the narrator's equivocal attitude toward these books, thirdly, one
detects a microcosm of his general intellectual ambivalence, shared by
Ariosto, whose visible *io* is comparable to Rabelais's acrobatic *je*. The

latter's list of past masterpieces, along with the contrast between two months and nine years, fourthly, attests to a sense of flux and temporal ferment, which is also present in the *Furioso*. Closely related to this awakening in and to time is the narrator's reference to the *Chronicque*'s utility ("le grand émolument et utilité"), an incipient meditation on the function of literature which permeates the prologues and exordia of both authors as well as their intrafictional art. Mention of the *Furioso* and *Robert le Diable*, finally, both of which focus upon an ambiguous and reversible madness, sets in motion that vast play of folly which dominates the *Tiers* and *Quart Livres*.

On the one hand, of course, it is small wonder that this particular comparison has been "cosa non detta." Far from being "nouveaultéz" or "propriétéz occultes," these similarities between Rabelais and Ariosto are, when taken individually, Renaissance commonplaces. Contradictory discourse is, first of all, characteristic of the Renaissance, from Petrarch's oxymoron and dialogue with Saint Augustine to Montaigne's mercurial self-portrait. Such is the broken form required to express the changing concepts and changing reality of this turbulent postmedieval era, in which absolute truths are being placed in question. Granted, the dialectical method is an important tool in medieval logic and, as such, is no great innovation on the part of humanists. Whereas the old dialectic functions within a closed system and moves toward a preestablished synthesis, however, that of the Renaissance unfolds as pure antithesis and interrogation, in an open and fragmented structure appropriate to the universe it reflects. For many of the same reasons the burlesque epic romance is also one of the period's most representative forms, stretching from Pulci and Boiardo to Cervantes. This "failed' epic must be understood as a function of the same culture that produced such epic failures as Petrarch's *Africa* and Ronsard's *Franciade*.[15] In different ways both forms reflect a simultaneous attraction for and uneasiness with the epic's stable, heroic universe, an ideal which proves itself inadequate and inauthentic in a period so fraught with conflict as the Renaissance. For the epic is the art form of a closed universe and homogeneous civilization, like that of the classical Greeks and medieval

15. Works dealing with the Renaissance epic's different manifestations include Robert Durling, *The Figure of the Poet in Renaissance Epic* (Cambridge, Mass.: Harvard University Press, 1965); Thomas Greene, *The Descent from Heaven* (New Haven, Conn.: Yale University Press, 1963); Michio Peter Hagiwara, *French Epic Poetry in the Sixteenth Century* (The Hague: Mouton, 1972); David Maskell, *The Historical Epic in France 1500–1700* (Oxford: Oxford University Press, 1973).

Christians, which are the antitheses of Renaissance openness.[16] In apparent recognition of this fact Rabelais and Ariosto incorporate into their works both the subjective yearning for essentiality and the empiric contradictions that, in this the dawn of the modern era, thwart such a goal. In this respect, their works are, like the *Don Quixote*, forerunners of the novel.[17]

As far as the set of themes and forms shared by the two artists is concerned, no one of them is unique to Rabelais and Ariosto. Neither can one say, however, that either artist is simply imitating some predecessor's rendition of the theme. Instead, theirs is an amalgam of many traditions, a panorama of their culture's countervoyage. The Rabelaisian and Ariostan voyage recalls, for example, both the humanistic Homeric voyage and the Middle Ages' transcendent quest; both Petrarch's labyrinthine wanderings in a *cieco legno* and the more contemporary voyages of discovery. While their numerous references to classical gods and demigods reflect a humanistic fascination with pagan mythology, evident in such works as Boccaccio's *Genealogie deorum gentilium* and in the graphic arts as well, so also does their mythic imagination run in nocturnal as well as diurnal directions, recalling both medieval bestiaries and the dark, hallucinatory menageries of Hieronymus Bosch. The burlesque, and even grotesque, nature of much of their fantasy at once echoes the derisory humor of Lucianic satire and the earthier comicality of the decadent romanesque epic tradition.

The multifaceted narrator of both mock epics, thirdly, may be considered a variation on both Petrarch's divided self and the *Decameron's* multiple storytellers. At the same time vestiges of the inspired Homeric and Dantian "I" coexist, in Rabelais and Ariosto, with the mere scribe's

16. For a discussion of "les civilisations closes," see György Lukács, *La Théorie du roman*, trans. Jean Clairevoye (Geneva: Gonthier, 1963), pp. 19–30. With regard to post-Homeric literary forms, he also tells us that "il n'y a plus de totalité qu'elles auraient seulement à assumer. Aussi faut-il, ou bien qu'elles rétrécissent et volatisent ce à quoi elles doivent donner leur forme, de façon à pouvoir le porter, ou bien qu'elles mettent en lumière d'une manière critique l'impossibilité de réaliser leur objet nécessaire et le néant intérieur du seul possible, introduisant ainsi dans l'univers des formes l'incohérence structurelle du monde" (p. 30). Rabelais and Ariosto, clearly, are beginning to do the latter.

17. Cf. ibid., p. 99; "Ainsi le premier grand roman de la littérature universelle se dresse au seuil de la période où le Dieu chrétien sommence [sic] de délaisser le monde, où l'homme devient solitaire et ne peut plus trouver que dans son âme, nulle part apatriée, le sens et la substance, où le monde, détaché de son paradoxal ancrage dans l'au-delà actuellement présent, est désormais livré à l'immanence de son propre non-sens."

more limited, even ignorant, viewpoint; and the epic poet's sublime, with the popular talespinner's low, vulgar style. Newly mobilized time, fourthly, is a capital theme throughout the Renaissance, its constructive side inspiring the myth of man-progressing and its destructive, negative one provoking a variety of reactions: a resurrection of Horace's *carpe diem* and transformation of life into pastime, as well as a nostalgic quest for eternity—be it orthodox heaven, biological procreation, or art. Each of time's contradictory faces finds its way into the Rabelaisian and Ariostan masterpieces, along with a meditation on creation that at once reflects the glorious blossoming of paintings, tapestries, and sculptures in the Renaissance, and recalls Petrarch's realization that the artist's *fama* is itself temporal and thus subject to change.

The theme of folly in Rabelais and Ariosto, finally, is the culmination of many conflicting currents. The word retains its negative connotations of vice and vanity from the medieval *speculum stultorum* and ship of fools, as well as its more positive connotations of joy and revelation from Erasmus's *Encomium moriae* and the Platonic-Christian tradition. Playing the fool themselves, Rabelais and Ariosto both mock folly in the name of humanistic rationality and praise it from an antiintellectual standpoint that is equally prevalent in the Renaissance.

Clearly this dialectic reaches its apex of contradiction in Rabelais and Ariosto, who sum up and unite the tensions of their age. Why this happens is another problem, about which one can only speculate. As we have seen, both the Ferrarese and French cultures are highly heterogeneous, sharply torn between the gothic and the modern, between tradition and invention, in such varied areas as art, religion, and politics. Each, moreover, is a crossroads between north and south, a curious mixture of the former's religious Renaissance and the latter's more hedonistic, pagan rebirth. Yet since no other French or Ferrarese writer produces such a conglomerate masterpiece of tension it is evident that cultural factors alone do not account for the countervoyage movement in Rabelais and Ariosto.

Undoubtedly, biographical variables also contribute to the Ariostan and Rabelaisian world view. Both were involved, the one directly and the other indirectly, in international diplomacy and its dialectical decision-making process. The Ferrarese artist represented his duchy upon several occasions at the Vatican, during the disputes that plagued northeast Italy, while Rabelais accompanied Jean Du Bellay on his mission to plead the case of Henry VIII to the pope. Moreover, the ambiguous relationship of each poet with regard to the Establishment must surely compound this tension. Traditionally the poet is a "fringe" figure, an outsider who nonetheless depends upon "insiders" for his livelihood. In the case of Rabelais and Ariosto this in-out situation is complicated by the fact that economically and politically the poet's calling is secondary to a more prosaic career. Ariosto is a functionary in the Estense court, while Rabelais supports himself as a physician and through patronage. Living witnesses of a new social mobility, they earn their livelihood as upholders of the system and thus are compelled to give it some kind of verbal support in their art. Their class origins do not make them inherent members of the ruling élite, however. Hence they retain the outsider's objectivity, coupled with the artist's "otherness." The result is a divided consciousness, which at once affirms and negates, praises and mocks its culture.

More important than this biographical bipolarity, however, is the historical moment itself. If the age of Petrarch was that of nascent, abstract contradictions, those ambiguities have bloomed into full-blown reality at the time of Rabelais and Ariosto. Abstract hopes of progress have been realized on one hand. In art one witnesses the humanistic splendor of Botticelli's and Michelangelo's masterpieces, which deify man's body as well as his soul. The invention of the printing press at the end of the fifteenth century has increased the possibility of *fama* for the artist. The voyages of discovery have realized, in a literal sense, the dreams of a new world.

Yet "progress" does not abate tensions or unite contradictions but rather brings them into sharper contrast. The voyages of discovery, physical as well as intellectual, not only give men new horizons but also upset their conceptual equilibrium, replacing Dante's stable universe with a kind of intellectual and spatial vertigo. The realization, moreover, comes that inventions can just as easily be harmful as productive. The firearms and gunpowder berated by both authors are examples of these negative advances, which are scarcely distinguishable from regression. France and Ferrara gain firsthand familiarity with these inventions in the peninsular wars of the late fifteenth century, another experience which reveals the limitations of progress. For there are some realities that scientific advances cannot touch: death, wars, poverty, suffering. Inasmuch as they contain these universals, the "new worlds" of Rabelais and Ariosto are but a different manifestation of the old, an affirmation of "nil novi sub sole."

It is to be hoped that this study will help elucidate this period of crisis—both in its specifics, as far as they can be determined through the analysis of topical themes, and in more general structural and conceptual terms as well. This, indeed, is the primary justification for a method that is itself almost "sans parragon," and not without reason. Logically, monothematic comparative studies allow for more depth of analysis and interpretative unity than multithematic approaches such as this. Yet the goal of this study, precisely, is to unite thematic and stylistic contradictions under the rubric of the countervoyage. Such a synthesis-in-antithesis, after all, is appropriate to the texts involved. For Rabelais and Ariosto themselves end their countervoyage and reconcile all differences in the definitional alterity of folly.

The analysis of multiple themes within a single system, moreover, also promises other "nouveaultéz." First of all, it not only promotes understanding of the specific figures involved but also enables one to see how the parts interact with and reinforce one another to form a coherent whole. While Lucien Goldmann refers to this structural unity as "le tout et les parties," quoting Pascal, the concept is equally consistent with the more Renaissance notion that the microcosm and macrocosm have parallel forms.[18] On the one hand, the relationship between textual themes and structures is synchronous; each trope, in Rabelais and Ariosto, is developed in a bipolar dialectical fashion, which reinforces and is reinforced by the ambiguous discourse. At the same time, however, this approach allows one to develop the themes diachronously, as part of a developmental sequence. Each theme can thus be viewed as a unit in a continuum, which begins with the transcendent voyage and culminates, eventually, in folly. As Panurge says, "tout est fol" (TL.XLVI.490). Within the mock epic context, moreover, this countervoyage into madness takes on a particular significance; it is the perfection of an antistructure, a perfectly paradoxical art form. Thus the analysis of themes shared by Rabelais and Ariosto, only one of three similarities between them, contributes to an understanding of the other two: style and genre. Moreover, its topical content accomplishes what a generic or stylistic study could do less well, enabling one to relate intratextual ambivalence to extratextual cultural manifestations.

To extend this multithematic analysis to a bitextual level is another variation on "le tout et les parties": it permits one to see not only the

18. Goldmann, pp. 13–31.

text but the culture as well as a coherent whole. To refer to the *Orlando furioso* and the Pantagrueline tales as synchronous manifestations of the High Renaissance, of course, is in itself a liberty. The two writers were, in essence, a generation apart, while their works themselves span a generation. The *Orlando furioso* was composed from 1507 to 1532, while the Pantagrueline tales date from 1532 to the 1550s. We are, moreover, talking about two different albeit similar cultures: the Ferrarese, where the Renaissance is already in full swing, and the French, which is just "awakening" in the early sixteenth century. This very geographical difference helps justify the temporal gap, however. While the French Renaissance is not progressing at the same rate as its Italian predecessor but assimilating and building upon the latter's experience, it nonetheless stands to reason that the great French mock epic should appear slightly later than its Italian counterpart. Not only does it take some time for the southern experience to be assimilated but one must also wait for the French Renaissance to arrive internally at its own state of contradiction: certainly the *affaire des placards* in 1534 and the escalating religious conflict that follows contribute to the increased negativity of Rabelais's later books. Since contradiction is the basis of comparison between the two authors, moreover, the temporal gap is somewhat diminished in importance. For contradictions necessarily develop through time, from instant to instant, within the time it takes to write a book, within the expanse of a lifetime.

Given the contradictions that time has unfolded between the sixteenth and twentieth centuries, finally, one might indeed venture that this study risks being more dialectical than the Pantagrueline tales and *Orlando furioso* themselves; but this is the essence of the critical relationship. Each critic takes with him his own particular culture and world view into every undertaking, however objective his method may be, and necessarily transforms (or deforms) the work. Because of their open, antithetical configurations, which yield so many possible "meanings," the texts of Rabelais and Ariosto lend themselves particularly well to this modernization. Nor can one feel that they would object too strenuously to this twentieth-century mask imposed upon them. For was not this, after all, the goal of every humanist, to create a work of art that would live forever?

In a very limited sense, one might even venture that our continued ability to identify with the *Orlando furioso* and Pantagrueline tales, over four centuries after their composition, realizes another of their ideals: that of prophecy. In their tension between the individual and society, ideals and reality, progress and changelessness we see not only a tableau of Renaissance culture but also an image of ourselves-made-object. In part it is because these tensions are universal, but there is also something compellingly contemporary in the era's utopian dreams and boasts of scientific advances. Like them, our civilization has discovered new worlds, celestial instead of terrestrial, and has sent men to the moon, not on a hippogriff but in a no less incredible monster—a spaceship drawn straight from the annals of science fiction. Nor has twentieth-century "progress" been a totally positive experience: we also have invented our own "machina infernale," in the form of missiles and antimissile missiles which are a grotesque realization of Gaster's antibullet device. Perhaps because of our own hope for, fear of, and disappointment with "progress," we then are more sensitive to the ambiguities of the Renaissance than critics of some other eras. This is not to say that it is the only "sense" there but it is one which corresponds with our own world view. It is in this particular structure of thought that we, children of communism and capitalism, existentialism and the "absurd," find our "semblable" and "frère."[19]

19. Charles Baudelaire, "Au lecteur," *Les Fleurs du mal*, in *Œuvres complètes*, ed. Y.-G. Le Dantec (Paris: Bibliothèque de la Pléiade), p. 6.

I. THE VOYAGE

By reason of their positive extratextual associations the voyages in Rabelais and Ariosto seem at first glance a vehicle for the encomium of contemporary progress. Not only do the physical journeys call forth images of Columbus and Magellan, but their symbolic association with the quest for knowledge, as evidenced by Gargantua's encyclopedic letter on learning (P.VIII) and Logistilla's self-evident symbolism, hails recent artistic and scientific achievements as a foothold on the suddenly accessible unknown.

In view of their many humanistic evocations the Rabelaisian and Ariostan voyages would appear to find ancestors in classical rather than medieval literature: in Odysseus's superhuman heroics, for instance, or in Aeneas's founding of a new civilization. Indeed, the narrative is teeming with reminders of Greek and Roman prototypes. Yet despite these superficial affinities the Rabelaisian and Ariostan odysseys do not unfold in the Homeric world of pure immanence, along a predominantly horizontal trajectory, but in a hybrid universe still conditioned by the transcendental consciousness of medieval Christianity. Not surprisingly, the ascending route of that age's allegories, pilgrimages, crusades, and quests also figures in the Renaissance epic. Ostensibly, amalgamation of such heterogeneous source material will provide for optimal expression of the Renaissance explorers' all-encompassing goals, uniting Homer's here with Dante's Christian beyond. In fact, however, the different forms prove contradictory rather than complementary, and their combination acts to undermine both the central voyage structure and its individual components.

Far from gratuitous, the theme's antithetical configuration is not an isolated by-product of indiscriminate syncretism, but also finds sustained echoes in discursive and stylistic ambiguities. So all-pervasive is this reflexive dialectic that one might well label it a voyage in its own right. To be precise, it is a countervoyage, which, despite its negative polemical structure, serves a positive function in the humanistic march toward truth. Analysis of this subversive current will show that ingenuous dreams of conquest have been coupled with self-critical inquest, and facile affirmation of human prowess with interrogation of the human condition.

THE GEOGRAPHICAL QUEST

Laud of the here-and-now strikes one, at the outset, as incompatible with the imaginary voyage form. Despite the generous measure of fantasy which embellishes most epic journeys, their life force is equally dependent upon the impression of reality the author manages to convey and the degree of credibility he establishes. The story usually purports to be true, contains a good measure of geographical realism, and finds at least partial substantiation in historical fact. Here, in this tenuous balance between fiction and truth, lies much of the genre's efficacy as a panegyric and didactic device. If Rabelais and Ariosto have exaggerated the fanciful elements in their work, so also have they apparently sought to ensure the aforementioned equilibrium by proportionately increasing references to and evocations of current discoveries.

The reader is dazzled by the enthusiastic display of place names, shipboard activities, and exotic descriptions which, inspired at least in part by contemporary voyage journals, communicate the sense of adventure surrounding these excursions. Particularly in the Renaissance, mere incorporation of the voyage motif into a work of art constitutes an automatic link with dynamic, present-day reality. Columbus had first landed in America just two years before the probable birth of Rabelais, when Ariosto was almost eighteen years old, and by the early sixteenth century, the ensuing vogue for travel lore was well under way. Not only do we see the publication of such fanciful odysseys as the *Pantagruel* and *Furioso* but Columbus writes letters about his journeys, Vespucci composes his memoirs, and opportunists fabricate firsthand accounts.[1]

1. *Mondus novus*, for example, the apocryphal Vespuccian accounts which Romeo Rosario discusses in *Le Scoperte americane nella coscienza italiana del cinquecento* (Milan: Ricciardi, 1971).

In a sense, the same might be said of Rabelais and Ariosto. As if to increase the journey's vividness and verisimilitude, they forsake the bard's impersonal narrative for an eyewitness guise. Seizing upon the old nautical metaphor's enriched potential in the Renaissance, Rabelais and Ariosto establish a spiritual affinity, if not total identity, between narrator and navigator.[2] "Je l'ay veu couleur changer . . . je l'ay veu certainement verdoyer" (QL.II.544–45), insists Alcofribas when he describes the "tarande" at Medamothi. Such affirmations of veracity, which are also found in Ariosto's fiction and in contemporary voyage journals, may be viewed in two lights.[3] Designed to strengthen the narrative by expressing incredulity and credibility in a single breath, they also signal an inherent weakness in the narrator and suggest a possible discrepancy between what he says and what he sees. Travelers-turned-storytellers are in fact faced with an inevitable communication barrier, which derives from a radically dislocated relationship between the voyagers, their word, and their world. Seeking to share their own awe, the more ebullient returning explorers revert not to dry observation but to poetic language, traditional myths, and spectacular embellishments.[4] Such, indeed, is the epic style. Yet the bard's tools, dulled by centuries of overuse and familiarization, prove inadequate to the task at hand. "Nouveaultéz" (QL.IV.550) such as Astolfo's hyperbolic whale ("la maggiore / che mai per tutto il mar veduta fosse" [VI.37]) and Columbus's new lands are necessarily devitalized by cliché-ridden language, which, in uneasy coexistence with the superlative, ineffable message it would express, smacks equally of fact and fiction.[5] Ariosto's defense against these charges of perjury, on the grounds that they reflect the public's ignorance, serves as a simultaneous self-indictment

2. Ernst Curtius summarizes the nautical metaphor's development from antiquity to the Renaissance in his *European Literature and the Latin Middle Ages*, trans. Willard R. Trask, Bollingen Series 36 (Princeton, N.J.: Princeton University Press, 1953), pp. 128–30.

3. In his letter of 15 June 1502 to the king and queen of Spain, Columbus writes: "¿Quién creyerá lo que yo aquí escribo? Digo que de cien partes no he dicho la una en esta letra." *Cartas de relación de la conquista de America*, ed. Julio le Riverend (Mexico, D.F.: Nueva España, [1945?]), p. 83.

4. In his *Storia letteraria delle scoperte geografiche* (Florence: Olschki, 1937), Leo Olschki shows that Columbus "non percepvia soltanto con spirito realistico le apparenze effettive del suo nuovo mondo, ma le interpretava sovente coi ricordi e i miraggi delle favole di fonte letteraria ed erudita" (p. 21).

5. Typical of Columbus's superlative style is the following description of a river, taken from the third "Indian" voyage: "No creo que se sepa en el mundo de río tan grande y tan fondo." *Cartas de relación*, p. 51.

and encourages our disbelief: "che 'l sciocco volgo non gli vuol dar fede, / se non le vede e tocca chiare e piane" (VII.1).

Although they are in truth imaginary, recounted neither by navigators nor intinerant bards, the Rabelaisian and Ariostan voyages do contain a wealth of topographical and nautical detail which, drawn as it is from the authors' own mental and physical travels, lends some measure of verisimilitude to the works. Local geography in both works, mapped out in Pantagruel's educational tour (P.V) and in Rinaldo's Italian itinerary, is undoubtedly drawn from firsthand experience. Not only did the artists travel extensively throughout Italy, one as Ferrara's ambassador to Rome and the other as physician to Jean Du Bellay, but they have voyaged with Ptolemy and Pliny, ancients and moderns, travelers and tale-spinners.[6] Free access to the Estense library, a veritable goldmine of geographical data, provided Ariosto an intimate knowledge of the regions we traverse with him and his paladins: England, Europe, Asia, Africa.[7] His detailed tribute in the fifteenth canto to specific feats of the conquistadores also helps pinpont what is perhaps the major source of his inspiration: he describes the routes of Columbus and Vasco da Gama (22), refers to Pizarro and others as "i capitan di Carlo quinto" (23), and even mentions Cortez by name (27). Contemporary records moreover indicate that Rabelais frequented nautical circles, whence his specialized vocabulary and grasp of New World geography. The Utopians' itinerary in the *Pantagruel* (XXIV) coincides loosely with that of recent Spanish expeditions, while the *Quart Livre* route (I.541–42)—which Rabelais proclaims superior to that of the Portuguese—appears to have been inspired by Jacques Cartier's quest for a Northwest passage.[8]

6. Ariosto's preference for armchair voyages is made clear in the *Satire*:

Chi vuole andare a torno, a torno vada:
vegga Inghelterra, Ongheria, Francia e Spagna;
a me piace abitar la mia contrada.
Visto ho Toscana, Lombardia, Romagna,
quel monte che divide e quel che serra
Italia, e un mare e l'altro che la bagna.
questo mi basta; il resto della terra,
senza mai pagar l'oste, andrò cercando
con Ptolomeo, sia il mondo in pace o in guerra.   (III.55–63)

7. "Gli studi della geografia erano alla corte estense favoriti dalla smania dei viaggi," says Bertoni (p. 184). See also Michele Vernero, *La geografia nell'Orlando furioso* (Torino: Bonio and Rossi, 1913).

8. In his *Les Navigations de Pantagruel* (Paris: Leclerc, 1905), Abel Lefranc

Benefits to navigator and narrator are mutual. Rabelais will glorify Cartier and company by spreading their fame, while inclusion of the explorers' names and achievements will lend an air of timeliness to the fiction. Literary realism and contemporary allusions are, one must remember, a trick of the talespinner's trade. His art is, at least in part, a consumer product, which must catch and hold the audience's interest; and, particularly in the Renaissance, colorful depiction of the popular voyage is one sure means to this end. Even for a modern reader archetypal tempest scenes appear enlivened by Rabelais's picturesque nautical jargon (QL.XVIII.593) and by both artists' animated accounts of shipboard activities (QL.XVIII–XXII; XLIII), while their fanciful portrayals of extraordinary animals and foreign civilizations add a touch of exoticism to the narration.

Here, as elsewhere in literature, voyage realism is less a diverting end in itself than a means to a potential meaning. It serves, first of all, to involve the reader in a spiritual odyssey with which he might not otherwise identify. If Dante's convincingly drawn panoramas and first-hand observations promote reader participation in his teleological progression, how much more authentic such realism appears in the epic of a worldlier period which at times seems to propagandize heaven on earth. That laud of the here-and-now implied in the voyage's mimetic descriptions and topical allusions is, however, counterbalanced by a simultaneous thrust toward the then-and-there. Retrogressive evocations of the medieval crusade and romance, along with flights of fantasy and *locus amoenus* scenes, effectively transport us to another time and place. This temporal and spatial fragmentation of the voyage is not purely polemical, all form and no substance, but rather brings to light new and equivocal facets of Renaissance aspirations.

Not all of the noncontemporary allusions are subversive, of course. Comparative reference to ancient heroics, seen in Ariosto's juxtaposition of Astolfo, Argonauts, and conquistadores ("io veggo uscire/ . . . nouvi Argonauti e nuovi Tifi" [XV.21]), is easy enough to reconcile

---

cites Jacques Doremet (*De l'antiquité de la ville et cité d'Aleth ou Quidalet, ensemble de la ville et cité de Saint-Malo et Diocèse d'icelle*): "Rabelais vint apprendre de ce Cartier les termes de la marine et du pilotage à Saint-Malo pour en chamarrer buffonnesques Lucianismes et impies épicuréismes" (p. 60). Cf. also L. Denoix, "Les Connaissances nautiques chez Rabelais," *Études rabelaisiennes* 7 (1953): 171–90; Lazare Sainéan, "Les termes nautiques chez Rabelais," *Revue des études rabelaisiennes* 8 (1910): 1–56; and Jacques Soyer, "A propos de quelques termes nautiques chez Rabelais," *Revue des études rabelaisiennes* 9 (1911): 109–24.

with the theory that these works are primarily panegyric. Apparently, it is only in the context of Hellenic idealism that the Renaissance artist can give tribute to his own heroes. Just as factual details lend an air of authenticity to the fiction, so does myth reflect reality itself. Thus allusions to Greek heroes, borrowings from classical sources, and choice of epic forms would all seem to communicate a thoroughly humanistic vision of life. Integrating past and present, the authors would transcend temporal oppositions to uncover the essence of man.

Medieval crusade elements, however, reflect still another facet of Renaissance bravado, as subversive references to the period's unpleasant realities, even when phrased negatively, testify to the humanistic voyage's deformation, to the transformation of exploration into exploitation, to a thirst for battle and bloodshed.[9] Documents of the period reveal that valor is still often gauged by the standards of the Crusades, which remain warm in the minds of sixteenth-century explorers. If Columbus would seem to regard himself as a soldier of Christ, it is small wonder that Jesuit missionaries inflicted innumerable atrocities in the name of militant Christianity.[10] Despite the humanists' high-minded deploration of war, reacquisition of the Holy Land remained a popular cause for battle and was touted by pope and poets alike. It will be to the Crusades, and not the voyages of discovery, that Tasso will look for the subject of his *Gerusalemme liberata*.[11]

Like his successor, Ariosto appears to toy with this particularly Christian vision of the Renaissance epic, strengthening Boiardo's reprise of Roland's fight against the Saracens with exhortations for a contemporary march on Jerusalem: "Perché di Cristo gli uomini uccidete? . . . / Perché Ierusalem non rïavete, / che tolto è stato a voi da' rinegati?" (XVII.75). Structural and stylistic undercurrents, however—such as the Christians' merciless invasion of Africa ("Omicidio, rapina e man violente / nel sangue e ne l'aver, trasse di botto / la ricca e trionfal città a ruina" [XL.32]), an echo of historical massacres—dispute the aggressive certainty of this attitude, as the self-critical eye turns to look objectively at its own vehement passion. Use of obviously pejora-

---

9. The Utopians "ne voyageoient pour gain ne traficque de marchandise" (QL.XXV.611), while Ruggiero's journey "non è per guadagnar terre né argento/ ma sol per farne beneficio altrui" (VI.80).

10. "Colombo destinava una parte dell'oro acquistato nelle isole alla crociata di Terra Santa," writes Olschki, p. 58.

11. By tradition and convention, of course, the epic deals with past rather than present history.

tive substantives such as "omicidio" and "rapina" suggests that the narrator's apparent enthusiasm is part irony, an irony which reflects on the preceding passage: not only attacking Italy's internal strife, Ariosto laments the loss of a symbolic Jerusalem by warring man.

Even further removed from the medieval epic is Rabelais's use of the crusade theme, which emerges briefly in the first two books, and both times as a source of the ridiculous. Pantagruel's humanistic exploits include a victory over the infidel Loup Garou in a burlesque duel which, like many in Ariosto, is clearly satirical. Even though Christianity does not appear a major issue in the Picrocholine War, Rabelais clearly mocks the enemy's fanatical, crusading spirit:

> —Ne tuerons-nous pas tous ces chiens turcs et mahumétistes?
> —Que diable (dirent-ilz) ferons nous doncques? Et donnerez leurs biens et terres à ceulx qui vous auront servy honnestement.
> —La raison (dist-il) le veult; c'est équité. Je vous donne la Carmaigne, Surie et toute Palestine.
> —Ha! (dirent-ilz) Cyre, c'est du bien de vous. Grand mercy! Dieu vous face bien tousjours prospérer! (G.XXXIII.100–101)[12]

Ironically, these would-be Christian soldiers occupy the same structural position that the Mohammedan Loup Garou did in *Pantagruel*, as Catholic ceases to signify "good" automatically.

Medieval romance elements, such as itinerant knights and fantastical landscapes, further this fragmentation of the heroic voyage. They

---

12. In his *Satira Seconda*, Ariosto hypothesizes an ecclesiastic's rise to the papacy and distribution of favors in similar terms:

Ah! che 'l disio d'alzarsi il tiene al fondo!
Già il suo grado gli spiace, e a quello aspira
che dal sommo Pontefice è il secondo.
 Giugne a quel anco, e la voglia anco il tira
e l'alta sedia, che d'aver bramata
tanto, indarno San Giorgio si martira.
 Che fia s'avrà la catedra beata?
Tosto vorrà gli figli e gli nepoti
levar da la civil vita privata.
 Non penserà d'Achivi o d'Epiroti
dar lor dominio; non avrà disegno
de la Morea o de l'Arta far despòti;

. . . .

 ma spezzar la Colonna e spegner l'Orso
per tòrgli Palestina e Tagliacozzo,
e darli a' suoi, sarà il primo discorso.　　　　(202–19)

suggest that escapism is an integral part of travel psychology, ill-distinguished from more positive elements such as quest, crusade, and reform. Granted, it would appear that the explorers' wanderlust is channeled toward constructive ends, such as commerce in the word's largest sense. Buying rare and indigenous gifts at Medamothi, where "c'estoit le tiers jour des grandes et solennes foires du lieu, èsquelles annuellement convenoient tous les plus riches et fameux marchans d'Afrique et Asie" (QL.II.543), Pantagruel shares his own discoveries with Utopians at home. Astolfo's magic stopovers in exotic lands such as Egypt and Ethiopia, moreover, call to mind the wonder of Marco Polo's visits and the opening of new trade routes between Eastern and Western civilizations.[13]

Yet Panurge's pre-*Quart Livre* invitation to Pantagruel appeals both to the "abysme de science" and to the *cavalier errante,* romance version of the eternal wanderer. "Je vous ay longtemps congneu amateur de pérégrinité et desyrant tousjours veoir et tousjours apprendre. Nous voirons choses admirables et m'en croyez!" (TL.XLVII.492). It is true, of course, that familiarity with nature is essential to humanistic pedagogical theory, as outlined by Gargantua; Panurge's "apprendre" plays second fiddle to "veoir," however, which is in turn detached from insight and directed toward "choses admirables." Similarly, Rinaldo and Astolfo are seduced by the marvelous "otherness" of Alcina, who beckons less to the knights' inquisitive minds than to their restless senses:

> Io vi farò veder, ne la mia caccia,
> di tutti i pesci sorti differenti:
> chi scaglioso, chi molle e chi col pelo;
> e saran piú che non ha stelle il cielo.   (VI.39)

To see, in this instance, is distraction rather than discovery; and as colors dazzle, odors intoxicate, and sounds hypnotize, the wanderer loses himself in exterior phenomena, in a world of pure sensation.

Matter, which Renaissance humanism seeks to revaluate after a period of excessive spiritualism, dominates man throughout much of the travelogues. Accounts of Medamothi and Ethiopia are more descriptive than meditative, more concerned with diverting, unusual form

---

13. Mario Apollonio and Pio Fontana, note to *L'Orlando furioso,* 2d ed. (Brescia: La Scuola, 1971), p. 735.

than with function, relations, or meaning. Such mindless displays of materiality are common in Renaissance literature and are well suited to the exotic tastes of aristocratic readers, who seek diversion no less than the fictional travelers. Thus what at first appears a tribute to physical reality in all its immediacy emerges as its own opposite. The vacuous descriptions are actually a vehicle for flight, which, coexisting uneasily with the works' equally strong reflective current, appear symptomatic of a developing chasm between self and object, spirit and matter, which will persist in later periods as well. It is when viewed in the light of modern poetry, in fact, that the voyage's evasive quality becomes most patent. Traveling "au fond de l'Inconnu pour trouver du nouveau," the ennui-ridden Baudelaire will also seek obliteration in the "other" and, hopefully, sublimation in some vast realm of essences.[14]

The antihumanistic implications of the imaginary voyage are supported by the occasional metamorphoses of people themselves into objects. As in Baudelaire, human language and manners merge with odd plants and animals in a spectacular landscape, thereby providing observers with potential steppingstones to some nebulous beyond. One's gaze does not penetrate the surface of being, dazzled instead by the power of words, exotic customs, and impressive costumes. Ariosto's reduction of British troops to faceless names and insignias (X) is already an exaggeration of epic enumerations. Like Rabelais's even more outrageous depiction of Quaresmeprenant as a mechanical monster (QL.XXX–XXXII.621–27), it points back to the dehumanization of man in an increasingly materialistic world.

Instead of domesticating matter, the viewer-voyager often tends to be mesmerized by it, in an apparent change of roles. The metamorphosis which animates the Andouilles and which, conversely, objectifies Astolfo, signals that the attraction of externality may well constitute a threat. The Utopian explorers are attacked by the surrealistic sausages, while Alcina magically petrifies Astolfo into the form of a tree. Symbolically linked to *voluptas*, these oneiric realms dissolve natural hierarchical boundaries, promising free access to infinity; but instead, the viewer risks annihilation of his critical faculties by the vision his senses engender.

Physical, sensual, and mental flights away from civilization and back

14. "Le Voyage," p. 127.

to nature, as indicated by recurring *locus amoenus* scenes and by scattered evocations of the Golden Age, both support an escapist interpretation of the voyage and allow for further investigation of the relationship between man and milieu. It is in implicit reaction to the tension of social life, stilted conventions, and perpetual conflicts that Ariostan knights seek refuge in calm pastoral landscapes and that Utopians depart for a more primitive, bucolic land:

> Mais je voy que ceste ville est tant pleine des habitans qu'ilz ne peuvent se tourner par les rues: doncques je les mèneray comme une colonie en Dipsode et leur donneray tout le pays, qui est beau, salubre, fructueux, et plaisant sus tous les pays du monde.
>
> (P.XXXI.303)

This exodus from court to country modifies, and is modified by, the two works' civilizing thrust. Their juxtaposition exaggerates the real-life tension between utopian treatises and arcadian literature, and serves to emphasize the humanistic voyage's irreconcilable goals.

As depicted in Rabelais and Ariosto, the flight from civilization is temporal as well as spatial. In effect, man would become a child again, reverting to a world of simple, instinctive pleasures which, as epitomized by rustic dances at la Saulsaie (G.IV.16), preexists Gargantua's birth. The voyage genre will in turn situate this dream in the geographical beyond, where the "good savage," a polemical reaction to overcivilized etiquette, reigns.

Rabelais and Ariosto undercut the idyllic lure of primitivism, however, by identifying natural man with the fool, an equivocal figure whose regression inspires pity and laughter in the reader. Incorporated into the life style that Panurge proposes and Orlando enacts are the traditional Golden Age absence of private property and reintegration of the individual with nature, God, and humankind.[15] The Chastellain de Salmiguondin verbally transports us to a communal paradise where "mine and thine" no longer exist ("de leurs propres personnes font part à leur patrie, part à leurs amis" [TL.II.336]), while the Ariostan paladin indeed owes his survival to the hospitality of shepherds and commonfolk (XXIII). The age of Saturn's social harmony, expounded

---

15. Harry Levin, *The Myth of the Golden Age in the Renaissance* (Bloomington: Indiana University Press, 1969), pp. 22, 28, et passim.

by Panurge in his "Éloge des debteurs,"[16] is succeeded by a state of divine providence in which the fallen god ("Saturne lié de belles chaînes d'or dedans une roche d'or" [TL.XXIV.416]) is "alimenté de ambrosie et nectar divin, lesquelz journellement luy sont des cieulx transmis en abondance par ne sçay quelle espèce d'oizeaulx (peut-estre que sont les mesmes corbeaulx qui alimentoient ès désers sainct Paul premier hermite)." If the notion of living on grass and roots ("de sallades et racines" [TL.II.337]) appeals to the Gallic fool, Orlando actually subsists on this crude fare, protected by "Fortuna, che dei pazzi ha cura" (XXX.15).

Although this return to nature is a common figure of Renaissance literature, its negation of cultural achievements and individual self-reliance is at odds with the basic tenets of humanism. To renounce all the achievements of civilization is to negate the value of reason itself, which, even though frequently disparaged by the authors, still distinguishes man from the lower species. Thus Orlando's consumption of acorns is not idyllic but pathetic, phrased in negative terms ("Senza il pane discerner da le giande" [XXIV.12]).[17] By reducing Orlando to a purely bestial existence, to a kind of "ignoble savagery," Ariosto has allowed the whimsical theme of nudity and primitivism to run its full self-destructive course. At his most primitive level, suggest both authors, man does not borrow but steals, pillages, and exploits his fellow man. "Ainsi," says Pantagruel, "est-ce grande vergouigne, tousjours, en tous lieux, d'un chascun emprunter, plus toust que travailler et guaingner" (TL.347.48).

The humanistic voyage is diverted not only elsewhere in but outside of time and space, moving at times to a realm of pure fantasy. Contemporary explorers already incorporate a good amount of hyperbole into their letters and journals, of course, just to render the account more vivid. In the artistic mythification of their exploits fiction plays an even more essential role, providing historic travels a panegyric much more effective than unadorned truth. Astolfo's hippogriff flights and Rabelais's fanciful variations upon well-known intineraries pay

16. "Vray Dieu, ne sera-ce l'aage d'or, le règne de Saturne, l'idée des régions olympicques ès quelles toutes autres vertus cessent, Charité seule règne, régente, domine, triumphe? Tous seront bons, tous seront beaulx, tous seront justes. O monde heureux!" (TL.IV.344).

17. In his First Satire, however, Ariosto admits to a strong personal attraction for this simple existence: "Io non ho molto gusto di vivande/ che scalco io sia; fui degno essere al mondo / quando viveano gli uomini di giande" (148–50).

metaphorical homage to recent Spanish and Portuguese accomplishments in a manner which pure veracity could not equal. An ingenious
blend of geographical fact and temporal exaggeration, the account
both mythifies contemporary discoveries and jolts myth into the realm
of possibility:

> Car sans naufrage, sans dangier, sans perte de leurs gens, en
> grande sérénité . . . feirent le voyage de Indie supérieure en moins
> de quatre moys, lequel à poine feroient les Portugaloys en troys
> ans, avecques mille fascheries et dangiers innumérables.
>
> (QL.I.542)

This agile modulation of truth into poetry represents a conscientious
refusal to immobilize progress, to repress aspiration with concrete
achievement. Negating the prosaic present, fantasy restores to the
voyage its becoming.

It is difficult not to credit narrative sincerity. Their natural sympathy
for such ambitious enterprises shines through the lyrical, almost im-
perceptible transmutation of fact into poetry. Exaggerated depictions of
animals, the whale and "tarande," for example, may be clichés, but they
are transformed by an aura of conquest. The ambiance has changed.
Aware that his exotic animals clutter the pages of ancient and medieval literature, Pantagruel affirms the modernity of his attitude
toward them, a feeling of marvel unmixed with fear: "Je m'esbahis
comment nos escrivains antiques les disent tant farouches, féroces et
dangereuses, et oncques vives n'avoir esté veues" (QL.IV.550). Transformed by a youthful zest for discovery, Ariosto's most banal itineraries take on cosmic dimensions and give testimony to a humanization
of the entire universe. As he traverses Italy in a single swoop of the
hippogriff's wings, Rinaldo seems to hold the globe within his dominion (XLIII.53–55).

Fantasy is, however, a double-edged sword, which, even while im-
plementing the voyage's forward progress, contravenes its credibility.
The only instrument capable of praising so dynamic a civilization, it is
at once the source of all human vanity and presumption, of the hopeful
delusions that blind man to his mortality. Instead of consistently sus-
taining the illusion, Ariosto and Rabelais spin fantasies only to destroy
them. For instance, the banal protestations of veracity, which open
one's mind to new possibilities, also call attention to the works' fictitious
nature.

Insertion of lyrical tributes to human conquests within a burlesque framework already belies total narrative sincerity. Rabelais and Ariosto seldom maintain an elevated tone for long periods of time but rather slide almost invariably into subtle mockery, aimed both at the characters' superhuman pretensions and at the momentary credence which the audience gave them. The "Éloge du pantagruelion" pits man's inflated self-image against common sense, bombarding the reader with a fanciful description of nymphal explorers and frightened gods:

> De mode ques les Intelligences célestes, les Dieux tant marins que terrestres, en ont esté tous effrayéz, voyans par l'usaige de cestuy bénédict Pantagruelion, les peuples arctiques, en plein aspect des Antarctiques, franchir la mer Athlanticque, passer les deux tropicques, volter soubs la zone torride, mesurer tout le zodiacque, s'esbatre soubs l'æquinoctial, avoir l'un et l'aultre pôle en veue à fleur de leur orizon. (TL.LI.509)

Similarly, the glorious ascent of man into heaven is dramatically realized by Ariosto's Ruggiero, who, in spiritually rejecting his place among mortals, becomes the epitome of presumptuous human vanity:

> Or veder si dispose altra campagna,
> che quella dove i venti Eolo instiga,
> e finir tutto il comminciato tondo,
> per aver, come il sol, girato il mondo. (X.70)

The injection of comic, earthy details alongside such hyperbolic praise knocks man off his newly acquired pedestal, restoring him to the common soil from which he sprang. Thus the world-conquering Mohammedan doubles as Bradamante's straying lover, an irresponsible adventurer who "ogni sera all'albergo se ne gía / schivando a suo poter d'allogiar male" (X.73). Insofar as they represent a descent from the sublime, Ruggiero's terrestial hotels, with their bawdy, materialistic associations, are little different from the humanized Olympian realms made accessible by the French doctor's hemp.[18] This drug will enable man to "envahir les régions de la lune, entrer le territoire des signes célestes, et là prendre logis, les uns à l'Aigle d'or, les aultres au Mouton, les aultres à la Couronne, les aultres à la Herpe, les aultres au

---

18. Dante also uses hotel imagery in his *Convivio* (IV.28) to distinguish terrestrial life from the heavenly: "Uscir le pare dell'albergo e ritornare ne la propria mansione" (p. 286).

Lion d'argent; s'asseoir à table avecques nous et nos Déesses prendre à femmes, qui sont les seulx moyens d'estre déifiéz" (TL.LI.509).

SPIRITUAL SYMBOLISM

Deflating tactics such as the above serve to mock both geographical exploration and the spiritual odyssey of which it is a figure. Clearly the physical journeys within the two works symbolize man's more general epistemological quest, his Promethean effort to unite opposites, resolve dilemmas, and humanize the universe with his mind as well as his might. This metaphorical link between the voyage and learning is not a creation of the Renaissance but rather finds roots in primitive initiation rites, the epics of antiquity, and the Middle Ages' allegorical progressions. Rabelais and Ariosto combine vestiges of this last genre with related themes and forms to reinforce the voyage's figurative value. Among the many symbols giving an intellectual flavor to their odyssey are Logistilla, Ruach, Ariosto's phial of wisdom, and the Dive Bouteille.

Undoubtedly, the voyage's metaphorical value is particularly well suited to the Renaissance. During that period, topographical discoveries constitute only one small step in a great chain of scientific, artistic, and intellectual advances. Old truths, frozen for so many years, seem to have suddenly thawed, allowing man to pass through the ancient Gates of Hercules. Classical studies are renewed; texts are freed from ecclesiastical interpretation; the Bible itself is open to perusal. One might even venture that Magellan and Columbus are only minor heroes in comparison with the scholars, who themselves seek to encompass the globe in one sweep of the intellect.

Study itself, for the Renaissance man, becomes a kind of pilgrimage, and pedagogical itineraries are rigorous. Gargantua would make of his own son an "abysme de science" (P.VIII.206), nourishing him with past and present, pagan and Christian, theoretical and practical materials. On a symbolic level, the hippogriff given Ruggiero by Atlante and trained by Logistilla gives wings to the paladin's mind as well as to his body. His choice to "gire / cercando il mondo" (X.72), and his desire to "sapere il tutto" (X.75) about what he sees, bear witness to a thirst for knowledge no less hyperbolic than that of Pantagruel. Again the authors are authoritative tour guides, belonging to "la famille de ces moralistes et de ces pédagogues dont les systémes ne sont en quelque sorte que des autobiographies, où l'auteur recommande aux autres ce qu'il a pratiqué lui-même."[19] Ariosto does not, of course, know Greek and, as an aspiring humanist, is clearly sensitive to this gap in his education; with an eye toward progress, he rejoices that his son "può senza me per le latine / vestigie andar a Delfi, e de la strada / che monta in Elicon vedere il fine" (*Satira* VI.145–47). Similarly, Gargantua praises those advances in learning which will elevate Pantagruel's intellectual stature above his own:

> Le temps estoit encores ténébreux et sentant l'infélicité et calamité dez Gothz, qui avoient mis à destruction toute bonne littérature. Mais par la bonté divine, la lumière et dignité a esté de mon eage rendue ès lettres, et y voy tel amendement que de présent à difficulté seroys-je receu en la première classe des petitz grimaulx, qui en mon eage virile estoys (non à tord) réputé le plus sçavant dudict siècle. (P.VIII.204)

Essentially melioristic, this boast of enlightenment appears to signal the possibility of positive change, into an upward generational spiral.

Voyage expectations are again overstated. By combining the sum of human science with his own intellectual faculties, Renaissance man ambitiously hopes to read the newly illumined universe like a book. Logistilla, who symbolizes rationality, promises a clairvoyance reminiscent of Saint Paul's religious "through a glass darkly, but then face to face" (1 Corinthians XII):

> L'uom sin in mezzo all'anima si vede;
> vede suoi vizii e sue virtudi espresse,
> sí che a lusinghe poi di sé non crede,
> né a chi dar biasmo a torto gli volesse. (X.59)

Her faith in man's intellect, further reflected in the magic book with which she arms Astolfo, is seconded by Panurge's belief that Homer and Vergil will tell him his destiny.

Knowledge, which represents an end in itself to some humanists, is only one element in the Renaissance myth of progress, which also presupposes the practical application of learning toward the betterment of everyday life. While their medieval predecessors thought perfection

19. Gabriel Compayre in preface to Albert Coutaud's *La Pédagogie de Rabelais* (1899; rpt. Geneva: Slatkine Reprints, 1970), p. iii.

possible in heaven alone, the contemporaries of Rabelais and Ariosto dream of approximating this state of illumination, felicity, and godliness on earth. As analysis of the geographical voyage has shown, Renaissance man seeks to know and harness natural resources, to become better attuned to the physical universe in which he lives. His growing interest in ethics, politics, and the arts may be viewed, secondly, as the cultural equivalent of the physical voyage, directed toward the improvement of society. Exploration is oriented not only toward the perfection of communal life, thirdly, but also toward self-knowledge, as reflected in the era's strong current of individualism, its introspection, and its use of the ancients for behavioral analysis. Far from limiting himself to secular pursuits, finally, the Renaissance explorer invades metaphysical realms as well to ensure his entrance into heavenly paradise should the earthly one elude his grasp. In their works Rabelais and Ariosto unfold each of these contemporary currents, without, however, realizing the goals or integrating them all into a single structure; instead, they choose to develop the contradictions themselves, pitting truth against beauty and wisdom against knowledge in a confrontation of Renaissance ideals.

Some confidence in man's ability to realize these aspirations is of course partially justified by the inroads he has already made on the unknown. Cities, castles, and ordered gardens stand, in the two works, as monuments to humanity's triumph over chaos. Nature is no longer inimical but apparently an ally, whose own artistry is matched by man's artifice. The lack of encircling walls at Thélème, like the merging of "materia" and "artificio" in Logistilla's paradise, attests to man's alliance with the elements, a passage from primitive defiance to conquest and utilization of environmental resources. More significantly, interhuman tensions are resolved in seemingly optimal governments. The Rabelaisian cloister would strike a perfect balance between man's basic libertarian instincts and the advantages of sophisticated communal living; even though their motto is "Fay ce que vouldras," the residents of Thélème do "tous ce que à un seul voyoient plaire" (G.LVII. 160). Even the enlightened despotism of the Ferrarese duchy, which Ariosto praises so highly in the *Furioso* for its polished life style and high level of cultural development, seems to flourish because of its similar kind of give-and-take relationship between the individual and the state. While the dukes were despots, they did, during much of Ariosto's lifetime, encourage religious freedom, some amount of poetic license, and original thought—all with the purpose of enriching the collectivity as a whole.[20]

Once again, however, the characteristic praise-mockery movement is effected through abuse of hyperbole and fantasy. On the one hand Rabelais's abbey and Ariosto's court are tributes to Renaissance civilization, its achievements and its aspirations. Not limited to fiction, ideal city-states spring up everywhere in the Renaissance, at least if we are to believe contemporary panegyrists. Yet analysis shows that utopian treatises, imaginary solutions to real problems, derive less from an admiration of contemporary achievements than from a heightened awareness, triggered by the "progress" itself, that what *is* is not what should be.[21] In Rabelais and Ariosto the poets' self-conscious exaggeration relegates this dream of a perfect society to its appropriate world of make-believe.[22]

Ferrara's claim to "tutte le grazie" (XXXV.5) is undermined both by its own hyperbolic impossibility and by Ariosto's running satire of the court. Similarly, the abbey's superlative inhabitants—"gens libères, bien néz, bien instruictz, conversans en compaignies honnestes" who "ont par nature un instinct et aguillon, qui tousjours les poulse à faictz vertueux et retire de vice" (G.LVII.159)—are rhetorically de-realized by inexpressibility topoi that relegate them to never-never land: "Jamais ne feurent veuz chevaliers tant preux . . . ," Rabelais insists, ". . . Jamais ne feurent veues dames tant propres, tant mignonnes" (160).[23] Instrumental in undermining the cities' real substance and

20. For a generally positive account of the Estense public policies and patronage of the arts, see Gardner, passim, and Gundersheimer, pp. 5, 173–228. The latter refers to the dukes, specifically, as "enlightened despots before the enlightenment" (p. 5).

21. It is, as Jean Servier points out in his *Histoire de l'utopie*, Collection Idées (Paris: Gallimard, 1967), the Renaissance's transitional status and resulting instability which underlie that period's explosion of utopian thought: "Aussi, lorsque l'homme des civilisations traditionnelles repense sa société, il ne peut se livrer à cette réflexion que dans un moment de crise spirituelle, sociale ou économique, alors que l'ordre existant chancelle et qu'un autre ordre apparaît à la conscience de tout un groupe" (p. 16).

22. For a slightly different interpretation of Thélème's "derealization," see François Rigolot, *Les Langages de Rabelais*, Études rabelaisiennes 10 (1972): 77–98. For a discussion of the form's necessarily imaginary and implicitly critical nature, see Servier; Massimo Baldini, *Il linguaggio delle utopie. Utopia e ideologia: una rilettura epistemologica* (Rome: Edizoni Studium, 1974); Claude Dubois, *Les Problèmes de l'utopie* (Paris: Archives des Lettres Modernes, 1968); Émile Dermenghem, *Thomas Morus et les utopistes à la Renaissance* (Paris: Plon, 1927); and *Utopisti italiani del cinquecento*, ed. Carlo Curcio (Milan: Colombo, 1944).

23. See Curtius, pp. 159–62, for a discussion of the inexpressibility topos as a

in awakening us to the fallacy involved is precisely this temporal paradox upon which they are founded. Ferrara's medieval "future," projected forward from the age of Roland, has become a less-than-ideal present, plagued by war and poverty, while Rabelais's cloister has moved from future to past, disintegrating like a dream. Following a cyclical pattern the Abbaye is first built and populated on the upswing, then stylistically evacuated and razed on the downswing; for when, at the end of the passage, the poet allows the inhabitants to "issir hors" for marriage and directs our attention back to the buildings' "fondemens" (G.LVII.160), he retraces his steps so as to deconstruct the entire edifice.

Evasive elements in the geographical quest are directly linked to this same intellectual idealism. Like romance and romantic heroes, the Renaissance explorer has also acquired his tastes in a library and constantly flees a reality which does not satiate him. The light of learning is a false glow. "J'entens et veulx que tu aprenes les langues parfaictement" (P.VIII.205), says Gargantua in his famous letter. Yet in the succeeding chapter Panurge's thirteen-tongued request for basic sustenance labels him—in terms of practicality, at least—a consummate idiot, an educated fool.[24] In this instance he might well have profited from the example of Ariosto, who forfeited the study of Greek to master a more practical idiom: "ché 'l saper ne la lingua de li Achei / non mi reputo onor, s'io non intendo / prima il parlar de li latini miei" (*Satira* VI.178–80).

Panurge's folly is one of misjudgment, a confusion of learning and life, a deformation of Gargantua's pedagogical notion of language as literary tool. Granted, Orlando's knowledge of Arabic, traditional to the romance figures from whom he is descended, appears to facilitate his pursuit of Angelica, allowing him to infiltrate the enemy camp as a native (IX.5).[25] Yet when seen in the context of the overall voyage,

---

rhetorical tradition. Cf. also this hyperbolic description of Alcina's court: "aveva la piú piacevol gente / che fosse al mondo e di piú gentilezza" (VII.10).

24. As Rigolot notes, of course, Panurge does triumph: "Par le détour d'un contenant linguistique privé de sens, il peut communiquer la vérité profonde de son caractère" (p. 36).

25. Orlando's linguistic background is further attached to folly in Canto XXIII, when the paladin reads of Angelica's infidelity:

Era scritto in arabico, che 'l conte
intendea cosí ben come latino
fra molte lingue e molte, ch'avea pronte,
prontissima avea quella il paladino.   (110)

the episode is revealed to be a detour, an ill-advised artifice which widens the gap between Orlando and his lady, and which initiates his withdrawal from reality. Significantly, since Ariosto usually refers to his hero as wise instead of learned, this detachment of knowledge from good sense appears symptomatic of nascent mental aberration.

A potential guide, the lamp of learning can also produce a dazzling glare. In describing the artistic glory of Ferrara, Ariosto reverts to a hollow language of parade and ostentation: "la piú adorna / di tutte le città d'Italia scorgo, / non pur di mura e d'ampli tetti regi, / ma di bei studi e di costumi egregi" (XXXV.6). This emphasis on brilliance rather than enlightenment suggests that humanistic "conquests" are mere ornaments, which change just the taste, and not the nutritive value, of man's daily fare: "Des ars libéraux," says Garantua to his son, ". . . je t'en donnay quelque goust quand tu estois encores petit" (P.VIII.205). Similarly, Ariosto will introduce his son to the same "dolci studi" (*Satira* IV.170) which, before their interruption by familial and civic duties, brightened his boyhood and which, in the *Satire*, represent a kind of mental *locus amoenus*. Thus associated with sweetness and light, academia takes on the idyllic quality of a child's paradise ("car doresnavant que tu deviens homme . . ."), which must cede to empiric truths such as war and family responsibility (" . . . il te fauldra yssir de ceste tranquillité et repos d'estude, et apprendre la chevalerie et les armes pour défendre ma maison" [P.VIII.206]).

Overdependence upon books tends to retard man's cognitive growth, by substituting the imaginary and the authority of others for personal experience. Associated with both reason and irrationality, Ariosto's "libro" is an ambiguous symbol which, more often than not, leads knights astray. It is not only the progressive source of Melissa's prophecy (III.21) and the figure of Logistilla's reason (XV.13) but also the regressive tool of Atlante (IV.17,25), who, serving as Ruggiero's parent and preceptor, is responsible for the paladin's prolonged state of innocence. The *negromante*'s book, which animates the unreal when opened, is complemented by a magic shield, which blinds knights to reality when uncovered.[26] This use of light to blind and knowledge to

26. This, of course, is the traditional function of the book, which, far from being original to Ariosto, is commonly linked with negromancy in the romance. Ariosto's innovation lies in his association of the symbol with Logistilla as well as with magicians. Thus polarized, it serves as a springboard for dialogue between reason and unreason, fantasy and reality.

stupefy signals a fracture between form and functionality. It is a characteristic step in the countervoyage and leads, in both works, to the transformation of apparent beacons into obstacles. No longer totally positive symbols, as they were in Gargantua's letter (P.VIII), light and learning have been endowed with negative connotations as well. "C'est belle chose veoir la clairté du . . . soleil," says Rabelais in the prologue to his *Tiers Livre* (319), initiating Panurge's intellectual odyssey with a suggestion that learning's artificial glow can obscure the pure light of truth. Taking a cue from Diogenes, who accused the learned Alexander of blocking his view, the Rabelaisian narrator shouts "hors de mon soleil!" to all the wise fools ("cerveaulx à bourlet" [328]) who criticize his writings.

Human constructions, with their multiple towers and corridors, have blocked man's ascension and made him confuse fiction with truth. Having discovered Daedalus's maze, a product of human ingenuity, Renaissance explorers cannot extricate themselves: "Vous, semblablement," says Pantagruel to Panurge, "efforçant issir . . ., plus que davant y demourez empestré" (TL.XXXVII.461). Panurge's marital consultations may well be compared to Atlante's magic castle, through which Ariostan paladins chase images and echoes of their ladies. Although they have many rooms, and thus many potential doors to Truth, both structures prove upon closer inspection to be closed unto themselves. The castle windows themselves enforce this closure: heavily draped on the inside, they serve not to illuminate the building but rather project false images outward, thus luring errant knights back inside. There the different chambers merge into a circuitous sameness which also characterizes the *Tiers Livre*. Like Ruggiero, who "revisto ha quattro volte e cinque / di su di giú camere a loggie e sale" (XII.19), the Rabelaisian reader also has the impression of covering the same ground many times. In effect, the two structures are mental labyrinths, which reflect man's enslavement to his own circular logic and imagination. If the castle walls are mirrors of the paladins' minds, so does Panurge only see his personal uncertainty reflected in Trouillogan's circumlocutions and Vergil's brilliant verses. On a larger scale each work may be likened in its entirety to a maze. The amalgamation of epic, allegory, and romance—of different subjects, styles, sources, and settings—complicates not only the heroes' journey but that of the reader as well: both they and we become entangled in the jungle of man's mind and his culture.

On a spiritual level the voyage yields neither a single revelation nor the progressive consolidation of knowledge. Particularly in Ariosto, it serves instead to alienate paladins from reality and sequester them in a world of their own making. Similarly, what should be intellectual commerce in the *Tiers Livre* develops into a meeting of mutually impenetrable minds. Taking on new meaning in this mock epic context, a predominantly insular topography not only suggests that each man is an island, exiled to his own fantasies, but also graphically depicts his loss of control over disconnected phenomena. Far from compounding their knowledge with each new encounter as did Dante, Panurge and the Ariostan knights depart from and return to point zero, following an interminable succession of dead-end leads. The closest approximations of apotheosis in the *Orlando furioso* and *Tiers Livre* are, ironically, Astolfo's mad lunar visit and Panurge's audience with the fool Triboullet. Like Épistémon's descent into hell, their only revelation is negativity itself. In both instances human science is neutralized and made to merge with its opposite. Just as Orlando's sense is found on the moon by a fool, so does Triboullet say that Panurge, the would-be sage, is mad.

And perhaps he is. Certainly, Panurge lacks the epic hero's strong sense of who he is and what he wants. "Il ne sçait le premier trait de philosophie, qui est: *Congnois-toy*" (TL.XXV.418), says Panurge as he belittles Herr Trippa; but Pantagruel has directed a similar critique at *him* ("N'estez-vous asceuré de vostre vouloir? Le point principal y gist" [TL.X.361]). He and Orlando jeopardize their physical well-being, neglect civic duties, and brave eternal damnation to pursue their extravagant ambitions. Although Panurge, like Orlando, is seeking to realize an inner virtuality, the externality of his quest contributes to a simultaneous diffusion of the ego and represents a negation of both his own identity and the human condition. In his Sixth Satire the Ferrarese poet lashes out at just this kind of enterprise, mocking those contemporaries who aspire to "saper troppo" (45) and suggesting that it is not man's lot to penetrate heavenly mysteries. Accordingly, Ariosto counters the excesses of Orlando and Astolfo with Rinaldo's moderation. Resisting Alcina's attraction (VI.41), renouncing the metaphorical Angelica (XLII.63), and rejecting an offer of absolute truth about his wife's fidelity, he appears to share Ariosto's belief that *mediocritas* is more compatible than extravagance with happiness ("Sin qui m'ha il creder mio giovato, et giova: / che poss'io megliorar per farne prova?"

[XLIII.6])[27] Even Panurge, his confidence shaken by a tempest, comes to echo his narrator's earlier praise of "médiocrité" (QL.prol.): "Adam c'est l'homme," he says, "nasquit pour labourer et travailler, comme l'oyseau pour voler" (QL.XXIV.607–08). In the universal hierarchy of being, man is midway between God and beasts. Recognition of this intermediate rank should provde him a sense of measure, an internal center of gravity, a stable viewpoint from which to judge.

Deviations from the middle road, however, also contribute to self-knowledge, which includes the extremes of human behavior as well as its means. The mediocrity of Pantagruel and Rinaldo is a cross between Panurge's and Orlando's excessive highs and lows; it is arrived at only by balancing, and not denying, their contradictory nature. From this standpoint extravagance may itself be viewed as an authentic and necessary expression of the self, inasmuch as it recognizes the godlike in man: "l'homme qui n'a jamais tenté de se faire semblable aux dieux," says Paul Valéry, "c'est moins qu'un homme."[28] One principal function of the voyage structure is to confront these inhuman aspirations with the characters' mortal limitations, thereby shedding light on the human condition. Far from being an absolute, authentic judgment does not preexist the voyage but can emerge only across its vicissitudes, its situational demands. In the *Quart Livre* prologue a woodcutter's prayer for the return of his lost axe appears judicious, in retrospect, because it was answered: "C'estoit chose médiocre," says the narrator. Yet a priori judgments—a dialectical balancing of sense and sensibility, logical thinking and imagination—are necessarily more problematic than a posteriori ones, since man recognizes or shatters his limits only by testing them. "S'il eust soubhaité monter ès cieulx dedans un charriot flamboiant comme Hélie," continues Rabelais, "multiplier en lignée comme Abraham, estre autant riche que Job, autant fort que Sanson, aussi beau que Absalon, l'eust-il impétré? C'est une question" (526). If Ariosto scoffs at his ancestors' expectation, based upon an old paradisaic myth, of reaching the moon from a hilltop (*Satira* III.208–231), he and Rabelais nonetheless give voice to the fantasy. And although Astolfo's lunar jaunt and Pantagruel's proposed trip there (P.XXXIV.

27. *Mediocritas* is a dominant motif in the *Satire*, providing the poet a situational ideal from which to criticize the immoderate ambitions and pretensions of others. Specifically, he voices a preference for plain food and transportation, unpretentious ecclesiastics and scholars, modest fortune, and wives of average beauty.

28. *Œuvres*, ed. Jean Hytier (Paris: Bibliothèque de la Pléiade, 1960), 2:486.

312) are primarily satirical, their historical coincidence with the voyages of discovery suggests a whimsical intuition on the author's part that such feats may one day be possible. History tells us, as it must indeed have told them, that *mediocritas* is a relative, changing measure.

Like Montaigne, Rabelais and Ariosto paint not "l'estre" but the "passage," using the voyage as a vehicle for self-analysis and the formation of judgment.[29] The constantly changing landscape reflects the mutations of an ego, which, like the fractured universe, is multiple. It is a perpetual play of variables and antitheses, which modulate through time and space. The different ports of call, castles, and kingdoms in each work correspond loosely to both external cultural or metaphysical realities and the narrators' and protagonists' own inner self. Ariosto's genealogies and art displays reveal to the characters their latent capacity for creation and generation, as do the last episodes of the *Quart Livre*. Particularly in Rabelais, it is obvious that this generative potential is entwined with its negative poles, destruction and degeneration: the "parolles gelées" include the cries of dying men and women; the "Maistre ès Ars" subsists on sacrifice; and the Island of Ganabin is an Anti-Parnassus, inhabited by thieves. Such encounters with fear are, of course, necessary in the cognitive process and appear in all epics and initiation rites. Monsters and battles not only provide classic tests for the hero, and thus a possible source of immortality, but also bring him face to face with his own mortality and the darker side of his character.

In the Rabelaisian and Ariostan voyages such antitheses are joined as different sides of a single coin, each indispensable to the other. The personality is unfolded not in a consolidative, straightforward progression: it is instead realized through a point-counterpoint interplay of antitheses. When Ariosto playfully personifies the "Gola, Avarizia et Ira, / Superbia, Invidia, Inerzia e Crudeltade" (XIV.81) that knights errant encounter many times during their journeys, he reveals them to be universal foibles which constantly threaten man's nobler impulses. In anticipation of his ambiguous *pro bono malum*, however, Ariosto at the same time demonstrates that evil can also be a generating force of goodness.[30] In the *Furioso* heroism owes its existence to comple-

29. "Du repentir," *Essais*, ed. Maurice Rat (Paris: Garnier, 1962), Bk. 3, Ch. 2 (2:222).

30. Cf. Baldessar Castiglione, *Il libro del cortegiano* (Milan: Hoepli, 1928), ed. M. Scherillo: "Niuno contrario è senza l'altro suo contrario. Chi non sa che al mondo non saria la giustizia se non fussero le ingiurie? la magnanimità se non

mentary acts of villainy, which produce wrongs to be righted. Ruggiero's rescue of Angelica from the sea monster, for example, sublimates a previous injury, which thereby becomes an integral part of its opposite. In fact, one motive for Ruggiero's "generous" act proves to be *cupiditas*, a desire to possess the lady himself. Similarly, the sadism of Basché reflects an already-demonstrated capacity for cruelty in Panurge, which has in this episode become inextricably linked to its antipode: to beat the masochistic Chiquanous is in fact a form of kindness.

During the course of the voyage there occurs both a counterbalancing and confusion of alternative moods, mores, and values. The principal allegorical thrust in each work involves a tension between heart and reason, court and cloister, Bacchus and Apollo. By fragmenting the symbolism of each allegorical figure with these different connotations, the authors allow the dialectics of the decision-making process to unfold in all its complexity. Analysis reveals that the two authors do not resolve, but rather vacillate between, the oppositions. Although the austerity of Logistilla and Quaresmeprenant appears to "correct" the sensual ebullience of Alcina and Panurge, in keeping with ascetic Christian values, this descending cycle reverses itself in the Rabelaisian and Ariostan odyssey. Not only is the modest Logistilla less well developed poetically than her more voluptuous sister, but she also instills a new kind of *superbia* in Ruggiero. By teaching him to master the hippogriff she unwittingly provides wings for his romantic flights and fantasies. Likewise in Rabelais, Lent gives way almost immediately to a more characteristic Carnival, initiating a debate between mind and matter that persists throughout the *Quart Livre*. The addition of new nuances to this old conflict serves to complicate and enrich the self-knowledge process, which is shown to be no less elusive than the external truth men more frequently seek.

Because of the questions and conflicts it engenders, the voyage upsets not only man's comfortable conception of himself but also the relationship he enjoys with God and his fellowman. During the Middle Ages scholarship tended to be sequestered in cloisters and universities, thus contributing to a considerable gap between the active and contemplative life. Within this controlled environment, in which scholarship was detached from experience and subordinated to metaphysics,

---

fussero li pusillànimi? la continenza se non fusse la incontinenza? la sanità se non fusse la infermità? la verità se non fusse la bugia? la felicità se non fussero le disgrazie?" (2:2, p. 119).

there occurred only minimal conflict between reason, on the one hand, and practice or faith, on the other.[31] In the sixteenth century academia's ivory tower is still there, but it has been transformed, enlarging its bases and spreading out in labyrinthine directions. If some Renaissance scholars still suspect, as did Petrarch, that the study of humane letters for its own sake is a worldly sin, so also do they develop new anxieties about the possible abuses of knowledge. Indeed the moment it becomes an instrument rather than an end in itself it enters the relativistic world of morality. Thus Gargantua advises Pantagruel that "science sans conscience n'est que ruine de l'âme" (P.VIII.206), while Ariosto insists that his son's tutor be virtuous as well as learned:

> Dottrina abbia e bontà, ma principale
> sia la bontà: che, non vi essendo questa
> ne molto quella alla mia estima vale.   (Satira VI.16–18)

Inventions such as firearms, abhorred by both authors, reveal that the real-world impact of knowledge is not necessarily positive. Yet even if Rabelais and Ariosto agree that the cannon is an "infernal machine" (XI.23;QL.LXII.710), they forestall absolute condemnation with a confusing series of ifs and buts. The Ferrarese artist's indignation is conspicuously absent when he speaks of his own duke's arms ("non quel de lo 'nferno, / ma quel del mio signor" [XXV.14]), an exception to the infernal rule. Whether the passage springs from a justified belief in his prince's goodness, partisan self-delusion, or compromise of ethics to livelihood is irrelevant. In suspending us between these contingent possibilities the poet reveals a strong awareness of morality's real-world complexity. Similarly amending his own condemnation of firearms, Rabelais tells readers that Messere Gaster "inventa l'art militaire et armes pour grain défendre" (QL.LXI.708). These defensive weapons are quickly turned to offensive use, however, by the very brigands against whom they were initially deployed. Gaster's subsequent improvement of his armaments, once again for "defensive" purposes, marks the beginning of military escalation in the world: to protect himself against the bullet, he creates an antibullet device. This transformation of effects into new causes also entails the substitution of situa-

---

31. "Entre la raison et la foi, l'équilibre est rompu," says Henri Busson in his Le Rationalisme dans la littérature française de la Renaissance (Paris: J. Vrin, 1957), p. 103.

tional ethics for absolute rights and wrongs. Rabelais's attribution of diabolic (firearms were created by "suggestion diabolicque" [P.VIII. 204]), divine ("Gaster, leur dieu" [QL.LX.707]), and human ("Gaster confessoit estre non dieu" [707]) characteristics to the "Maistre ès Ars" interrogates the source of these muddied values, questioning man's liberty and the mere possibility of morality on earth.

Instead of emerging as the one straight path among many crooked ones, goodness itself—how, what, and why—enters into the epistemological debacle. Ariosto and Rabelais confront moralistic ideals with subversive, equivocal situations, bending Grandgousier's pacifism to Picrochole's aggression and Bradamante's integrity to Brunello's hostility in a contest of ends versus means. "Quantunque il simular sia le più volte / ripreso, e dia di mala mente indici," says Ariosto, "si truova pur in molte cose e molte / aver fatti evidenti benefici" (IV.1). The notion that virtue always finds its "just" reward is furthermore placed in doubt by the workings of indiscriminate chance or indifferent fate, as "innocents" die and the brigands thrive during Rabelais's plague: "ces diables pilleurs et meurtriers oncques n'y prindrent mal," says the narrator. "Dont vient cela Messieurs? Pensez-y je vous pry" (G.XXVII. 83).

In an attempt to hypothesize the initial cause of these frequently baffling effects, Rabelais and Ariosto direct their explorations toward metaphysical realms as well. Such interest in the beyond is certainly not surprising in the sixteenth-century context of budding reform and evangelism, when purification of scriptural texts and the revival of mystical works such as the Cabala promised the revelation of new truths. If religion appears to play a more important role in the Gallic monk's life than in that of the Italian court poet, it must be remembered that Ariosto also held minor orders in the church and served as ambassador to the Vatican. And while Italy will be spared the violent religious conflicts that plague France during the Reformation, the intellectual ferment which has accompanied the peninsular Renaissance from its origins, and of which Ferrara is a center, is no less innately metaphysical than its northern counterpart.

More than topical in its evocations, however, the transcendental thrust is a constant of human aspirations, the traditional end of man's epistemological drive. Such, at least, is the Platonic contention which Dante expounds in the Convivio:

> Io dico che non solamente ne l'acquisto de la scienza e de le
> ricchezze, ma in ciascuno acquisto l'umano desiderio si sciampia,
> avvenga che per altro e altro modo. E la ragione è questa: che lo
> sommo desiderio di ciascuna cosa, e prima da la natura dato, è lo
> ritornare a lo suo principio. E però che Dio è principio de le nostre
> anime e fattore di quelle simili a sé . . . essa anima massimamente
> desidera di tornare a quello.   (IV. 12, p. 250)

For Rabelais and Ariosto Christianity is no longer merely a goal to
which man aspires, as in the medieval epic, but a possible means which
must be tested under fire. Structural equalization of *Quart Livre* sects
and gods or of French and Arab forces in fact reduces religious differences to a nominal cultural phenomenon. Prebattle invocations to
Christ and Mohammed, Bible and Koran are purposefully symmetrical,
implicitly undermining the entire crusade thrust.[32] The war between
Christians and Moslems is counterbalanced by their symbolic union,
through love, in the figures of Ruggiero and Bradamante. This proposed
marriage of "opposites" is moreover rendered highly ironic by the
Mohammedan's Christian birth. Paternal opposition to the union,
couched in legalistic terms, reflects a widespread confusion of form
and faith:

> Ma se gli è stato inanzi che cristiano
> fosse Ruggier, non vo' che me ne caglia;
> ch'essendo ella fedele, egli pagano,
> non crederò che 'l matrimonio vaglia.   (XLV.110)

Like Rabelais's Papimanes, the Duke of Amone considers his own religion the "Unicque," when perhaps it is really the "Eunuque"—a
deformed and impotent effigy of the truth.

In the manner of Lucian, Swift, and eighteenth-century "relativists,"
the authors have transformed the voyage into a first-rate satirical vehicle. The confrontation of Christianity with its objectified other self—
transformation of the "we" into the "they"—both reveals the ills of
deformed Christianity and blurs qualitative differences between sects.
If, on the one hand, it appears that the One truth has been fragmented
into the Many, all relatively equal, Rabelais and Ariosto balance this

---

32. In quel del nostro è la vita perfetta
    scritta di Cristo; e l'altro è l'Alcorano.
    Con quel de l'Evangelio si fe' inante
    l'imperator, con l'altro il re Agramante.   (XXXVIII.81)

hypothesis, on the other hand, with implications of a much more rigid, restrictive religion. Ariosto's mention of a predetermined group of "dannati" (XXXIV.90) and Rabelais's reference to predestination moreover support this interpretation, while frequent allusions, within this context, to the "camin dritto" from which paladins stray remind one that "narrow is the path and strait is the gate."[33] Certain theologians of the Middle Ages and Renaissance—notably such reformers as Luther and Calvin—professed that salvation was accorded not to all Christians but only to the "chosen," to those who had been predisposed to believe. The voyage of life ostensibly tests this inner light, as vicissitudes separate the wheat from the chaff.

To a certain extent earthly successes themselves become a reflection of faith. "Toutes-foys je n'espère en ma force ny en ma industrie," says Pantagruel, "mais toute ma fiance est en Dieu, mon protecteur" (P. XXVIII.284). Inseparable from a ruse to deceive the enemy, however, this apparently ingenuous demonstration of piety is at least partially staged for a departing prisoner's benefit, as a camouflage for pure human cunning ("j'ay donné entendre à ce prisonnier . . . mais cependant mon intention est . . ." [285]). Though a virtue in the ancient epic, deceit such as this condemned Odysseus to Dante's hell.[34] Similarly, a carefully veiled irony—the burlesque quality of Astolfo's revelation (XXXVIII) and the too-opportuneness of Ruggiero's conversion (XLI) —catapults Ariosto's praise of faith into the same ambiguous domain as that of Rabelais. Just what is this nebulous property, and how does one distinguish it from natural and psychological contributing factors? The prowesses of both books' heroes waver between the purely humanistic and the divinely facilitated. Astolfo's invocation of divine aid, which enables him to effect a rather burlesque transformation of stones into horses, recalls the ancient hero's prayer to pagan gods as well as Christian miracles, while the metamorphosis itself harks back to Ovid's tale of Pyrrha and Deucalion.[35] In this comic, syncretic atmo-

33. Notably, Orlando is punished "perché torse / dal camin dritto le commesse insegne" (XXXIV.62)

34. He was also condemned for his worldly ambition—in Dante's *Inferno*, for his "ardore . . . / a divenir del mondo esperto" (XXVI.98–99) and in Petrarch's *Triumph of Fame*, because "desió del mondo veder troppo" (II.18). *Rime, Trionfi, e poesie latine*, ed. F. Neri and others (Milan: Ricciardi, 1951), p. 537. This aspect of the Ulyssean theme is implicit throughout the *Furioso*, while Rabelais ironically includes the Greek hero in Épistémon's hell (P.XXX.294). See also W. B. Stanford, *The Ulysses Theme: A Study of the Adaptability of a Traditional Hero*, 2d ed. (Oxford: Blackwell, 1968), pp. 175–210.

35. *Metamorphoses* 1:367–413. See Rajna, p. 549.

sphere, Ariosto's glib Biblical paraphrase—"Oh quanto a chi ben crede in Cristo, lece" (XXXVIII.33)—lends itself to literal and ironic interpretations.[36] Pantagruel's equivocal battle tactics moreover supplement faith with works in illustration of the old adage that "God helps those who help themselves."

At the same time they explore orthodox religious paths toward epistemology, Ariosto and Rabelais turn also to the occult, which, with its oracles and mages, seems to promise more direct contact with the beyond. The works are so constructed that these attempted divinations are endowed with a certain narrative logic. Since the goal of Panurge's quest is situated in the future, it is only natural that he should first consult supernatural sources of knowledge: the Vergilian lottery, dream analysis, and the sibyl. Likewise, the futuristic visions of Melissa, Merlin, Atlante, and Malagigi are not so much celebrations of the occult as vehicles for the introduction of contemporary encomium within an historic framework. Nonetheless, magic is both a convenient poetic hypothesis for Ariosto and a theme in its own right, which has been developed in a detailed and contradictory fashion. Merlin's grotto, where the amazon "si vede in sacre loco" and sends "preghi a Dio," is for example a mixture of Breton fantasy, Christian supernaturalism, and picturesque witchcraft:

> E perché da li spirti non sia offesa,
> le fa d'un gran pentacolo coperchio,
> e le dice che taccia e stia a mirarla;
> poi scioglie il libro; e coi demoni parla. (III.21)

In a world where man and the cosmos appear joined through mysterious alchemical rapport, and the heavens filled with both demons and angels, such confusion of domains is less religious heresy than mere exploitation of the God-given possible. In speaking of a diviner Pantagruel says, "et peut estre que celluy homme estoit ange, c'est-à-dire messagier de Dieu envoyé, comme feut Raphaël à Thobie" (TL. XVI.385).

Narrative reservations toward magic and divination arise less from religious scruples than from a current of humanist rationalism on record in Gargantua's famous letter: "laisse-moy l'astrologie divinatrice et l'art de Lullius, comme abuz et vanitéz" (P.VIII.205). Not surprisingly, traditional symbols of the occult are divested of

36. Cf. Mark ix.23.

their magic power and "rationalized." The force behind Panurge's "philosopher's stone" (TL.XVII.243), which has degenerated into a hollow metaphor, is no longer alchemy but man's ingenuity. Similarly, Angelica's charmed ring, an old symbol of the irrational, has been given a new signified to fit the times: "Chi l'annello d'Angelica, o piú tosto / chi avesse quel de la ragion" (VIII.2).[37] Derision of the occult is, however, tinged with a faint "perhaps" which in itself serves to justify the voyage: "Que nuist sçavoir tousjours et tousjours apprendre, feust-ce d'un sot, d'une gedoufle, d'une moufle, d'une pantoufle" (TL.XVI.384), demands Pantagruel.

Endowed with an inquisitive but incredulous critical sense, however, both authors proceed to mock "revelations" produced by this venture into the occult. The reliability of "supernatural" media is repeatedly placed in doubt, through satirical presentation and interrogation of motives. Truth and self-interest, inspiration and charlatanism merge into mockery when Épistémon asks Panurge if he has brought the *Tiers Livre* sibyl "le rameau d'or," a mystical symbol inherited from Homer and Vergil which Panurge degrades with materialistic connotations. By linking the golden bough with a gold ring and coins to be used as payment, he clearly suggests that the gold's monetary value, and not its magical force, will inspire the witch's "prophecies."[38] And in spite of the apparent gifts of Melissa and Malagigi as fortune tellers, magicians frequently find themselves the target of Ariosto's denigrating wit. They are demystified by the comicality of their miracles, their capacity for mistakes (XVIII.174–75;XXVII.2), and Ariosto's irreverent reduction of negromancy to banal professionalism. His affirmation that Malagigi (XXVI.128) and Melissa (XLIII.21) are no less proficient in their trade than any other self-respecting magus, for example, serves not to exalt the occult figures, as the content would lead us to believe, but rather to deflate them through a process of narrative condescension and over-familiarization.[39]

37. While Giulio Ferroni is right to say, in his "L'Ariosto e la concezione umanistica della follia" (*Atti dei convegni lincei* ([Rome: Accademia Nazionale dei Lincei, 1975], pp. 73–92), that Angelica's antimagic ring is a "metafora della ragione" (p. 84), it is no less magic than the spells it combats and thus emerges, like the *negromante*'s book, as a simultaneous figure of irrationality.

38. "Nous ne aurons d'elle response aulcune, car nous n'avons le rameau d'or. "—Je y ay (respondit Panurge) pourveu. Je l'ay icy dedans ma gibbesière en une verge d'or acompaigné de beaulx et joyeulx carolus" (TL.XVII.388).

39. He "sa d'ogni malia / quel che ne sappia alcun mago eccellente" while she "sapea d'incanti e di malie / quel che saper ne possa alcuna maga." Ariosto's satiric comedy *Il negromante* and Rabelais's parodic *Prognostications* and *Al-*

Agilely turning to explore their own critical spirit, Ariosto and Rabelais nonetheless leave open the mystical road to truth, at least on a theoretical level. Ironically, it is perhaps man's own rationality, the product of a modern age, which blinds him to the answers he derives from traditional, irrational sources. Bradamante's common sense, supported by circumstantial evidence linking Ruggerio to Marfisa, persuades her to discredit a vision in which the paladin reaffirms his fidelity to her (XXXIII.62). The "falso sogno" that she sees with "closed eyes," however, proves to be more accurate than the deceiving appearances perceived by her open eyes. Communication between mortal and supernatural realms is just as problematic in Rabelais, as Panurge both seeks the sibyl's advice and fails to take it seriously, ridiculing her at least in part because she is "different" ("elle ne parle poinct christian" [TL.XVII.389]). Much of the scene's comicality moreover arises from the gap between the hermetic sign and its intellectualized interpretation, between eight crude verses and their four pages of ludicrously documented commentary.

This inability to follow the occult path to its end is not without psychological basis, since divination is potentially a portent of misfortune. Thus Panurge's strong predispositions—in this instance, for a perfect marriage—blind him to any conflicting truths: "Mais ô que chose rare est son malheur propre prædire, cognoistre, prævoir et entendre" (TL.XV.383), says Épistémon when dream analysis fails to yield an answer compatible with Panurge's desires. Conversely, both he and Bradamante, whose fears outweigh her hopes in the above episode, are suspicious of overly auspicious edicts. Even when accurate, these positive prophecies are furthermore repugnant in their metaphysical ramifications. To see the future in its entirety, theoretically a step toward the divine, ironically implies predestination, loss of liberty, and condemnation to mortality itself.

GUIDEPOSTS AND STEPPINGSTONES

One key to this metaphysical journey's failure is man's inability to decipher the universe's hermetic language. While Panurge questions the interpretation of his *Tiers Livre* dream, reading both cornucopia

manachs (pp. 896–917) bear further witness to the authors' skeptical attitude toward magic and divination.

and cuckoldry into the horn, he never doubts its ultimately significant nature. This symbolic consciousness finds its immediate roots in the Middle Ages and that period's peculiarly Christian conception of the world:

> In God nothing is empty of sense: *nihil vacuum neque sine signo apud Deum*, said Saint Irenaeus. So the conviction of a transcendental meaning in all things seeks to formulate itself. About the figure of the Divinity a majestic system of correlated figures crystallizes, which all have reference to Him, because all things derive their meaning from Him. The world unfolds itself like a vast whole of symbols, like a cathedral of ideas. It is the most richly rhythmical conception of the world, a polyphonous expression of eternal harmony.[40]

Far from being exclusively occult or religious in their associations, signs and symbols are an integral part of everyday life for Renaissance figures. Names, emblems, and colors help consecrate their voyage, by encapsulating amorphous existence in reassuring forms and establishing each man's place in the cosmic order. The use of emblems to achieve social and temporal integration is of central importance in both Ariosto and Rabelais. Gargantua's rings renew "le signe antique de noblesse" (G.VIII.30), while Ruggiero's white eagle, dating from Trojan times, places him in a long line of valorous warriors. A vivid sense of stability and familiarity is traditionally derived from this formalization of the individual's "essence" in collective and personal terms.

Ostensibly serving as anchor and compass, this semiological framework is intended to channel the voyage movement, to tell man—both readers and hero—where he is and where he is going. Not only those symbols generated spontaneously by the subconscious, such as the horns of Panurge's dreams which are overtly employed for purposes of divination, but institutionalized blasons and emblems as well are potential portents of the future, bridging all three dimensions of time. Like Bradamante's phoenix, which anticipates her marriage and illustrious progeny, the drinking vessels on Pantagruel's ships are less expressive of being than of becoming:

> Ainsi estoit nommée la grande et maistresse nauf de Pantagruel, ayant en pouppe pour enseigne une grande et ample bouteille, à

40. Johan Huizinga, *The Waning of the Middle Ages*, trans. F. Hopman (1924; rpt. New York: Doubleday Anchor Books, 1954), p. 202.

> moytié d'argent bien liz et polly, l'aultre moytié estoit d'or esmaillé
> de couleur incarnat. En quoy facile estoit juger que blanc et clairet
> estoient les couleurs des nobles voyagiers et qu'ilz alloient pour
> avoir le mot de la bouteille. (QL.I.539)

Already, however, multiple interpretations of the emblems transform
absolute signification into mere hypothesis: "personne n'estoit . . . ,"
continues the narrator, "qui . . . ne dist que les voyagiers estoient tous
beuveurs, gens de bien; et ne jugeast . . . que le voyage . . . seroit en alai-
gresse et santé perfaict" (540). If the first clause of this passage reduces
the emblems to a wine-bibbing sailor's fancy, the second is proved false
by later events, such as the tempest, Panurge's fears, and Pantagruel's
tears (QL.XXVIII.619).

Characteristically, the authors subversively divert signifier-signified
rapports even as they are proposed, restoring to traditional signs their
myriad paths of possibility. In describing Gargantua's blue and white
livery, Rabelais rejects the medieval color symbolism "foye" and "fermeté" for a new interpretation: "diray en un mot que le bleu signifie
certainement le ciel et choses célestes, par mesmes symboles que le
blanc signifioit joye et plaisir" (G.X.37). The juxtaposition of opposing
signifieds for the same sign is less a process of negation and affirmation
than of mutual mystification and interrogation, since the critique of one
is equally applicable to the other: "Qui vous dict que blanc signifie
foy et bleu fermeté? . . . Quiconques il soit, en ce a esté prudent qu'il n'y
a poinct mis son nom" (G.IX.31).[41]

In Ariosto, Ginevra's symbolically white garments, ostensibly indica-
tive of her virtuous character, become a disguise for treacherous Dalinda (V.47). On a purely structural level, this association of one color
with both faith and deceit fractures its functional value, transforming
it into mere decoration: even Ginevra is described more often in terms
of beauty than of purity. Similarly, the conflict between Ruggiero and
Mandricardo about the "aquila d'argento"—claimed by one because of
heredity, by the other because he has won it—undermines emblematic

41. In his "Richness and Ambivalence of the Symbol in the Renaissance" (*Yale French Studies* 47 [1972]), André Stegman discusses "the multiple symbolism of colors of diverse origins and often having contradictory meanings" (p. 18). For a further discussion of color symbolism in these two works, see Gérard Defaux, "Rabelais et son masque comique," *Études rabelaisiennes* 11 (1974): 117–27; Jean Paris, *Rabelais au futur* (Paris: Seuil, 1970), pp. 111–31; François Rigolot, "Craty-lisme et pantagruelisme," *Études rabelaisiennes* 13 (1976): 118–22; and Abd-el-Kader Salza, "Imprese e divise d'arme e d'amore nell' *Orlando furioso*," *Giornale storico della letteratura italiana* 38 (1901): 310–63.

symbolism through fragmentation of lineage from valor, and not through disputation of mystical man-emblem rapports (XXVI.99–100).

Not only do Rabelais and Ariosto mystify the reader by alternating different values for the same sign, but they also bait him with paradoxically nonsignificant symbols, designed to further circumvent his straightforward spiritual voyage. As they loosen meaningful figures from their traditional settings, the authors place at least equal stress upon superfluous materialism as upon mysticism, jolting the "signs" into an autonomous realm of decoration and appearance. Gargantua's image—which, with its blend of Platonic and Christian evocations, lends itself to various spiritual interpretations—is also presented in disquieting terms of weight, not devoid of economic overtones: "Pour son image avoit, en une platine d'or pesant soixante et huyt marcs, une figure d'esmail compétent" (G.VIII.29).[42] Narrative irony and comic deformation moreover strengthen the distance between the object and its purported sense. Amidst a detailed description of Pantagruel's sailing emblems, Rabelais confuses "presme d'émeraulde" with "sperme d'émeraulde" (QL.I.539), and Ariosto places a surrealistic broken chair and cleft mountain into his tenth-canto parade of standards, which, along with an impressive list of legendary names, seem to exist gratuitously, devoid of hermetic meaning.

Instead of constituting part of a divine network of analogies, the countervoyage emblem takes on a more exclusively human cast, as it fits into the vast network of institutional games.[43] In his portrait of young Gargantua, Rabelais mocks the idea that natural origins should be attributed to humanly consecrated, nonessential modes of fashion: "Lors commença le monde attacher les chausses au pourpoinct, et non le pourpoinct aux chausses: car c'est chose contre nature, comme amplement a declaré Olkham sus les *Exponibles* de M. Haultechaussade" (G.VIII.27). The subversive effect of the strategically placed name Haultechaussade demystifies the authority of Olkham just as the narrator's own name in a similar context ("le tout fut faict par le capitaine

---

42. *Les Grandes et inestimables chronicques du grant et énorme géant Gargantua*, appendix in *The Tale of Gargantua and King Arthur* by Frances Girault, ed. Huntington Brown (Cambridge, Mass.: Harvard University Press, 1932), pp. 103–28: "Gargantua avoit ung signet d'or en ung de ses doys, auquel avoit troys cens marcs d'or dix onces et deux deniers et demy; et y avoit ung rubiz enchassé dedans ledict signet qui estoit merveilleusement bien estimé, et pesoit cent trente livres et demye" (pp. 117–18).

43. See Huizinga, *Homo Ludens: A Study of the Play-Element in Culture*, trans. R. F. C. Hull (London: Routledge and Kegan Paul, 1940).

Chappuys et Alcofribas" [G.VIII.30]) reduces Gargantua's emblems to the realm of whimsical fiction.

The promise of meaning in Rabelais's nomenclature moreover parallels that in his emblemology, as the names Gargantua ("que grand tu as"), Panurge ("homme à tout faire"), and Pantagruel ("tout altéré") seem mystically linked to their bearers' characters, aspirations, and destiny. The obviously contrived etymologies (Gargantua and Pantagruel, for example, preexist their "meanings"), however, transform any signification into ill-concealed artistic flummery, a trap for the overly credulous. When he delves into the multiple, largely banal origins of plant names, Rabelais slyly undermines his own previous assertions, fragmenting unilateral sign-meaning paths into a contingent semiological network:

> Je trouve que les plantes sont nommées en diverses manières. Les unes ont prins le nom de celluy qui premier les inventa . . . Les aultres ont leur nom par antiphrase et contrariété . . . Les aultres, par les admirables qualitéz qu'on a veu en elles.   (TL.L.502–04)

Similarly, the purported signification of Angelica, an epistemological symbol that leads many knights astray, is deflected both by psychological penetration of a nonangelic character and by the ironic connotations of her superficial "angelico sembiante." No less contrived than this etymological signal of inner worth, moreover, are the reputational edifices surrounding the names of Ariosto's knights, living legends which precede their bearers like banners. Marfisa wants to meet Orlando, "e far esperienzia se l'effetto / si pareggiava a tanta nominanza" (XVIII.134).

Indeed, the social as well as mystical import of emblems is placed in doubt by this explosive exploration of semiology. Since design, like language, can serve as a means of communication and self-expression, knights who carry the crest of love are ostensibly only formalizing an inner sentiment (XVII.72). Signs with positive communicative potential may also be diverted for negative purposes, however. In Rabelais and Ariosto costume wavers between the realm of symbolism and that of mask and illusion. When Panurge, loath to make war, casts aside his "magnificque braguette" for a long robe or toga (TL.VII), the confusion between expression and deceit effectively neutralizes positive meaning. While Panurge claims that the codpiece is "première pièce de harnoys pour armer l'homme de guerre" (354), and the toga a sym-

bol of peace by virtue of its opposite historical associations, Pantagruel misses the robe's figurative value and merely calls it a "desguisement estrange" (352). And although armor often identifies knights to
their peers in the *Furioso*, it is just as frequently used for mystification
and disguise; Ruggiero "eletto avea combatter tutto armato," says
the narrator, "perch'esser conosciuto non vorrebbe" (XLV.64).

Traditional guideposts point back to the labyrinth, and unenlightened
mortals cannot emerge from its thralls without the guidance of an
initiate into the cosmic mysteries. Our faith is, however, shaken. Theologians and scholars, magicians and logicians have been disparaged,
leaving room for the writer alone to serve as initiator. Just as Rabelais
and Ariosto suspend the meaning of society's figurative language—
its colors, emblems, and names—so do they fragment those literary symbols which traditionally ordain the voyage's ascent, thereby
subverting their own sign-making function. Most promising as authorial guideposts are the water-wine imagery, the metaphorical woman, and the insular or earthly paradise. Yet each of these themes undergoes so diffuse a development that meaning becomes lost in its
own maze of virtualities.

Exploiting the multiple connotations of thirst, traditionally linked
with Bacchic inspiration, Socratic and scriptural verity, Rabelais and
Ariosto unite liquid and lady in a metaphorical quest for truth.[44] Rinaldo
will drink or spill his magic brew, depending upon his wife's fidelity
(XLII.103). Similarly, Panurge's "Doibve-je me marier" is initiated by
drinking imagery, as witnessed not only by the *Quart Livre* emblems,
but also by the *Tiers Livre* prologue's "tonneau":

> Sus à ce vin, compaings! Enfans, beuvez à pleins guodetz . . .
> Ainsi demeurera le tonneau inexpuisible. Il a source vive et vène
> perpétuelle . . . C'est un vray cornucopie de joyeuseté et raillerie
> . . . Bon espoir y gist au fond, comme en la bouteille de Pandora.
> (327–28)

Notwithstanding its hopeful tone, the preceding text already anticipates
later epistemological ambiguity. The cornucopia prefigures Panurge's
confusing dreams, while Pandora's box reminds us that human misery
was born of excess curiosity. The tub's multipronged symbolism, with

---

44. For a discussion of wine and women in Rabelais, see Florence Weinberg,
The Wine and the Will (Detroit: Wayne State University Press, 1972), and Michael
A. Screech, *The Rabelaisian Marriage: Aspects of Rabelais's Religion, Ethics, and
Comic Philosophy* (London: Edward Arnold, 1958).

its Christian, pagan, poetic, and purely natural evocations, furthermore questions the ultimate source of truth, stalling our quest at a man-God-nature juncture.

Obviously, traditional drink symbolism is developed in not only positive directions but along negative lines as well. Rinaldo's rejection of the truth-bearing liquor echoes the perverted relationship between wine, water, and knowledge in two preceding death scenes. By insisting that the "mirabil acqua" (XXIX.18) in which she bathes herself will render her invulnerable to physical attack, Isabella induces the drunken Rodomonte to decapitate her "experimentally." Her description of this test as a "saggio" (24) which "può dotte far le gente grosse" (23) moreover endows the episode with epistemological overtones. While Isabella's "baptism" presumably immerses her in the heavenly wisdom of death, it produces an ironic "hydrophobia" in her would-be seducer: he goes mad, builds an aquatic monument to Isabella, and is finally transported spiritually to the "squalide ripe d'Acheronte" (XLVI.140). Somewhat more lighthearted is Ariosto's account of two Christians, both linked with liquid in life, who die by drowning during Rodomonte's assault on Paris:

> Getta da' merli Andropono e Moschino
> giú ne la fossa: il primo è sacerdote;
> non adora il secondo altro che 'l vino,
> e le bigonce a un sorso n'ha già vuote.
> Come veneno e sangue viperino
> l'acque fuggia quanto fuggir si puote:
> or quivi muore; e quel che piú l'annoia,
> e 'l sentir che ne l'acqua se ne muoia. (XIV.124)

Fearing a similar fate, Panurge associates drink with drowning in the *Quart Livre* tempest scene: "nous ne boirons tantoust que trop, à ce que je voy" (QL. XVIII.593), he remarks.

Nor are the symbol's purely biological implications neglected, as both authors draw upon popular banquet tradition. Granted, Pantagruel's shipboard feast may begin with epistemological discussion ("tous problèmes . . . doibvent estre certains" [QL.LXIII.715]), but it concludes in ambivalent comedy: "Advisez, amis, si vos doubtes sont à plein résoluz (LXIV.719). . . . Remède jusques à præsent n'a esté trouvé contre la male femme" (LXV.720). Ironically, this uncertain "femme," object of Panurge's quest as a metaphor for absolute truth, and the materialistic play on words—"plein" as indication of full stomach, "femme" as near-homonym of "faim"—produce a seesaw debate between spiritual appetite and biological appeasement. Between Socratic initiation and anticipated apocalypse, drink becomes a way to "haulser le temps," to make "bon cher" within tragic confines. Related as they are to death, both banquets at the end of the *Furioso* form part of a physical as well as literary cycle. The first follows Brandimarte's funeral (XLIII) and provides bodily consolation to the mourners, thereby redirecting the voyage in more creative directions. Occasioned by the marriage of Ruggiero and Bradamante, the last feast begins on a jubilant, generative note and terminates with the death of Rodomonte (XLVI).

The traditional romance conception of woman is also evoked in both Orlando's and Panurge's quests. On a superficial level, undoubtedly, the Italian and French poets would appear to stand on opposite sides of the fence post. While the idealized Angelica is a travesty of courtly convention and the *donna angelicata*, Panurge's Gallic obsession with cuckoldry, which Rondibilis moreover seconds, stems from a popularly held pejorative attitude toward women. It is because of her dual symbolism, however, already polemicized in the *Querelle des Femmes*, that the woman provides Rabelais and Ariosto a perfect vehicle for both voyage and countervoyage. She is the "other" who is at once the same, who enjoys both negative and positive connotations.

To all intents and purposes, Panurge is also pursuing an angelic lady, an unspecified paragon of virtue who is, ironically, no more ephemeral than Orlando's conception of Angelica; and if the Gallic monk's celebrated antifeminism is tinged with romance idealism, so does his Italian predecessor mock woman's overspiritualized symbolic value by depicting her as a fallible, flesh-and-blood creature. Moreover, complementary and contradictory characters enforce the fragmentation of prototypical females. A sympathetic portrait of Gargamelle (G.III,IV,VI) and evocation of virtuous womanhood (TL.XXX.438) counterbalance Rondibilis's derision, while evil women such as Gabrina and heroic ones such as Bradamante and Marfisa add realistic complexity to Ariosto's borrowed metaphor. Far removed from their courtly counterparts, the Cretan women (XIX–XX) who kill their sons and lovers also serve a double polemic function: on the one hand, they reverse the laws and social codes which discriminate against women, while, on the other hand, they effectively neutralize the *donna angelicata's* positive symbolic value. The mystical lady's epistemological promise, as epitomized by Dante's Beatrice, is furthermore undermined by references to Eve (XI.22,XXVII.13), whose excessive thirst for knowledge merited expulsion from the Garden of Eden.

Woman is traditionally linked with man's exile from the Absolute, be it Eden, the Androgyne, or the womb itself. In this context, one notes the recurrence of mother-child imagery in Rabelais and Ariosto, used to express both initial security and the pathos of cleavage.[45] Even as his voyage goes forward, man seeks a return to this idyllic past through reintegration with the female. "Nous voyons bon nombre de gens tant heureux à ceste rencontre," says Pantagruel, "qu'en leur mariage semble reluire quelque idée et repræsentation des joyes de paradis" (TL.X.361). Not only do Panurge and Orlando seek ideal partners, but the entire utopian venture revolves around this proposed recoupling of the sexes, which the voyage both promotes and postpones. Panurge, Ruggiero, and Pantagruel all defer their nuptials until the end of their odysseys. This hesitation to marry may be partially explained by the experience of Orlando, whose idealistic commitment to Angelica makes him vulnerable to a comparable degree of disenchantment. Both Panurge's desire for happiness and his fear of disillusionment, symbolized in both works by the lover's potential infidelity, are projected onto his future wife. If marriage is sometimes a paradisiac state, says Pantagruel, so can it be equally hellish: "Aultres y sont tant malheureux que les diables qui tentent les hermites par les désers de Thébaïde et Monserrat ne le sont dadventaige" (361).

At best, marriage is the defective temporal equivalent of prelapsarian unity and, as such, involves a commitment to reality incompatible with the characters' youthful dreams and desires. Accordingly, the residents of Thélème pass their adolescence in the cloister, leaving both the abbey and their childhood behind when they wed. In his Fifth Satire, Ariosto advises men to marry at the age of thirty (194) to a woman of "mediocre forma" (170), far removed from the idealized object of his characters' immature passions. In the Furioso, the postvoyage marriage involves an acceptance of human fallibility on two levels. In refusing to question his wife's fidelity, Rinaldo accepts the possibility that she may be unfaithful. Intended as it is for a generational perpetuation of the self, secondly, Ruggiero's marriage implies a

45. I.34,53;XII.1–2;XVIII.14–15;P.III.181–82; and TL.XLVIII.497.

recognition of individual mortality and, thus, a reaffirmation of the original Fall.

References to original sin, together with utopian elements and the recurring *locus amoenus*, help articulate the voyage as a quest for lost paradise. Several motifs often associated with this theme are scattered throughout both works. The kingdoms of Alcina, Logistilla, and Saint John the Evangelist, like many of the *Quart Livre* ports of call, are characterized by idyllic landscapes, fertile territory, remoteness in time and space, and gem-studded castles which have become part of the Earthly Paradise tradition in literature.[46] And while these topoi are not united in any single Rabelaisian kingdom, with the possible exceptions of Thélème and Lanternois, it is interesting to note their separate diffusion throughout the *Quart Livre*. Utopian explorers are struck by the salubrious landscapes of Cheli ("grande, fertile, riche et populeuse" [X.566]) and Gaster's realm ("tant plaisant, tant fertile, tant salubre et délicieux" [LVII.695]); by the Papimanes' ornate temple ("couvert de fines et précieuses pierres" [XLIX.671]) and abundance of food ("la repaissaille feut copieuse et les beuvettes numereuses" [LI. 676]); and by the exotic animals ("divers animaulx, poissons, oizeaulx et aultres marchandises exotiques" [II.543]) at Medamothi. Rabelais's choice to balance this commonplace portrait of bountiful nature with desert scenes, in the lands of the Macræons ("par la forest umbrageuse et déserte" [XXV.610]) and the Papefigues ("le pays estoit resté désert" [XLV.661]) moreover strengthens the paradisiac thrust of his voyage by creating a tension between the prelapsarian and the postlapsarian. The old Macrobe's version of the Fall, the war with the sausage-serpents, and the Papefigues' eternal punishment for the sins of their fathers (661) serve as reminders of man's alienation from Eden. Conversely, the above-mentioned topoi, along with specific, albeit negative, allusions to the Earthly Paradise ("que je pensoys estre le vray Jardin et Paradis terrestre" [695]) and Parnassus ("mons Antiparnasse" [LXVI.725]), constantly posit the Garden as an implicit and perhaps even unconscious goal of the quest.

The ultimate object of this Edenic venture is the restoration of primordial harmony and the reconciliation of such postlapsarian oppositions as celestial and terrestrial, innocence and experience, infinity

---

46. See A. Bartlett Giamatti, *The Earthly Paradise and the Renaissance Epic* (Princeton, N.J.: Princeton University Press, 1966), pp. 11–93.

and the finite. By diffusing paradisiac scenes over a variety of kingdoms Ariosto and Rabelais do not resolve these contradictions but rather affirm conflict and separation. The existence of false paradises, which promise revelation but result in deception, is not of course unusual in allegorical or epic literature.[47] Of this variety are Alcina and the *Quart Livre* islands, which all derive whatever semblance of harmony they may possess from the abnegation rather than authentic unification of contradictions. The sensual fate's idyllic life style effectively excludes the rational and the spiritual, while the Papimanes' homogeneity of beliefs is achieved only by suppressing the Papefigues' skepticism; and Panigon's peace, only by stifling hostilities under an elaborate code of etiquette. Far from affording man a glimpse of the transcendent reality he seeks, these artificial paradises merely enfold their inhabitants in terrestrial illusions. Likewise, their internal stability derives not from the sublimation of conflicts in infinity but from the banishment of antitheses to the outside of these closed structures. Their "other" is to be found in the realms of Logistilla, Basché, and the Papefigues.

If the false paradise is a trap, it is also a natural and necessary part of the traditional allegorical progression, which generally outlines a period of purification and self-analysis. Although this voyage, epitomized by the *Divine Comedy*, may take its external form from the Earthly Paradise myth, it is also aimed at the moral beatification of the voyager—the creation of a "paradise within"—and at preparation of the soul for the celestial paradise. From this perspective it is necessary that Ruggiero and Astolfo experience the worldly pleasures of Alcina before rejecting them for the nobler Reason, embodied by Logistilla. Likewise in Rabelais such clearly symbolic ports of call as Quaresmeprenant, Mardigras, and Ruach may also be viewed as stages of the soul's internal odyssey. Yet the poet's own artistry contravenes the potential teleological progression that tradition would lead us to expect. As the talespinner warms to his subject, he "neglects" allegorical logic and gives free reign to autonomous fiction, seduced by his own false paradises. Although Logistilla supersedes her sister chronologically, Alcina's longer and more detailed description ensures her continued ascendancy in the reader's mind. Despite her apparent godliness, Logistilla's short-livedness, insipidity, and apparent use of artifice (X.60) suggest that she too may be a false, or at least imperfect, paradise. More radically, Rabelais blocks the moral valuation of one

47. The term is borrowed from Giamatti, pp. 85–86 et passim.

realm over another by subordinating the islands' allegorical value and content to diversional forms and unbridled satire. His propensity for these nontranscendent elements precludes the sustained movement toward or the establishment of any paradise other than a purely verbal one.

Astolfo, of course, arrives at the Earthly Paradise en route to the moon (XXXIV), while Messere Gaster's kingdom, near the end of the *Quart Livre*, is explicitly compared to the Garden (695). Thus these two episodes may well be regarded as apices of the paradisiac thrust. Both kingdoms are attained after long, strenuous climbs, finding their historical roots in longstanding geographical (Astolfo ascends from the Nile) and theological ("duquel tant disputent et labourent les bons théologiens" [LVII.695]) speculation. The incorporation into these descriptions of attributes generally associated with paradise does not ensure their transcendence but rather finds justification in contemporary reality. Renaissance explorers kept watch for this legendary spot and even used it as a yardstick to measure their concrete discoveries. Conversely, the authors "upgrade" their visions of paradise by making it comparable to their own highly developed civilization. The materialistic realization of these two scenes is no less utopian than paradisiac and reflects a revaluation of the terrestrial typical of the age. Ariosto's vivid external description of Saint John's garden, like Rabelais's tribute to the Maistre ès Ars, appears more laudatory of human achievements than anticipatory of the divine. This apparent willingness to visualize a heaven not too different from Renaissance culture may, however, be translated, less positively, as an inability to visualize anything else. Their overemphasis of pure physicality—Ariosto's allusions to banal human necessities ("Poi ch'a natura il duca aventuroso / satisfece di quel che se le debbe" [XXXIV.61]) and Messere Gaster's "tout pour la trippe!"—act to negate the sublime, mocking man's every effort to transcend.

The revelations that emerge from the paradisiac quest are, characteristically, of ambiguous import. Far from being resolved in the kingdoms of Gaster or Saint John the Evangelist, basic antitheses—creation and destruction, wisdom and folly, free will and predestination—are thrown into self-reversing uncertainty. Astolfo's netherworld, an apparently Christian realm of merit and reward, is incongruously graced by the Fates (XXXIV.89); and the monstrous Gaster, who creates and devours, could, like most of the initiators, embody either God or man.

Not just here, but throughout the entire allegorical sequence, the authors suspend readers between metaphysical and purely terrestrial interpretations, between figurative and literal readings of the text. In Quaresmeprenant, "fouetteur de petitz enfans" (XXIX.620), Rabelais not only satirizes hypocritical devotion and tyranny but also conjures up visions of a merciless god; and the fate Alcina, the figurative representation of *voluptas*, doubles as a flesh-and-blood woman.

Because of their anomalous development and unstable symbolism, the multiple preparadises are never eclipsed by or subordinated to successive episodes in the progression but generate a tension reflective of the artists' own uncertainty. Try as one may to mold the myriad realms into a meaningful hierarchical sequence, no schema ever quite fits. Just as the writer can never differentiate between terrestrial and celestial, sensual and intellectual ideals, neither can he integrate them all into a single, lasting vision. Although intrigued by Eden, the reign of Saturn, and the Mount of Virtue, the poet is himself at a conceptual loss. How can he even imagine a flawless world, having experienced only the defective?

Normally an imaginary voyage evades or transcends; yet Rabelais and Ariosto use the fantastic to unveil reality, not only mythfied heroics but life's more dismal aspects as well. For the elusive other—sought after in exotic lands, utopian dreams, and the fiction itself—is never totally realized, even in the most far-fetched scenes.[48] Alcofribas Nasier's gastroworld inquest reveals a haunting replica of his own land, where workers struggle to earn a living and where "l'on se meurt . . . tant que le charriot court par les rues" (P.XXXII.307). Similarly, the netherworlds which Épistémon and Astolfo visit, like those of Lucian, are merely reflections of a mixed-up world which man can neither alter nor escape; and the *Quart Livre* islands are caricatures of our universally close-minded societies.[49] They are mirrors, but not of the transcendent, Platonic-Christian variety. The voyage is a constant confrontation of man and his other self—his "semblable" and "frère"—in a dome-like world which rebuffs all quests for the Ideal.

A reversal of traditional heroic quests, the Ariostan and Rabelaisian

48. Similarly, Rabelais's letter to Jean Du Bellay from Lyon, in regard to his visit in Rome, reveals his failure to find "otherness" and "newness" in the Italian city: "Plantas autem nullas, sed nec animantia ulla habet Italia, quæ non ante nobis & visa essent & nota" (p. 969).

49. Alfred Glauser, *Rabelais créateur* (Paris: Nizet, 1966), p. 239.

odysseys are less progressive than self-negating; stymied on earth, the here-and-now quest must seek outlet in the beyond, while the transcendental thrust is deflected back down to reality. This circular voyage structure, however, does not fail to communicate an "apocalyptical" message of its own. The recurring cruelty and death are not merely reflective of the sixteenth century but take on the exaggerated relief of superreality. The Franco-Italian conflicts of the Renaissance have merged with Charlemagne's defense of Paris, with Picrochole's attack on Utopia, with the Andouilles' magical maneuvers; and only War, the raw essence, remains. Accordingly, the "past time" which Astolfo and Épistémon retrieve is not paradisiac innocence but eternal and self-perpetuating folly. All oppositions—heaven and hell, good and evil, laughter and tears—are swallowed up by the vast organism of life itself, as the "island" earth (like Alcina's whale) is jerked from apparent fixity, thrust out into chaos, and transformed into one mammoth Ship of Fools.

II. MYTH AND FANTASY

The Renaissance's most celebrated examples of myth and fantasy are, justifiably, the classical gods, goddesses, nymphs, and heroes that flourish in the art of that era. Poliziano's *Stanze* and *Orfeo*, Botticelli's *Birth of Venus* and *Allegory of Spring*, Michelangelo's *Bacchus*, and Jean Lemaire de Belges's *Illustrations de Gaule et Singularitéz de Troye* are only a few of the numerous manifestations of this phenomenon. Quite clearly, this "resurrection" of the pagan divinities is concomitant with the renewed surge of humanism and contributes to Renaissance man's own mythification. For while much classical myth does survive during the Middle Ages, subordinated to Christian philosophy, it undergoes a radical transformation during the succeeding era.[1] Certainly the ancient fables continue in many instances to function allegorically but they also gain new appreciation as artifacts to be honored for their antiquity and esthetic value alone. In both their form and content, moreover, they serve as both the inspiration for and the instrument of a new mythology—that of man-conquering and man-progressing. The influence of classical art helps restore to man his spark of divinity; he models gods in his own image, borrows names from ancient heroes, and traces his lineage back to Greece and Troy. These contemporary practices are reflected in Rabelais and Ariosto, who not only compare their protagonists and princes—Pantagruel and the Estensi—to gods and heroes, but also count Hercules and Hector among their ancestors.

Intertwined with this Olympian constellation of forms and figures in Rabelais and Ariosto are rudiments of the Middle Ages' intellec-

1. See Jean Seznec, *The Survival of the Pagan Gods*, trans. Barbara F. Sessions, Bollingen Series 38 (Princeton, N.J.: Princeton University Press, 1953).

tualized allegory and variations on a number of standard initiatory motifs. Combined as they are with the Renaissance myths of knowledge, progress, and humanism itself, these diverse traditions will ostensibly coalesce to generate a new mythology which is at once transcendent and authentic. Ideally, it will affirm man's stature, resolve his moral and metaphysical problems, and provide him a vision for the future which is consistent with past and present experiences.[2]

For the Gallic and Ferrarese artists, however, this overmythification constitutes an inverse demystification. By juxtaposing ascending and descending symbolism, deforming classical figures and sequences for satirical purposes, and consistently destroying positive or solar archetypes, the poets restore negativity to a frequently overoptimistic world view. While authorial irony, on one level, appears to signal a victory of the nonmythic over the mythic consciousness, on another level one may attribute this subversion of collective fantasies to a war between the different kinds of myth themselves: between the rational and the imaginative, the negative and the positive, the meaningful and nonmeaningful, the truthful and the untruthful. Myth is, after all, ontologically ambiguous. If, on the one hand, it is thought to be a symbolic code for some higher meaning, it may also be defined as nonsignificant narration or fantasy instead of fact.[3] It is by exploiting this definitional multiplicity that the poets mock their culture's fondest illusions and, in so doing, provoke in the reader a critical reaction to what he assumes to be fact.

2. "On the one hand, a myth always refers to events alleged to have taken place a long time ago. But what gives the myth an operational value is that the specific pattern described is timeless; it explains the present and the past as well as the future." Claude Lévi-Strauss, "The Structural Study of Myth" in "Myth, a Symposium," *Journal of American Folklore* 78 (1955), 428–44; rpt. in *Structural Anthropology*, trans. Claire Jacobson and Brooke Grundfest Schoepf (New York: Basic Books, 1963), p. 209.

3. "Mitologies" are defined, for example, as "fabuleuses narrations" in the *Briefve Déclaration* (p. 737). Some ambiguity is generated by the term "fabuleuses," however, which, like "myth," enjoys meaningful and nonmeaningful connotations. On the one hand, Edmond Huguet defines "mythologiser" positively, as "expliquer allégoriquement" (V.388), but its synonym "fabuleux" has patently negative associations: "fabulosité" is defined in one sense as "mensonge" (IV.2). *Dictionnaire de la langue française du seizième siècle*, vols. 4 and 5 (Paris: Didier, 1950 and 1961). For an outline of myth's multiple definitions, see Harry Levin, "Some Meanings of Myth," *Daedalus* 88, no. 2 (Spring 1959): 223–31; rpt. in *Myth and Mythmaking*, ed. Henry A. Murray (Boston: Beacon Press, 1968), pp. 103–14.

GODS, HEROES, AND BEASTS

During the Renaissance classical antiquity comes to represent a kind of absolute, and its figurants idealized points of reference which facilitate the artist's encomium of sixteenth-century achievements. Particularly fascinating to the humanists are the ancient gods and goddesses, whom they enthusiastically restore to an honored place in contemporary art and literature. And while this transposed pagan mythology must obviously not be taken literally, as a substitute for the Middle Ages' Christian beliefs, neither is it purely ornamental. The classical divinities do function as ideals which help Renaissance man develop and express, figuratively, his own modern, and apparently heroic, mythology. Since man, in the "Éloge du pantagruelion" and in the aerial odysseys of Ruggiero and Astolfo, is depicted as a volatile, aggressive creature, one logically expects that his "patron" divinity or hero will be equally solar. Superficially, at least, Rabelais and Ariosto do not disappoint us: for if Prometheus is noticeably absent from their works, Apollo, Jupiter, Hercules, and Mars recur time after time, as do, to a lesser extent, prototypic voyagers such as Jason, Ulysses, and Aeneas. More important than the mere quantitative dominance of these seemingly positive figures, however, is their qualitative use within specific passages and their overall juxtaposition with aquatic, vegetative, and generally less positive myths.

Since the Ariostan and Rabelaisian odysseys are, to some extent, based upon those of the ancient mythographers, the author's attitude toward these epic heroes quite naturally reflects upon Renaissance man, in a manner which, however, varies. Encomiastic comparison of the Argonauts and modern-day explorers (XV.21), one of Ariosto's best-known classical allusions, is in fact atypical in its perfect and positive analogy, and is moreover rendered ambiguous by a network of related, although contradictory, myth. If the mention of Jason conjures up glorious travel images, it also brings to mind the cruelty of Medea (III.52,XXI.56) and sorrowful visions along the route:

> Non piú a Iason di maraviglia denno,
> né agli Argonauti che venian con lui,
> le donne che i mariti morir fenno
> e i figli e i padri coi fratelli sui,
> sí che per tutta l'isola di Lenno
> di viril faccia non si vider dui.   (XXXVII.36)

A similar literary fate befalls Rabelais's Ulysses, who makes his first appearance in the *Pantagruel* on a note of inferiority (Panurge's adventures "sont plus merveilleuses que celles de Ulysses" [IX.213]) and then reappears in a sequence of unfavorable contexts. He is a harvester in hell (P.XXX.297), a murderer (G.XXXVI.108), foodless (TL.II.336), absent and thus potentially cuckold (TL.L.502), a prisoner (QL.VIII.560), dependent upon the waves of fortune (QL.XXI.600), and degraded by the obscene deformation of his bag of winds (QL.XLIII.657).

Fragmentation of heroic models also occurs at Olympian levels, as commonly accepted symbols of strength and valor are toppled from their pedestals and their analogical value neutralized. Ariosto's various references to Mars provide a capital example of this syndrome. Despite their quantitative predominance encomiastic similitudes used to elevate warriors by association with the god of war, such as Marfisa's belief that the valiant Ruggiero "fosse Marte / sceso dal quinto cielo in quella parte" (XXVI.20), are offset by two significant negative allusions. Astolfo's rather burlesque trapping of Caligorante is, first of all, compared to the ensnarement of Mars by Vulcan (XV.56). While such an analogy might be expected to elevate Asolfo's exploit to an Olympian level, the latter is itself quite literally debased: using the same bantering style that comicized the paladin's heroics, Ariosto emphasizes the physical details ("già piedi e mano/ avea legate a Venere et a Marte") of the divine lovers' entrapment and "builds up" to their prone position ("insieme ambi nel letto"). The parallels between Astolfo's trapped giant and Mars further implies an ascendancy of Renaissance man over the classical gods, an interpretation which finds support in a second textual reference to the war god: Orlando's feats are of such a magnitude "da far tremar nel ciel Marte" (IX.79). While this human threat to Olympia lacks the burlesque development it will find in Rabelais's "Éloge du pantagruelion" (TL.LI.509), the conceptual structure underlying both passages is the same.

Even more striking, in Rabelais, is the ambivalent literary treatment of Hercules, the adopted forefather of Gallic humanism.[4] Like other contemporaries of his, the French monk exploits the demigod's hyperbolic infancy, transmitting it hereditarily to Gargantua and Pantagruel (P. I.175). The most explicit verbalization of this analogy, how-

4. For a discussion of Hercules and Renaissance humanism, see Marc-René Jung, *Hercule dans la littérature française du XVIe siècle*, Travaux d'Humanisme et Renaissance 79 (Geneva: Droz, 1966).

ever, proffered by Panurge during Pantagruel's duel with Loup Garou, tips the balance in Renaissance man's favor and is uttered in a language and tone so irreverent that humanism's overall deification of the ancients is satirically undermined: "—C'est (dist Panurge) bien chié en mon nez; vous comparez-vouz à Hercules? Vous avez, par Dieu, plus de force aux dentz et plus de sens au cul que n'eut jamais Hercules en tout son corps et âme" (P.XXIX.289).

On the one hand, this vulgarization of classical myth, a simultaneous familiarization and degradation, is an end in itself, a polemic rejection of the Renaissance's obsessive interest in trumped-up genealogies, of their indiscriminate valuing of antiquity over modernity. By varying the context of their myth and regenerating tragic as well as heroic fables, failures as well as successes, Ariosto and Rabelais restore inflated ancient prototypes to an existential setting; and stylistic deformation furthers the demystification process, as irony and vulgar contexts create a critical distance between reader and classical allusions. When he places ancient stories in the mouth of Medoro, a simple Arab shepherd (XVIII.185), Ariosto at once strips the fable of its sanctity and parodies the equally incongruous cult of classical myth in the sixteenth century. The satirical implications of this misplaced myth are made more explicit in Rabelais, where Panurge and the narrator persist in "materializing" epic figures, in contaminating them with mercenary and biological overtones. At their hands the golden bough is reduced to monetary dimensions (TL.XVII.388), allusions to the judgment of Paris used to court the "haulte dame de Paris" (P.XXI.261), and the Trojan horse associated with Pantagruel's regurgitation of some man-powered capsules:

> Pantagruel se parforce de rendre sa gorge, et facillement les mist dehors, et ne se monstoyent en sa gorge en plus qu'un pet en la vostre, et là sortirent hors de leurs pillules joyeusement—il me souvenoit quand les Gregeoys sortirent du cheval en Troye;—et par ce moyen fut guéry et réduict à sa première convalescence.
>
> (P.XXXIII.311)

Frequently, the apparent denigration of heroes and gods merely enforces the poet's aggrandizement of his own characters and, by extension, of contemporary man. It is in keeping with the narrator's hyperbolic propensities, in fact, that he should supplement comparisons of equality with those in which mortals, and not heaven, are the superlative term. Such is the case in several of the preceding examples, including Rabelais's mockery of Hercules, Orlando's potential intimidation of Mars, and the anticipated unseating of Olympian gods in the "Éloge du pantagruelion." Both authors have restructured the "antica guerra" (XI.46), pitting the new Titans now against the sky (TL.LI.509), now against the oceanic divinities:

> Rimbombano al rumor ch'intorno s'ode,
> le selve, i monti e le lontane prode.
>
> Fuor de la grotta il vecchio Proteo, quando
> ode tanto rumor, sopra il mare esce;
> e visto entrare e uscir de l'orca Orlando,
> e al lito trar sí smisurato pesce,
> fugge per l'alto occeano, oblïando
> lo sparso gregge: et sí il tumulto cresce,
> che fatto al carro i suoi delfini porre,
> quel dí Nettunno in Etïopia corre.   (XI.43–44)

Thus one infers that the denigration of ancient divinities, heroes, and heroics reflects doubly upon contemporary feats, not only depreciating them through similitude but also, as in this instance, glorifying them by force of contrast.

Mythical prototypes serve as a referent not only to physical prowess but to ideals of wisdom and beauty as well. In his third canto, however, Ariosto establishes "Pallade" as a symbol of strength and sagacity only to deflate her force and, by extension, that of Bradamante:

> —Se tu fossi . . . Pallade o Marte,
> e conducessi gente alla tua paga
> piú che non ha il re Carlo e il re Agramante,
> non dureresti contra il negromante.   (66)

Here the Renaissance myth of strength and reason is undermined by its irrational double, a belief in negromancy and magic. The meaning of this dichotomy is, however, somewhat obscured by the magus's alternate connection with books, potential figures of reason, and by his rational opponent's concomitant association with the irrational *maga* Melissa. Similarly ambiguous is Rabelais's *Tiers Livre* reference to Minerva, which appears to ordain the value of studies as a weapon in the "antica guerra":

Quant les géantz entreprindrent guerre contre les Dieux, les Dieux
au commencement se mocquèrent de tels ennemis, e disoient qu'il
n'y en avoit pas pour leurs pages. Mais, quand ilz veirent par le
labeur des Géantz le noms Pelion posé dessus le mons Osse et jà
esbranlé le noms Olympe pour estre mis au dessus des deux, feurent tous effrayéz. Adoncques tint Juppiter chapitre général. Là
feut conclud de tous les Dieux qu'ilz se mettroient vertueusement
en défence. Et pource qu ilz avoient plusieurs foys veu les batailles
perdues par l'empeschement des femmes qui estoient parmy les
armées, feut décrété que, pour l'heure, on chasseroit des cieulx
en Ægypte et vers les confins du Nil toute ceste vessaille des
Déesses desguisées en beletes, fouines, ratepenades, museraignes
et aultres métamorphoses. Seule Minerve feut de retenue pour
fouldroier avecques Juppiter, comme Déesse des lettres et de
guerre, de conseil et exécution, Déesse née armée, Déesse re-
doubtée on ciel, en l'air, en la mer et en terre.   (TL.XII.367)

The qualitative and quantitative hyberbole of this Olympian fable inevitably conjures up its own negation, however, in Panurge's reaction
to Pallas from a human standpoint, in his slur upon her beauty and
common sense: "Ce sort dénote que ma femme sera preude, pudicque
et loyalle, non mie armée, rebousse, ne écervelée et extraicte de cervelle
comme Pallas" (368). Venus's own contradictory connotations in the
Furioso also reflect Renaissance man's ambiguous attitude toward the
ideals she represents. Upon one occasion she is a gauge of feminine pul-
chritude (I.52), yet upon another she appears as a symbol of that sloth-
ful decadence associated, contemporarily, with courtesans (XXXV.21).[5]

At this point our initial hypothesis concerning the predominance of
solar deities must be slightly modified. If the poets do speak most often
of Jupiter, Hercules, Apollo, and company, they also incorporate myriad other gods into their fiction, mobilizing the Olympian ideal and
descending the gamut of its hierarchy. Despite their apparently positive rank, Venus and Minerva are already departures from the diurnal

5. Although Venus tends to undergo a positive reincarnation in the Renaissance,
as witnessed by Botticelli's Venere, her negative connotations do of course preexist the Furioso. As Seznec indicates (p. 22), she is decried by Polidoro Virgilio,
in his De rerum inventoribus (Venice, 1499), for teaching the courtesans their art
(III.17). For an interesting discussion on the "twin Venuses"—Venere Celeste and
Venere Volgare—of Neoplatonic philosophy and related works of art, see Erwin
Panofsky, Studies in Iconology (1939; rpt. New York: Harper Torchbooks, 1962),
pp. 129–69.

mode, inasmuch as they are female, thus possessed of an ambiguous, mutable, and potentially negative symbolism. Equally subversive are the clusters of aquatic, biological, and vegetative deities. Neptune, Proteus, and the Tritons on one hand, Ceres and Bacchus on the other, are all anthropologically associated with cycle and recur throughout the text. This deification of impermanence itself, a potential tribute to Renaissance dynamism, takes on ironic overtones when viewed in a broader mythological context. One of myth's primary functions is to transcend the temporal by intuition of the eternal, to serve as an antidote for change.[6]

Mere mention of nonsolar gods, in itself, of course, is not conclusive proof of subversive intentions on the narrator's part. Undoubtedly, such references are frequently more ornamental than meaningful and seem more clearly connected to the artist's momentary fancies than with discursive or metaphorical exigencies. In itself, however, this alienation of the gods from their significant origins constitutes an act of apostasy, a radical step toward the "floating" of absolute values. Rabelais and Ariosto have not even animated the pagan deities as characters within their fiction, as do a number of Renaissance writers, but rather only use them rhetorically as names. Thus refusing to be seduced by the classical divinities or to grant them any degree of textual autonomy, the artist maintains a critical distance toward, and hence mastery over, them. If the writer appears to draw inspiration and dignity for his work from the stellar figures, it is more accurately he who is in command and they who owe their resurrection to his whim.

The poet is God and the gods his slaves—rhetorical figures which he has pulled from his bag of literary tricks. This subordination of classical sources to the Renaissance poet's imagination is particularly evident in the following passage, a description of Angelica's flight from Rinaldo, which finds its origins in Ovid's tale of Jupiter and Europa:

6. See Gilbert Durand, *Les Structures anthropologiques de l'imaginaire*, 2d ed. (Paris: Presses Universitaires de France, 1963), p. 405: "Recherche du temps perdu, et surtout effort compréhensif de réconciliation avec un temps euphémisé et avec la mort vaincue ou transmutée en aventure, paradisiaque, tel apparaît bien le sens inducteur dernier de tous les grands mythes." Cf. Philip Rahv, "The Myth and the Powerhouse," *Partisan Review* 20 (1953): 635–48; rpt. in *Myth and Literature*, ed. John B. Vickery (Lincoln: University of Nebraska Press, 1966), p. 111: "The one essential function of myth stressed by all writers is that in merging past and present it releases us from the flux of temporality, arresting change in the timeless, the permanent, the ever-recurrent conceived as 'sacred repetition.' Hence the mythic is the polar opposite of what we mean by the historical, which stands for process, inexorable change, incessant permutation and innovation."

Per tirar briglia, non gli può dar volta:
piú et piú sempre quel si caccia in alto.
Ella tenea la vesta in su raccolta
per non bagnarla, e traea i piedi in alto.
Per le spalle la chioma iva disciolta,
e l'aura le facea lascivo assalto.
Stavano cheti tutti i maggior venti,
forse a tanta beltà, col mare, attenti.   (VIII.36)

Stripped of both its classical figurants and its medieval allegorical
meaning, this borrowed tableau serves in one sense as an incidental
embellishment and, in another, as a primitive carving which the Renaissance artist sculpts to perfection.[7]

It is not so much the content as the form of the artist-God rapport
which interests us, and which, by virtue of its reversibility, belongs to
that same network of mutating values manifested within the Olympian
spheres. This pulverization of the Great Chain of Being and the implicit
equalization of antitheses is further extended to the animal level. The
artist is just as likely to compare his hero to a beast as to a god, metaphorically vacillating between the extreme terms of existence. Granted,
the use of zoological similitudes is itself a borrowing from the classical
epics, in which the lion or wild boar served as affirmative figures of
strength and courage. Ariosto's version of this analogy is so phrased
that his heroes "outdo" the diurnal beasts and, implicitly, the classical
heroes that are merely their equals: "Non si vanno i leoni o i tori in
salto / a dar di petto, ad accozzar sí crudi, / sí come i duo guerrieri al
fiero assalto" (I.62). Already in the second canto, however, the substitution of "can mordenti" (5) for the animals commonly used in such
a comparison acts to reduce the duelers' stature. By virtue of its originality the new metaphor seeks its field of reference not in its positive
classical models but in the negative theme of bestiality.

Just as the gods vary in Rabelais and Ariosto, so does their menagerie
contain within it the most disparate beasts, which differ in both size
and symbolism. Victims in both works are compared to frogs (IX.69,
XIV.46;P.XXIX.294), which, because of their reptilian mutations and

7. As Panofsky points out (pp. 29–30), the Renaissance version of the scene
is far removed from its medieval allegorization in the *Ovide moralisé*, which gives
the *Metamorphoses* Christian interpretations. Both life and sensuality are restored
to the myth by Poliziano and Dürer, for example—by the one in his *Giostra*,
(I.105–06) and by the other in a drawing inspired by the Florentine's stanzas.

the fluctuating waters in which they are found, are traditional figures of cycle and instability.[8] Nor do their conquerors always fare substantially better. Both Panurge and Pantagruel are likened, upon occasion, to members of the lower species, one to a "chat maigre" (P.XIV.227) and the other to an "asne qu'on sangle trop fort" (P.XIII.225). This second analogy is, of course, a burlesque variation upon the more positive horse symbolism, which is further perverted in both works. Instead of man being equated with the metaphorical horse, which has been personified and highly valued in medieval literature, one finds him being upstaged by and subordinated to his own beast of burden. Rinaldo's stallion Baiardo, who "avea intelletto umano" (II.20), leads his master to Angelica, while, similarly, Gargantua's prowess is demystified through transposition to a horse (G.XXXVI.107), or worse still, to a horse's *tail* (G.XVI.52–53).

Taking this descending metaphorical pattern out of context, one would conclude that the authors are merely satirizing the Renaissance's overaggrandizement of man, a judgment which is, however, only partially correct. This downward metamorphosis of man must be coupled with its upward twin, the Olympian comparisons, and considered as part of an heuristic, if self-negating, system. In other words, gods and animals are the ultimate figurative terms of an inquest into the stature of man—into Rabelais's problematic "propre de l'homme," which will find philosophical expression more than a century later in the *Pensées* of Pascal: "L'homme ne sait à quel rang se mettre."[9]

This quantitative and qualitative dialectic corresponds to the contrasting syndromes of gigantification and "gulliverization," which

---

8. Durand, p. 430.

9. *Pensées*, ed. Léon Brunschvicg (Paris: Garnier, 1948), no. 427, p. 177. For Pico della Mirandola, of course, man's indeterminate rank is a measure not of his misery but of his dignity: "Statuit tandem optimus opifex, ut cui dare nihil proprium poterat commune esset quicquid privatum singulis fuerat. Igitur hominem accepit indiscretae opus imaginis atque in mundi positum meditullio sic est alloquutus: 'Nec certam sedem, nec propriam faciem, nec munus ullum peculiare tibi dedimus, o Adam, ut quam sedem, quam faciem, quae munera tute optaveris, ea, pro voto, tua sententia, habeas et possideas. Definita ceteris natura intra praescriptas a nobis legis coercetur. Tu, nullis angustiis coercitus, pro tuo arbitrio, in cuius manu te posui, tibi illam praefinies. Medium te mundi posui, ut circumspiceres inde commodius quicquid est in mundo. Nec te caelestum neque terrenum, neque mortalem neque immortalem fecimus, ut tui ipsius quasi arbitrarius honorariusque plastes et fictor, in quam malueris tute forman effingas. Poteris in inferiora quae sunt divina ex tui animi sententia regenerari.' " *Oratio de hominis dignitate*, ed. Eugenio Garin, trans. Elizabeth Livermore (Lexington, Ky.: Anvil Press, 1953), pp. 3–4.

frequently distinguish diurnal and nocturnal thought patterns.[10] Instead of working within one modality, however, Rabelais and Ariosto vacillate between the two world visions, in an exploratory and inquisitive manner. In their works man soars not just to Olympia but unseats Zeus himself, appears as both giant and dwarf, and is metamorphosed not merely into an animal but into mammal, amphibian, and even insect:

> Simil battaglia fa la mosca audace
> contra il mastin nel polveroso agosto,
> o nel mese dinanzi o nel seguace,
> l'uno di spiche e l'altro pien di mosto:
> negli occhi il punge e nel grifo mordace,
> volagli intorno e gli sta sempre accosto;
> e quel suonar fa spesso il dente asciutto:
> ma un tratto che gli arrivi, appaga il tutto. (X.105)

Rabelais pursues this insect analogy to its differential extreme, uniting both ends of the Great Chain of Being in a single, subversive simile: "A ces motz, tous les vénérables Dieux et Déesses s'éclatèrent de rire comme un microcosme de mouches" (QL.prol. 533).[11] In this vision one sees that not only man but gods as well are subjected to definitional scrutiny.

THE DEFORMATION OF STANDARD QUEST FORMS

If comparisons with figures from classical mythology do not affirm the superhuman stature of man, neither do allegorical or initiatory motifs and sequences arrive at their anticipated end. Although they appear consistent with the Renaissance myths of knowledge and

---

10. Durand, pp. 223–27.
11. Folengo is also fond of frog and fly imagery:

> Quali praestezza tordus se in rete viluppat,
> sive ad porrectum trat rana golosa boconem
> moscaque multipedis gathiatur compedi ragni,
> tali veschiatur Bertae Tognazzus amore. (VII.76–78)

Il Baldo, ed. Giampaolo Dossena (Milan: Feltrinelli, 1958), 1:250–53. In his *Iliad*, moreover, Homer also uses insect similes (II.469, IV.131 XVII.570), largely to provide what Richmond Lattimore calls an "escape from the heroic." Introduction, *The Iliad of Homer* (Chicago: University of Chicago Press, 1951), p. 43. These comparisons are doubtless familiar to Rabelais and Ariosto, if only by way of Lucian's satiric tribute to *The Fly*.

progress, one must recall that the changing reality that gave birth to these goals also complicates their realization. Not only were multiple and divergent philosophies in circulation during that period but increased social, physical, and mental mobility rendered problem-solving ever more difficult. Thus the integrative myth structures that effectively represented the ethos of closed societies in the past are no longer adequate to the needs of a disjointed world. The Renaissance poet finds a more authentic mode of expression in the mock epic, a ruptured form which communicates both the heroic ambitions of that age and the peculiar problems of initiation in so complex and dynamic a culture.[12]

Although the traditional quest motif undergoes so diffusive and uneven a development as to be partially obscured by other threads of the narrative, its general outlines are still maintained by the presence of several characteristic figures: departure-initiation sequences, initiatory gods and goddesses, the telling of tales, duels and battles, encounters with monsters, netherworld visits. The fact that Rabelais and Ariosto have derived these recurring consistent units of myth from the epic and romance somewhat complicates interpretation of their "mythology." Theirs are not spontaneous expressions of a primitive consciousness but highly stylized works of art in which mythemes are often used, in part for ornamental and satirical purposes. Yet while the sophisticated literary combination of these units is far removed from their more simplistic articulation in folklore, they are still intended to serve an epistemological function in addition to their diversional value. Like a sentence, myth ideally makes a coherent statement, constructed upon logical principles, which aims at the resolution of basic contradictions surrounding human experience.[13] And if the specific form that this structure takes varies according to the exigencies of each particular society or generative consciousness, it is these variations that render the myth meaningful within any given historical context.

Another factor which appears to make the Ariostan and Rabelaisian mythology problematic is its fractured syntax, the linear progress of

<hr/>

12. In his *Imagination symbolique* (Paris: Presses Universitaires de France, 1964), Durand notes that "plus les sociétés dialectiques se compliquent, plus les schémas symboliques se contredisent" (p. 102).

13. Although myth is, according to Cassirer's theory, a prerational form of conceptualization, it nonetheless resembles reason in both its use of symbols and its logical processes: Lévi-Strauss hypothesizes that "the kind of logic in mythical thought is as rigorous as that of modern science" (p. 230).

which has been diverted through a process of division and overlap. More specifically, the departure or separation stage of the voyage recurs and regenerates itself time after time, superimposing epos upon epos. A certain repetition of figures for emphasis or to express different nuances of meaning is not uncharacteristic of myths in oral and written literature, it is true. And within the Renaissance context, one might expect that the repetitive, spiraling narrative would be a capital vehicle for the representation of man's progress through time.[14] Such is not the case in Rabelais and Ariosto, however. In their works the technique tends to constantly reroute the voyage movement, thereby depriving it of its forward momentum. The original core of Rabelais's work, which depicts Pantagruel's growth to manhood, loses much of its positivity when viewed from the vaster temporal perspective afforded by its sequels—the earlier education of Gargantua, Panurge's unresolved *Tiers Livre* inquest, and the even less decisive *Quart Livre* voyage of "discovery." Thus amended, initiation becomes an ebb-and-flow generational process, which, beginning with Gargantua's break with scholasticism, moves without really progressing. Repeated returns and redepartures, trials and errors moreover alter the initial portrait of the Renaissance hero, as epitomized by Pantagruel. Originally characterized by his optimistic thirst for knowledge, he develops into a rather stoic figure, whose principal virtue is equanimity in the face of mounting frustration and adversity.

More kaleidoscopically, Ariosto fragments his story spatially instead of temporally. Shifting his focus successively from one protagonist to the other, he diverts the reader's attention from the medieval epic's central crusade theme to the overlapping odysseys of Rinaldo, Astolfo, Ruggiero, and Orlando. The fact that these romance-flights-turned-Renaissance-quests may be interpreted negatively as irresponsible, purposeless, and fruitless vagaries, however, renders the broken syntax potentially subversive. For while repetition of the heroic voyage might generate an upward spiral, symbolic of human progress, repetition of the circular voyage that goes nowhere tends to reinforce the alternate theme of unprogressive regeneration.

14. On the spiral growth of myth, see Lévi-Strauss, p. 229: "Since the purpose of myth is to provide a logical model capable of overcoming a contradiction (an impossible achievement if, as it happens, the contradiction is real), a theoretically infinite number of slates will be generated, each one slightly different from the others. Thus, myth grows spiral-wise until the intellectual impulse which has produced it is exhausted."

This diffusion of the quest among different figures and generations is compounded in both works by the layering of topical voyages—physical, intellectual, and metaphysical—upon the basic structure. This cubistic effect acts to devitalize each quest's directional thrust and, at the same time, provides a metaphorical commentary upon the curiosity of Renaissance man, whose aspirations are no less diffusive than those of the fictional knights errant. Analysis will further show that a similar disintegration occurs within the individual symbols and mythemes as well. Yet the deformation of these structures at the hands of Rabelais and Ariosto does not diminish but increases their epistemological importance, inasmuch as it sustains the countervoyage movement. For here, as in all myth, it is not so much the manifestation of archetypes as deviations from expected norms which shed light upon the tale's originality, the author's world view, and the idiosyncrasies of his culture.[15]

Like many earlier mythographers, Rabelais and Ariosto have centered their initiation quests around a mother-wife-goddess and father-god-husband paradigm. While the mytheme should contribute to revelation, Rabelais and Ariosto choose to develop it dialectically, using it to explore tensions that are prevalent in all societies, particularly those involved in transition from one ethos to another. The characters' division between different initiators, first of all, reflects their uncertainty as to the source of true wisdom. In Rabelais, Pantagruel is the regressive side of the Janus head, explicitly linked to both father and mother, while Panurge, conversely, instigates the search for both mate, in the *Tiers Livre*, and male godhead in the *Quart Livre*. The ambiguity of the initiators themselves furthers this fragmentation. As a tyrannical ogre, for example, Quaresmeprenant represents both potential threat and salvation for the sailors, serving at once as monster and possible mask of God.[16]

Similarly, Ariosto also divides Alcina and Angelica into simultaneous siren (negative) and goddess (positive). On the one hand, the fate is Circe reincarnated. Seducing voyagers with her sensuality, she in-

15. Charles Moorman indicates that it is not the "closeness to the known pattern," but the "changes which the poet effects in that pattern," which should "constitute the proper aim of the myth critic." "Myth and Medieval Literature: Sir Gawain and the Green Knight," *Medieval Studies* 18 (1956): 158–72; rpt. in *Myth and Literature*, p. 175.

16. The term is taken from Joseph Campbell, *The Masks of God* (New York: Viking, 1959).

troduces them to sin and metamorphoses them into lower forms of being. On the other hand, her fisherman stance (VI.38) vibrates with mystic and even Christian overtones which, in uneasy coexistence with her siren symbolism, leaves both voyagers and readers in an epistemological quandary. Also in Ariosto there exists a conflict between parent (past) and mate (future) as initiators. This structure appears in the episodes concerning Bradamante and Ruggiero, each of whom is torn between a regressive father figure—the Duke of Amone and Atlante, respectively—and a progressive surrogate mother in the person of Melissa. While the death of Badebec in Rabelais and Ariosto's maternal imagery link the biological mother with death and separation, it is her replacement, a second female, who will initiate the characters into the cosmic mysteries by reintegrating them into the realm of natural cycle and flux.

Another, albeit secondary, deformation of the quest movement occurs in the telling of tales, a process which traditionally occurs between sequestration and physical initiation of the young warrior, and which serves as both entertainment and preparation for the trials to come.[17] Ariosto's most dramatic diversion of the prototype from its hero-building function occurs in the sixth and seventh cantos, when, after Astolfo's lengthy warning to Ruggiero about Alcina, Ruggiero proceeds to become embroiled in the same trap. By so clearly juxtaposing identical errors, the poet casts serious doubt upon man's ability to learn and progress. If this repeated "fall" reveals an innate human weakness, so are the Rabelaisian tales basically negative in content. Both Panurge's history, which precedes the trials in the *Pantagruel* (XIV), and the *Quart Livre's* similarly placed Basché-Chiquanous story (XII–XV) find their mainsprings not in heroism but in comic cruelty. The semantic perversion of the recounted experience is compounded by its formal displacement, manifest in Pantagruel's battle with Loup Garou and in the entire *Quart Livre*. In the first situation, the doubling of the prince's trial with Panurge's "fables de Turpin" (P.XXIX.290) serves to equalize fiction structurally with feat; and in the second, stories clearly outnumber physical confrontations, enforcing the stories' inner theme of not prowess but game and illusion.

The battles themselves, which traditionally function as a testing ground for virtues, tend to present man in a burlesque rather than

17. Charles W. Eckhert, "Initiatory Motifs in the Story of Telemachus," *The Classical Journal* 59 (1963): 49–57; rpt. in *Myth and Literature*, pp. 161–69.

heroic light. In medieval and classical epics the hero's prowesses generally carry the weight of his character as well as his bodily strength. If it is in such scenes that his moral and physical presence is most strongly felt, however, the opposite holds true in the *Orlando furioso* and the Pantagrueline tales. Replacing the classical model's intense force of reality are hollow men who generate only bemused fascination in the reader. Unlikely weapons such as Frère Jean's cross and kitchen humor ("te hascheray-je comme chair à pastéz" [P.XXIX.293]) in Rabelais, along with the characters' burlesque positions ("Pantagruel print Loup Garou par les deux piedz et son corps leva . . . en l'air" [293],[18] transform potential pathos into comedy by diverting attention away from the spiritual to the material realm of existence. Such is also the effect produced by the narrator's glib accounts of massacre and mutilation. The dismembered bodies which inspire horror in readers of the classical and medieval epic have been removed to the carnival stage, transformed by Ariosto and Rabelais into sideshow spectacles ("fa restar con mezza gamba un piede" [XVI.22]) and ludicrous courses in anatomy:

> Lors d'un coup luy tranchit la teste, luy coupant le test sus les os petrux et enlevant les deux os bregmatis et la commissure sagittale avecques grande partie de l'os coronal, ce que faisant luy tranchit les deux méninges et ouvrit profondément les deux postérieurs ventricules du cerveau; et demoura le craine pendent sus les espaules à la peau du péricrane par derrière, en forme d'un bonnet doctoral, noir par-dessus, rouge par dedans. Ainsi tomba roidde mort en terre.   (G.XLIV.128)

Conversely, rhetorical attempts to give epic dimensions to such earthy episodes not only provide a foil for the unheroic action, which appears even more comic by force of contrast, but are themselves comicized by overuse, deformation, and misapplication. Rabelais's invocation of divine aid (P.XXVIII.288), both authors' evocation of clas-

---

18. Like Pantagruel, mad Roland also grasps his enemy by the foot and swings him around:

> Il pazzo dietro lor ratto si muove:
> uno ne piglia, e del capo lo scema
> con la facilità che torria alcuno
> da l'arbor pome, o vago fior dal pruno.

> Per una gamba il grave tronco prese,
> e quello usò per mazza adosso al resto.   (XXIV.5–6)

sical events and personages, and Ariosto's repeated references to the battles' cosmic reverberations polarize the duels by invoking an ideal at odds with the situation. Despite its comicality, this rupture between the ideal and the real, mind and matter, is also possessed of social and metaphysical resonances. Not only a polemical effort to humanize the hero, this burlesque rendering of his prowesses at the same time dehumanizes him. Animal similitudes suggest that warring man is in fact bestial, while Rabelais's allusion to a "fondeur de cloches" (292) and "forgeron" (293) during the battle with Loup Garou reflects the mechanical, robotlike nature of armed and armored knights. In view of the narrator's amused distance from the action, their stilted behavior not only provides a satirical commentary on the Renaissance's increasingly mechanized warfare but also hypothesizes, on another level, that man is a marionette of the gods. Thus the battle interrogates rather than solidifies the hero's stature.

Instruments of battle are likewise diverted from the ascending or affirmative symbolic network to which they usually belong. Particularly in Rabelais, knights fight more frequently with trunks and masts than with lances, sabers, and conventional weapons.[19] If, on the one hand, this innovation signals a high degree of resourcefulness on the warrior's part, it also, on the other hand, comicizes his heroics. The duel's most inherently positive symbol, the sword, furthermore undergoes a deformation which reflects on the hero. Ariosto transfers the blade from human to magic mandate, so exaggerating its fetishistic value that the disputed Durindana becomes an end as well as a means of battle. This development of the sword's original personification into an ironic valuation of weapon over warrior, or matter over man, both interrogates the source of heroism and satirizes the symbolic and materialistic abuses upon which this reversal of roles is founded. At the same time the sword's value as a vehicle of justice is undermined by the pagan's usurpal of Durindana for use against the Christians and by Rabelais's utilization of the weapon as an instrument of Panurge's tricks (P.XVI.238).

Lying midway between the physical trial and the underworld descent in its symbolism is the swallowing whale, a recurring figure of the epic tradition. It represents a meeting and merging with the Other

19. This technique is also favored by Boiardo. For example, he tells us that "il crudel Orione . . . con l'arbore occide molta gente" (I.iv.57). *Orlando innamorato*, ed. Pio Rajna (Milan: Istituto Editoriale Italiano, n.d.), 1:114.

and thus is implicitly associated with introspective integration of the self.[20] Meaning, however, appears largely subordinate to fantasy in the initial manifestations of this motif. Rabelais first substitutes a giant for the sea mammal and allows his narrator to be engulfed in his own creation (P.XXXII), while Astolfo goes floating off toward Alcina on an island-turned-whale (VI.37). Although both these episodes enforce the theme of flux and illusion, the explorers' enthusiasm bespeaks a forceful sense of wonder which dominates any existential vertigo. Thus the engulfment itself into Alcina's secular society, or into the mouth of metaphorical giants, is filled with positive expectations, with the promise of integration between man and the humanized world of his dreams. Further penetration of the pit, however, reveals death and decadence, producing a disillusionment reflected in reactions to the second, literal whale—the monstrous "orca" (VIII, X, XI) and "physétère" (QL.XXXIII). The explorers' initial gullibility is transformed by experience into mistrust, and hope into momentary terror.

This fear of being consumed also translates, more positively, into a desire to consume—to slay and, ideally, eat the whale or monster. This consumption, or destruction, of the devouring monster is also an archetypal step in youth's entelechy and represents the necessary ebb and flow of the cognitive faculties.[21] Man must balance the diffusion of self into the universe with an integration of it into him, as each mirrors the other. The complex circularity of the two episodes is indicated by analysis of their inward-outward dialectics. Significantly, the internal kingdoms in Rabelais and Ariosto reflect the outside world, and vice versa. The civilization inside Pantagruel's mouth and inside Alcina's realm are more realistic than many of the monsters revealed by the external voyage, which appear colored by, if not drawn from, the psyche. It is by introspecting and developing his subjectivity (the metaphorical whale) that man sees reflected the external universe (Alcina and the gastroworld), while, conversely, this exterior reality (the literal whale) must be reintegrated into his ego. Characteristically, this second and definitive step of cognition is never totally consum-

20. Joseph Campbell, *The Hero with a Thousand Faces* (New York: Pantheon Books, 1949), pp. 247–48.
21. Cf. ibid.: "The hero, whether god or goddess, man or woman, the figure in a myth or the dreamer of a dream, discovers and assimilates his opposite (his own unsuspected self) either by swallowing it or by being swallowed" (p. 108). The two forms of the myth may also coexist and appear sequentially, as they do in Eskimo folklore. There, the hero Raven escapes from the whale's belly and enjoys a blubber feast (pp. 207–09).

mated in Rabelais and Ariosto. The "orca" which Ruggiero slays is merely one of Proteus's considerable "gregge," while Pantagruel's consumption of the "physétère" is diverted to a mercenary level: its fat will not be eaten but sold (XXXV.634).

Their structural similarity notwithstanding, the particulars of this motif differ considerably in Rabelais and Ariosto. Not only Alcofribas, but pilgrims (G.XXXVIII) and encapsulated workmen (P.XXXIII) as well, enter the giants' bodies in *Gargantua* and *Pantagruel*. Because of their religious and medicinal associations, these figures may also be viewed as manifestations of Rabelais, who is at once artist, monk, and doctor. Their interiorization in the first two books is moreover counterbalanced in the *Quart Livre*: there, it is religion, matter, and art which threaten to swallow the Utopian explorers. Just as the motif has a tripartite construction in Rabelais, so it is fragmented among three characters in Ariosto: Astolfo, who first rode the whale to Alcina's kingdom, later kills the monster Orrilo (XV); Ruggiero, who has also been entrapped by the fate, goes on to slay the whale that threatens Angelica (X); and Orlando, entering the whale's mouth only to affix an anchor there, kills the monster to free Olimpia (XI). It is interesting to note the cycle's reversal in this last instance. Orlando, the only paladin who fails to explore the otherness of his psyche before destroying it, will later succumb to the ultimate alterity of madness.[22]

An even more dramatic fracture of significative forms occurs in the netherworld episodes, those descents into otherness which complete the hero's own partial existence and unite him with the whole. Rabelais's and Ariosto's unorthodox exploitation of the mytheme's antithetical structure, however, is the satirical force which finally subverts the heroic apotheosis. Once again the motif undergoes cell division. Rabelais doubles his initial mirror-world, that discovered by the wise Épistémon, with an extended *Quart Livre* voyage through the looking glass, precipitated by the fool Panurge. Similarly, the wise Orlando's mad otherness parallels his opposite's lunarworld jaunt. This frag-

22. The hero's madness is in fact symbolically related to both underworld descents and encounters with swallowing monsters: "D'un certain point de vue, on peut homologuer la 'folie' initiatique des futurs chamans à la dissolution de la vieille personnalité qui fait suite à la penetration dans le ventre d'un monstre ou à la descente aux Enfers. Dans tous ces contextes, nous avons affaire avec une immersion totale dans les ténèbres. Chaque aventure initiatique de ce type finit toujours par créer quelque chose, par fonder un 'monde' ou un nouveau mode d'être." Mircea Éliade, "Le Symbolisme des ténèbres dans les religions archaïques," in *Polarité du symbole*, Etudes carmélitaines (Bruges: Desclée de Brouwer, 1960), p. 22.

mentation of the netherworld visits into two components is moreover compounded at the interior of at least two of the new subdivisions, where a confusing combination of reflection and refraction renders "illumination" meaningless. Within Épistémon's hell and Astolfo's lunarworld one finds a miniature model of terrestrial antitheses, a new split between *follia* and *senso*, between *les grands* and *les petits*. This inability to transcend opposition is manifested not only by the netherworld's infinite reversibility but also in the Janus-like rapport which exists between its initiates. It is Panurge who, playing the sage for a moment, restores the philosopher's head to his shoulders (P.XXX. 295), while Astolfo does essentially the same for Orlando, effecting an exchange of roles.

This element of return is critical to the initiatory myth and ideally results in an integrated hero who communicates his experience to society so that they may benefit from it. Although Épistémon and Astolfo emerge from their descents in Rabelais and Ariosto, what follows is, in essence, a shift back to normality, not unification or progress but reversal. Ariosto informs us that Astolfo will in time return to his folly (XXXIV.86), while Pantagruel, after suggesting that his companion's "singulier passetemps" in hell does not even merit narration, expresses his preference for a good drink (XXX.301–02). The coming back, in other words, appears to negate the voyage. In the *Divine Comedy*, the myth's highest literary expression, it is through the storyteller that postquest expectations of reform and reappraisal are realized, in a union of epic hero and poet. Similarly, the ill-resolved *Quart Livre* voyage points back to the narrator himself, a potential survivor, whose experience bridges not only the quest for Bacbuc but the entire fictional netherworld. Like the Ariostan storyteller, Rabelais's narrator is himself a participant in the characters' madness, the true medium between us and otherness, and, as such, receives the protagonists' torch in his turn.

Ostensibly in order to explicate his intuitive synthesis of the universe in a rational manner, the narrator imposes upon the primitive myth structure, already intellectualized, an allegorical facade which will appeal to the intelligence of modern, thinking man as well as to his imagination.[23] Because the intellective and imaginative currents are

23. The distinction between myth and allegory indeed forms part of the works' more global dialectic between reason and unreason: "Tandis que le foisonnement des mythes récrée un univers mystérieux et étonnant, étranger à la sèche ration-

not consubstantial, as they were in Dante, however, the result is conceptual chaos instead of consolidation. Just as the narrator parodied epic forms to undermine the stature of man, so does he deform the medieval allegory to subvert moral hierarchies and, with them, their spirit of system. This end is manifested specifically in a repeated positing and withdrawal of sense, in the purposeful creation and destruction of allegorical forms.

By virtue of their symbolic names, attributes, and function within the narrative, many of the authors' kingdoms and characters elicit allegorical rather than purely literal interpretations. The different weight of reality between protagonists and larger-than-life figures such as Alcina and Logistilla, Quaresmeprenant and Mardigras automatically tends to place these latter personages on a figurative plane. Indeed, the incongruity of these isolated psychological abstractions within a superstructure which by and large defies a sustained allegorical reading already puts the personifications on an unsure footing. The reader's inability to reconcile them with coexisting currents of geographical realism and, conversely, diversional fantasy prohibits the consolidation of different interpretative levels, fostering instead a rupture between them and a consequential liquification of meaning.

The rather traditional opposition of values between Alcina and Logistilla, Quaresmeprenant and Mardigras appears to idealize man's double postulation or vacillation between sensuality and austerity. Whereas Ariosto's progression from the former to the latter gives voice to the standard Christian valuing of virtue over *voluptas*, the allegory has already been secularized in Rabelais's reverse sequence from Quaresmeprenant to Mardigras and Messere Gaster. Ariosto achieves a similar perversion not only in the lengthier depiction of Alcina but also, twenty-five cantos later, in his condemnation of chastity to hell. For if Astolfo is petrified for *lussuria*, so is Lidia eternally damned, in a second travesty of Dante, because of her unnaturally chaste behavior. Such neutralization of expected schemas serves to satirize both previous allegory and the artists' own pretensions toward the kind of positivism underlying that genre. Just as Ariosto goes full circle, neutralizing the ascendancy of Logistilla, so does Rabelais de-

alité," says Guy Demerson, "l'allégorie pénètre le monde d'un système cohérent d'explications modelées sur la logique du comportement humain, sur les rapports de parentage ou d'opposition." *La Mythologie dans l'œuvre lyrique de la Pléiade,* Travaux d'Humanisme et Renaissance 119 (Geneva: Droz, 1972), p. 37.

stroy, in a balancing of Gaster's positive artistry with his negative value as false god, the earlier victory of Carnival over Lent.

In many traditional allegories, of course, Reason is a central character whose role should logically be enlarged in the Renaissance and imbued with new, humanistic connotations. Use of the allegorical form itself denotes, in fact, a certain esteem for man's ability to explain his cosmos rationally, a goal which at first glance appears consistent with the Renaissance voyage of discovery. But one must recall that sixteenth-century reason, unlike her medieval counterpart, is exploratory rather than synthetic, diametrically opposed to the spirit of system which is, on the other hand, the essence of allegory. Not surprisingly, then, the traditional form's closure disappears with that of medieval society, diffusing into a more authentic, open structure that corresponds to the modern world. By the same token spiritual kingdoms such as Ruach— which means "vent" or "esprit" in Hebrew ("Briefve déclaration," 743)—and Logistilla are undermined by their own deficient attributes, internal ambiguities, and external conflicts. Part of this tension is more-over related to reason's old value as temperance and spirituality, the antipode of Renaissance sensuality and hedonism. Logistilla's noncorporeal chastity and Ruach's ethereal, nonmaterial life style are obvious variations on this traditional symbolism, which, in their opposition to the more sensual Alcina and Mardigras, strike the reader as inauthentic and unsatisfactory responses to the human condition.

Absent in Alcina's reign are the "suoni, danze, odori, bagni e cibi" (X.47) which rendered her sister so appealing. Now it is one's heart and not one's body that is nourished, with intangibles such as "costumi santi, / bellezza eterna et infinita grazia" (X.45). One sees ("si puon veder") rather than smells the gardens' "odoriferi arbuscelli" and "maturi frutti" (X.61), in an eidetic explosion which bespeaks at once emptiness and a new kind of *voluptas*. Similarly, the citizens of Ruach dine not upon sausage but upon "vent," a nothingness which is at the same time inebriating when equated with its near-homonym "vin." Indeed, one key to the interpretation of Ruach lies in this opposition between wind and wine, since the latter is used by Rabelais as a figure of both the popular and philosophical banquet, as a symbol of the one's physicality and the other's rational quest for *veritas*. While on the one hand Rabelais ridicules the old value of Reason as temperance, then, suggesting that man cannot live by spirit alone, he also mocks the sophists' wit, which is little more than hot air. Just as bon vivants philosophize about their wine—and philosophers, about truth —so the inhabitants of Ruach "disputent de la bonté, excellence, salubrité, rarité des vens" (QL.XLIII.655); and their discourse, like "rational" man's rhetoric, is substanceless. Not unexpectedly, the ascendancy of both authors' spiritual symbols is subsequently destroyed or sublimated by contradictory figures in the allegorical progression: Logistilla, by lunar wisdom, and Ruach, by Messere Gaster.

It is imperative to note, however, that the symbol's loss of internal univocity and its frequently fanciful realization tend to diminish the distinction between realms at first deemed diametrically opposed. The descriptive verve with which allegorical symbols are realized not only diverts them from their implicit didactic direction but also, in the case of Logistilla and Alcina, results in a meeting of internal characteristics. Their lush gardens, luminous castles, and cultivated life styles seem, in fact, more reflective of Renaissance culture than of significative exigencies. Closer analysis reveals that Quaresmeprenant's unnatural austerity is merely a reversed sensuality, which excretes rather than consumes an array of rich foods that rival the Andouilles in culinary appeal.[24]

It is during the wars, or the confrontation of opposite abstractions, that one is most forcibly struck by this subversion of content by form, an effect which is due not only to the poetic élan of such scenes but also to their juxtaposition within a particularly dense mass of meaningful material. Both authors are clearly building allegorical expectations into these scenes. To portray a war between man and monsters is already a conscious appeal for figurative interpretation, since animals come equipped with their own acquired network of symbolism. Ostensibly, then, what one is seeing in the seventh-canto menagerie is an attack upon Ruggiero's virtuous defenses by the abstract forces associated with Alcina: adulatory monkeys, simulating cats, and violent centaurs, all pitfalls of excessive worldliness.[25] The *Quart Livre* Andouilles are obvious, if less conventional, figures of sensuality and its

24. For example:

S'il crachoit, c'estoient panerées de chardonnette.
S'il mouchoit, c'estoient anguillettes sallées.
S'il pleuroit, c'estoient canars à la dodine.
S'il trembloit, c'estoient grands pâtés de lièvre.
S'il suoit, c'estoient moulues au buerre frais. (QL.XXXII.626)

25. Apollonio and Fontana, p. 151. See also William J. Kennedy, "Ariosto's Ironic Allegory," *Modern Language Notes*, 88, no. 1 (Jan. 1973): 44–67.

seductive attraction: "Andouilles sont andouilles, toujours doubles et traistresses" (XXXVI.637), says Xenomanes, verbalizing the threat to Utopian sailors.

Notwithstanding the built-in symbolism of these creatures, discursive comments create a critical distance between the reader and the allegory and force him to view it ironically. On the one hand, this end is achieved by the excessively rational treatment of an already over-intellectualized genre, or, more specifically, by reflexive comments on the creative process of appellation, and by a subversive confrontation between literal and figurative levels of interpretation. Rabelais's documented inquest into Andouille names (XXXVII.639–42) is clearly parodical; and its comicality derives from the incongruous application of logic and historical considerations to what seems, initially, pure creative fantasy. Logic, here, is tinged with *ludus* and thereby placed in critical perspective:

> Je suys tout confus en mon entendement quand je pense en l'invention admirable de Pythagoras, lequel par le nombre *par* ou *impar* des syllabes d'un chascun nom propre, exposoit de quel cousté estoient les humains boyteulx, bossus, borgnes, goutteux, paralytiques, pleuritiques et aultres telz maléfices en nature: sçavoir est assignant le nombre *par* au cousté guausche du corps, le *impar* au dextre.   (640)

Less blatant in his deformation of the genre, Ariosto nevertheless indicates that elaborate allegorical nomenclature is merely a game, as he relegates his own figures to a purely hypothetical level: "e tal saria / Beltà, s'avesse corpo, e Leggiadria" (VI.69).

Equally central to this subversive process is the symbolic instability of the pseudoallegorical monsters, triggered by their physical hybridity. It is as if the Andouilles and seventh-canto bestiary, all half-man and half-thing, had one foot in allegory and the other in mimetic fiction. A similar ambiguity structures their rapport with adjoining kingdoms and serves not to delineate definitional boundaries but to blur lines of demarcation between Logistilla and Alcina, Quaresmeprenant and Mardigras. If Astolfo originally identifies the animal army with Alcina (VI.56), the fate's own servant, personified Beauty, relegates it to the realm of avaricious Erifilla (VI.79), who in some ways is closer in affinity to Logistilla than to her voluptuous sister. In other words, Beauty and Bestiality have changed places. Likewise, the Andouilles' threat to the voyager is not just sensuality but duplicity, an ambiguity which is first manifested on a "military" level: "Ces andouilles vénérables vous pourroient, par adventure, prendre pour Quaresmeprenant" (XXXVI.636), prophesies Frère Jan with a premonition which proves to be true. Instead of attacking the Tapinois king, these subjects of Mardigras turn against the friendly Utopian crew, momentarily impeding its progress toward Carnival.

This prototypical war between "opposites," designed to settle the hero's psychological and moral quandary, gives way to total chaos. Andouille-soldiers are metamorphosed into Andouille-food, then killed with cooking utensils. Such mutation is of course appropriate to the sausage-serpent, whose reptilian molting recurs on a symbolic level: "Le serpens qui tenta Eve estoit andouillicque" (XXXVIII.643), says Rabelais, linking eroticism with cerebrality in this obscene allusion to the tree of knowledge.

From an esthetic point of view, this comic distortion, social satire, and unbounded fantasy complicate the potential psychological significance of each island. While the preceding episodes offer the most striking examples of allegorical promise and deception, a kindred process is evident in each of the other "symbols." If Melissa's confrontation with Alcina appears to represent man's inner conflict between spiritual and profane love ("pensò di trarlo per via alpestre e dura / alla vera virtù, mal grado d'esso" [VII.42]), the mage as a fully realized character both conjures up devils (XLVI.78) and destroys a knight's marriage (XLIII.20–49), in an ironic departure from idealized Christian spiritualism. Similarly, Messere Gaster's gluttonous motto, "tout pour la tripe," neutralizes his generous qualities. Instead of emerging as an end in the psychological or moral progression, this would-be structural climax of the *Quart Livre* is, like Ariosto's netherworld, if anything more equivocal than preceding episodes and stymies the expected hierarchical ascension.

Horizontal perversion of the epos is supplemented by its vertical subdivision into three possible levels of interpretation. Because the voyage is at once geographical, metaphysical, and introspective, many of its ports of call enjoy a correspondingly polyvalent symbolism. The ensuing coincidence, often within a single figure, of psychological abstraction, potential mask of God, and terrestrial monarch gives the dialectic between opposing figures different shades of meaning. On one level, it outlines the protagonists' inner struggle between contradictory priorities and tastes; on the second level, it effectively communicates man's difficulty in visualizing God; and on the third level, it represents the conflict between different customs and mores. Animated abstractions by virtue of their names, the *Quart Livre* islands are also presented as rival kingdoms, with different beliefs and ways of life, which also worship different images of God. These multiple levels interact in a divisive rather than integrative fashion, however. Gaster's people think him a god, he claims to be a man, and we know he is only a figment of the imagination. Likewise, the Andouilles and Papimanes worship unrelated images of God, the sanctity of which is undermined not only by their disparity but also by their comic material depiction. The multiplicity of these masks of God proves them to be relative to the society in which they appear and to the mind that generated them. The godhead's supremacy is thus modified by his simultaneous role as terrestrial monarch and psychological abstraction: for is not religion to some extent a function of both national custom and personal fantasy?

By confusing these three levels of interpretation, the poets in both works question the origin of values, religion, and social structures. In Ariosto, the allegorical Alcina and Logistilla also enjoy supernatural powers as fates and live in terrestrial palaces, as do the magus Atlante and even Saint John the Evangelist. Alcina's intellectualized association with *voluptas* and *lussuria*, moreover, is given added contours by her two complementary roles as queen and goddess. Thus Ariosto not only immobilizes sensuality as sin but, by bringing into play the elements of divine and natural determination, postulates both the tyranny of the passions and their possibly sacrosanct nature. Similarly, the fear embodied by monsters is variously linked to a devouring god, a repressive society, and a troubled psyche. There is some suggestion that the whale, a totally natural phenomenon, derives his "supernatural" force not from the invisible Proteus but from the superstitions of a culture which perpetuates this myth. The narrator admits his own doubt about the "cosa di Proteo" (VIII.58), while the inhabitants of Ebuda actually resent Orlando's efforts to destroy the monster to which they sacrifice their beauty and youth (XI.46–48).

In effect, the artist is conducting, on a symbolic level, a philosophical inquest into the functional relationship between the individual, God, and culture, which, with its constant dialectics, embraces the innumerable structures of Renaissance thought. By positing each of the

three levels of reality in a triangle, in which each angle is generated by
the other two, one approximates the dynamics of this hybrid and unstable mythology:

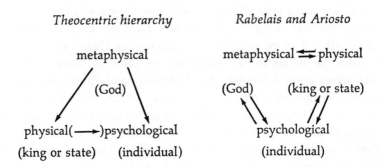

Theocentric hierarchy   *Rabelais and Ariosto*

By confusing rather than consolidating the three ontological levels of
their narrative, Rabelais and Ariosto have mobilized the theocentric
world's relatively stable morals and mores, which derive their justification from an absolute God. In the medieval epic and allegory, the
psychological, social, and metaphysical levels of interpretation are
generally consubstantial, united in the vast pyramidal system of Christian values and beliefs that emanate down from an immovable and immutable Supreme Being. Yet "in the sixteenth century, the hierarchy of
perspectives that had enabled Dante and Chaucer to unite potentially
contradictory modes of vision was in crisis."[26] With the decline of
feudalism, the Empire, and the Church's prestige during the late Middle
Ages and Renaissance, there rise up new, independent forms of government such as the communes, republics, princedoms, and nationalistic
monarchies. This gradual shift in the power structure of Europe is concomitant with an attitudinal change, a liberation and reevaluation of
man and his culture outside the rigid conceptual framework provided
by medieval Christianity and feudal society.

In their satire and fantasy, neither of which is subordinate to any
fixed ideology, Rabelais and Ariosto give evidence of this exploratory
attitude toward social structures and the human psyche. The alternating
dominance in their works of psychological, social, and metaphysical
currents generates a literary tension not unlike the real-life rivalry between the individual, the State, and the Church. The resulting mythol-

26. Durling, p. 67.

ogy is less anthropocentric, as one might expect in the Renaissance, than decentralized. Reflective as it may be of the period's philosophical dialectics, this structure is not a system but an antisystem, and it is geared not toward resolution but toward unending interrogation. Just as horizontal fragmentation of the mythos formulates man's quest for the One among the Many, so does its fractured vertical symbolism pose corollary problems, such as fate versus free will, seeming versus being. Is man the master of both nature and heaven, or is he predestined by his physical and metaphysical milieu? Is man a product of God's imagination, or are He and nature a reflection of man's?

THE DIALECTICS OF FACT AND FANTASY

Consideration of fantasy within a philosophical or even significative context appears, of course, to constitute a contradiction in terms, a negation of art's autonomy. It may be argued that the authors, by neutralizing the original value of preexistent myths and using them as rhetorical devices, are merely engaged in what many consider to be the highest form of artistry—the production of "pure poetry." According to this interpretation, the works' unity would derive not from the exigencies of a rationally imposed system, but rather from the writer's own liberated subconscious and artistic sensibilities, which together generate a purely affective disposition of sounds and images. Yet even if one holds to the thesis that the romances are politically and morally unengaged, their ambiguous symbolism necessarily reflects a personal mythology, no less "meaningful" than rational discourse, which is moreover at least partially situational. Be it conscious or subconscious, the comparison of heroes to both gods and beasts clearly formalizes an existential and epistemological crisis peculiar to the artists' sociohistorical milieu.

Generally, however, Rabelais and Ariosto do not require psychoanalytical interpretations but rather reflect consciously upon their own imaginations. To project one's own fantasy onto the written page is, after all, to objectify it, to intentionalize the illusion. Thus even the most surrealistic of Rabelaisian and Ariostan fauna, such as the "pourceau Minerve enseignant" (QL.XLI.652) and the hippogriff, are to some extent intellectualized, either in conception or in realization. Invention is inevitably mixed with imitation, creation necessarily conditioned by the artist's previously acquired stock of mythical and literary sources. As if in recognition of this fact, Rabelais borrows from Pliny and Lucullus to describe his far-fetched flying pig and even takes its ambiguous emblem, so apparently reflective of his own hybrid fantasy, from the Greek proverb ΤΣ ΑΘΗΝΑΝ ("hog teaching Minerva"). Juxtaposing this improbable animal with Ariosto's "destrier alato," a descendant of Lucian's hippogriff, one grasps the consummate irony of both symbols.[27] Despite that hybridity which renders them peculiarly Rabelaisian and Ariostan the two winged monsters both conjure up recollections of Pegasus, thereby negating the signified, imagination, through use of an imitative signifier.

This subversive pairing of invention with imitation is paralleled on an ontological level by the fiction's contingent rapport with convention. Just as folly is always defined in terms of sanity, so is the imaginary only relative in value, an adjunct of the real. To communicate their most obviously fanciful visions, in fact, Rabelais and Ariosto revert not to that language of the ineffable which embellishes their realistic episodes but instead rely heavily upon concrete comparisons. The overall inverisimilitude of Rabelais's pig is offset by a series of natural similitudes while Ariosto augments scientific documentation with the insistence that his hippogriff is real: "Non è finto il destrier, ma naturale, / ch'una giumenta generò d'un grifo" (IV.18). On one hand, the veristic description of this obvious illusion constitutes a tribute to the humanistic imagination, which enables man to fully realize God's creation, to rival it with his own art, or to replace it with solipsistic fantasms. Yet on the other hand, to insist that a lie is true calls attention to its falsity; and in talking about fantasy, albeit affirmatively, Rabelais and Ariosto destroy the illusion and, with it, the autonomy of their own fiction.

Not merely a subjective structure, the imaginary has become an objectified theme, a capital vehicle for satire. To submerge oneself in this fantasy world is not to escape reality but to see it more clearly, through the detached and disoriented eyes of an outsider. And instead of masking unpleasant realities, the fiction ironically unveils the masks and masques which comprise our culture. Episodes which appear to be the most far-fetched, such as Épistémon's vision of hell or Astolfo's visit to the lunar netherworld, prove on closer analysis to be satiric reorderings of terrestrial existence. Rabelais's ironic transfor-

27. For sources of the hippogriff, see Rajna, pp. 114–20.

mation of rich and famous people into beggars (and vice versa) not only attacks specific institutional ills—as witnessed by the inclusion of numerous popes in hell—but also interrogates the mythical foundations of social stratification:

> En cette façon, ceulx qui avoient esté gros seigneurs en ce monde icy guaingnoyent leur pauvre meschante et paillarde vie là-bas. Au contraire, les philosophes et ceulx qui avoient esté indigens en ce monde, de par de là estoient gros seigneurs en leur tour.
> (P.XXX.300)

Given the inherently parasitic nature of wealth and glory, even relatively untarnished figures are necessarily condemned for exploitation and sins of omission. Both Alexander and Nero undergo equally degrading metamorphoses, as merit and chance become opposite if indistinguishable sides of the same coin. Historical or mythical types are thus freed from time-honored identities and developed according to latent virtualities.

Mockery of *les grands* is transmitted with equal force across Ariosto's depiction of the moon, where riches and honors crumble to ruins before one's eyes:

> Passando il paladin per quelle biche,
> or di questo o di quel chiede alla guida.
> Vide un monte di tumide vesiche,
> che dentro parea aver tumulti e grida;
> e seppe ch'eran le corone antiche
> e degli Assirii e de la terra lida,
> e de' Persi e de' Greci, che già furo
> incliti, et or n'è quasi il nome oscuro.   (XXXIV.76)

Far from limiting himself to historic examples, moreover, Ariosto extends his satire to more contemporary ambitions, through explicit reference to "signor," "sofisti," "poeti," and courtiers. As in Rabelais, the satirical "bite" arises not only from the condemnation of specific abuses—such as the patronage system, with its petty politics and constant play-acting—but also from a far-sighted equalization of all acts and all lives in their ultimate vanity; the net result is a near-tragic satire which, in reversing and devaluating the givens of all existence, deprives them of their eternal necessity.

In the same vein, the inordinate amount of fantasy in both works reflects on society's own lies and illusions. Just as imaginary detours in the *Furioso* are no more fictitious than the "truths" with which they are juxtaposed, so is courtly etiquette—clothes, manners, and language—little more than an elaborate mask, an institutional game which distorts nature and stifles instinct. One primary result of Astolfo's netherworld visit is the brutal demystification of life's artifice and facades, classically expressed in the metaphor of women's makeup: "Vide gran copia di panie con visco, / ch'erano, o donne, le bellezze vostre" (XXXIV.81).

Similarly, the make-believe, theatrical worlds of the Rabelaisian *Quart Livre* are consciousness-awakening devices, which signal the mutually exclusive nature of culture and truth. On the island of Cheli, for example, the "courtoisie et coustume du pays"—denounced by Frère Jan in the following passage—are mere caricatures of sixteenth-century French conventions and, in a larger sense, of all social edicts:

> Corpe de galline! . . . j'en sçay mieulx l'usaige et cérémonies que de tant chiabrener avecques ces femmes, *magny, magna, chiabrena,* révérence double, reprinze, l'accollade, la fressurade, baise la main de vostre mercy, de vostre majesta, vous soyez le bienvenu, tarabin, tarabas. Bren, c'est merde à Rouan! (QL.X.567)

In case the ironic barb should be missed in this mockery of "alien" affectations, the satire is immediately transferred to a "realistic," explicitly French setting and is further actualized by allusion to a "seigneur de Guyercharois." This gentleman adheres so mechanically to etiquette and is so blinded by deceptive appearances that one night he mistakes the "paiges endamoyselléz" for ladies, and "les baisa tous en grande courtoysie et révérences magnificques" (567).

This perpetual dialogue between fact and fantasy not only reflects on society's artificiality but also upon some of its "incredible" truths. In Ariosto's vivid battle scenes there is just enough realistic detail to evoke reminiscences of contemporary conflicts, an association moreover reinforced by explicit narrative comments on firearms. Seen in the overall fictional context, true-to-life elements, such as diabolical gunpowder and tyrannical aberrations, seem no less fantastic than the *Quart Livre*'s most surrealistic hallucinations or Ariosto's most preposterous illusions. Insertion of wars, murder, and plunder into the "marvelous" and comic, mock-epic atmosphere softens their immediate emotional impact, it is true, in establishing a comfortable fictitious

barrier between reader and intrigue. Yet on the other hand, this distance elicits critical, objective reactions to "everyday" atrocities which,
artistically regenerated, are endowed with a full measure of irrationality
and absurdity.

More disquieting than the fantasy's satirical reference to reality are
the ontological implications of this constant flux between fact and
fiction. Not only do the artists objectify the imaginary, but they also
poeticize the real and, in so doing, point back to the necessary subjectification of externality during the process of perception. Tinged
with just enough objective realism to make us aware of its distortion,
Ariosto's deliberate *sfumatura* and Rabelais's crescendo of surrealism
make us dramatically conscious of the distance between their worlds
and ours. Comparison of the two mock epics, so similar in structure
and dissimilar in their particulars, helps illustrate this point. That two
artists with such like sociohistorical stimuli and world views should
produce such vastly different works signals the unique manner in
which each man perceives and reflects reality. The fact that we are
dealing with art, or reworked rather than immediate impressions, does
not invalidate this interpretation but serves instead to strengthen it.
For each time we view our surroundings are we not unconsciously
recreating them in our mind's eye, orienting nature in a distinctively
personal way? In this sense the authors' mythology is not so very
different from our own. On a larger scale the stylized universes of
Rabelais and Ariosto, which are obvious deformations of God's World
and Word, emerge as structural parallels to other, less overtly fictitious, human constructions: socioreligious institutions, heroes, and
myths are revealed to be products of the collective imagination, while
objective reality degenerates into a thousand shades of personal fantasy.

This latter effect derives not only from the gap between reader and
artist but also from a purposeful fragmentation of narrative affinities
within the text itself. Repeated shifts of the center of consciousness
and its objective focal points serve to heighten awareness of multiple
subjectivities. The Rabelaisian narrator enlarges the "established"
perspective with a guided tour of his master's gastroworld, while
Atlante's illusory castle, one learns, is seen by each knight in a distinctly personal way (XII.20). On the one hand, the closed, labyrinthine
quality of human consciousness, as dramatically revealed in Rabelais's
and Ariosto's respective hallucinations, points hopelessly to the individual's inevitable sequestration from his peers and from the exterior

"truth" which he seeks. Yet mere artistic awareness of universal solitude or solipsism, accompanied by a paradoxical desire to communicate this discovery to others, constitutes a Promethean attempt to break down the prison walls, to enlarge the limits of perception through literary and psychological commerce.

This disintegration of the center of consciousness into multiple parts, combined with a constant confrontation of fact and fantasy, serves to demonstrate the subjective conditioning of "objective" reality and, hence, its relativity. More radical than this perversion of ontology within a single dimension of time is its total liquefication through history as well, an effect which results in the implicit unification of past, present, and future, chronicle and legend, in a no-man's land somewhere between fact and fiction. In the anachronistic conflict between Orlando and Proteus's forces (XI), for example, rhetorical figures have been superimposed upon the primary fiction and come to life within it. This is not only to say that the monsters are "realized" but rather that, by contagion, all other figures are automatically fantasized. The apparent tautology of this observation is abated, and takes on meaning, when one recalls that the fictitious Ariostan paladins, like Gargantua and Pantagruel, double as real-life men, thus serving as mediators between reality and fantasy. When they move from one realm to another, man's standard ontological and chronological definitions, which give order to existence, are cast into fluctuating confusion.

To understand the full import of this transmutation, it is helpful to delineate the different levels of myth that coexist within the romances and to observe the sequential progression from absolute fantasy to totally objective reality. The following chart will clarify this categorization:

	Rabelais	*Ariosto*
Pure fantasy	Messere Gaster	Erifilla, Caligorante
Preexistent myth	Gargantua	Proteus, Merlin
Mythicized history	Underworld figures	Charlemagne, Orlando
Mythicized current event	Cartier, Jannequin	Artists and explorers

It is the protagonists, and, to a greater extent, the narrator, who link the various domains within a fictitious netherworld and thereby serve as catalysts in the hierarchy's dissolution.

Not only are fact and fantasy equalized by mere force of juxtaposition, but, at the same time, each is infected by the other's ontological value. The authors endow some of their most fantastic fauna, first, with not only graphic realizations but with pseudoscientific genetic justifications as well. When Ariosto tells us that the hippogriff is descended from a griffin and a mare, and when Rabelais looks to Switzerland and the Gallic provinces for historical analogies with the Andouille-warriors (QL.XXXVIII.643), they not only lend credibility to their fantasy but also draw reality into the fictitious whirlpool. This same technique of cross-contamination is applied to both the crusading legends in Ariosto and to the tale of Noah's ark (P.prol.176–77) in Rabelais. In each case the removal of presumed fact to an overtly imaginary stage serves to question the original story's authenticity and to label it—no less than the fiction per se—as myth.

This derealization of history, on one level, reminds us that fact becomes fiction once it has passed; and within this conceptual schema, the artists' equalization of fact and fantasy is not only esthetically justified but possessed of its own interior logic. Moreover, it casts a double reflection upon contemporary ancestor-worship and exaltation of antiquity. Common abuses of veracity, even as they are satirized, become insignificant in the face of history's unreality. This is not to say that the hybrid genealogies, both of which are part fact and part fiction, negate biological determinism. Rather, they affirm that while man is a physical product of his historical heredity, he is also conditioned, mentally, by his personal stock of myth, and that, on a creative, existential level, he is free to choose his own roots. In ostentatiously endowing his figures with an outlandishly gigantic heritage, Rabelais —as Renaissance man—is consciously espousing a set of gigantic standards to correspond with his own ideals and goals. Similarly, as he furnishes the Estensi with a hyperbolically heroic family tree, Ariosto —far from making a claim to historical accuracy—is at once proposing elevated expectations to Ferrara's rulers and, like God, recreating the world in his own image.

Fictionalization of the past, artistically speaking, is merely one step removed from a similar transformation of the present. Comparison of contemporary man to mythical heroes and antique divinities who never existed constitutes, by rational analogy, an exercise in self-negation. If Jason and Ulysses are fallible, we have seen, so are their modern-day counterparts. Thus, if Ruggiero and Pantagruel are imaginary, is not the ascendancy of their real-life referents, Columbus, Magellan, and company, ontologically undermined? Rabelais, indeed, has not only infected the voyages of discovery with his myth, but geographical fact as well, by implicitly equalizing Utopia ("nowhere") and France. Beauce is a product of Gargantua's chivalric exercises (XVI.53), and the river of Saint Victor, a result of Panurge's vengeance against the "haulte dame de Paris" (P.XXII.267).

By constantly remythifying reality, Rabelais and Ariosto appear to neutralize their own efforts at demystification. Closer analysis, however, reveals that the two thrusts are complementary, both conducive to critical reflection upon human thought processes. Even as the authors satirize the sacrosanct lies of Renaissance civilization, their own outrageous fantasies remind the reader that illusion is inherent to one's very being, and that conceptualization is itself an act of mythification.[28]

Myth, at the hands of Rabelais and Ariosto, thus becomes a capital instrument of demystification. By alternating classical and animal comparisons, running the gamut of mythical allusions, and treating the whole as meaningless rhetoric, the two poets do not eulogize but rather mobilize the analogy's second term. Renaissance man inherits not only the positive connotations of preexistent mythology but the negative connotations as well. Concurrent deformation of the cohesive quest structure serves, secondly, to interrogate man's cognitive efforts and to illustrate the complexity of truth. Finally, this subversive process finds completion in the dialectics of fact and fantasy, a paradoxical discourse which demystifies by means of remythification. Within this structure it is not only the givens of culture which are undermined but, more importantly, the myth of knowledge itself.

28. "But what are concepts save formulations and creations of thought which, instead of giving us the true forms of objects, show us rather the forms of thought itself?" Ernst Cassirer, *Language and Myth*, trans. Susanne K. Langer (1946; rpt. New York: Dover, 1953), p. 7.

III. THE NARRATOR

Within conventionally didactic works the act of telling represents a conquest of the highest order, the union of man and milieu in a single Logos. The instrument of this union is the inspired speaker, who translates celestial mysteries into mortal terms and renders God's word intelligible to human ignorance. In works designed to entertain the audience or express the poet's own inner sentiments, the narrator still serves as a mediator, but the paradigm's end terms have changed. Within these new structures the reader is transported toward a world of fantasy or brought into contact with the poet's inner self. Ideally these three narrative functions will coincide, as they appear to do within Dante's *Divine Comedy*. There entertaining fiction, celestial vision, and personal confession have merged into a single integrative superstructure.

Such is not, however, the case in Ariosto and Rabelais. Instead of effecting a stable balance between expressive, instructive, and diversional elements, they pit each against the other, mobilizing the narrative center of consciousness. Not only does the speaker assume a stance between sincerity and insincerity, *plaire* and *instruire*, but he moreover confuses each intentionality with its diametrical opposite, thereby casting the reader into an interpretative quandary. This fragmentation of the narrative functions is compounded by a mobilization of both voice and perspective, as the narrator ceases to mediate between heaven and earth, fact and fantasy, self and the other. Instead, he explores each of these contrasting poles and, in so doing, infects each of these values with his own definitional uncertainty.

That Rabelais and Ariosto, writing at the apex of the same cultural upheaval that produced Petrarch's divided ego, should recount their epic romances from an even more fragmented viewpoint is not surpris-ing. These mythographers of a new era have not restricted themselves to old narrative conventions but seek instead to reintegrate esthetics and epistemology. Their constant metamorphoses, then, are neither unintentional gaucheries nor meaningless experiments but rather con-stitute a sustained reflection of and inquiry into the changing struc-tures of knowledge. Analysis will reveal that narrative ambiguity, a source of consternation to seekers of the "sustantificque mouelle," is also a mainspring of the countervoyage and, as such, contributes to the two works' conceptual unity.

THE MASTER SHOWMAN, YOUR HUMBLE SERVANT

The Renaissance poet does not abdicate his affirmative post as a visionary or mage, which was theorized by Plato in his *Phaedrus* and *Ion* and kept alive through the Middle Ages. Instead, he updates it, using old epic and apocalyptical devices to serve a contemporary end. Turning his fictional mirror of truth earthward, he unveils utopias which seem mere reflections of sixteenth-century civilization; and current event, as exemplified by the timely voyage motif, becomes both subject and source of the poet's inspiration. Admittedly, Ariosto and Rabelais call upon Apollo (III.2) and Calliope (P.XXVIII.288) respec-tively for their furor, but only in a half-jesting, rhetorical manner, which negates the need for assistance. Nor do they evoke a medieval God for guidance, as their immediate predecessors were wont to do.[1] Instead, Ariosto opens his epic with a "prayer" to Ippolito d'Este, patron of the arts and figurehead of humanism's reign.[2] Yet this "hu-manized omniscience" is in fact a contradiction in terms, which con-tributes to fragmentation of the narrative "focalization" into two radi-cally opposing poles, the omniscient or unrestricted perspective and the restricted, unomniscient viewpoint.[3]

At first glance, the two perspectives appear joined as one, signaling

1. For a discussion of medieval "sources" of poetic inspiration, see Curtius's chapters entitled "The Muses" and "The Poet's Divine Frenzy," pp. 228–46, 474–75.
2. Rajna, p. 67.
3. There are actually two types of unomniscient focus, since the narrator may know the same as or even less than the characters. See Gérard Genette, *Figures III* (Paris: Seuil, 1972), pp. 206–11. In the Ariostan and Rabelaisian narratives, however, they are both opposed polemically and semantically to the omniscient point of view.

a reunion of the real and the ideal. Liberal use of the words "veoir" and "vedere" supports the eyewitness stance of both voyager and visionary. The two postures complement each other, the one by lending credence to the inspired poet's revelation and the other by sublimating contemporary accomplishments. The *Quart Livre,* which doubles as a geographical and netherworld odyssey, is filled with the narrator's insistence that he saw ("Je veidz" [IX.564]) the spectacle, while Ariosto explicitly unites the two stances in both his vision of modern Argonauts (XV.21) and his eidetic voyage ("Ma mi par di veder, ma veggo certo" [XLVI.1]) toward an afterlife graced by the stars of Renaissance culture. Simple firsthand observations are given an apocalyptic flavor not only by the narrator's rhetorical claim to inspiration but also by the arcane, privileged nature of the information he imparts. It is because of his occult powers as an "abstracteur de quinte essence" that Alcofribas is called ("Je . . . y fuz appelé" [G.I.8]) to decipher Gargantua's invisible genealogy ("practicant l'art dont on peut lire lettres non apparentes" [8]) so that the world may "see" ("ainsi que veoir pourrez" [9]). The mysteries which he reveals to us are not limited to the giant's lineage but, according to the prologue, concern religion, government, and the economy (5). If Ariosto poses less openly as a magus, it is nonetheless through the implicit association of his prophetic powers ("quel profetico lume che m'inspiri" [III.2]) with those of Merlin ("il profetico spirto di Merlino" [III.9]) and Melissa that the Estense family tree as well as predictions about Ferrara's future come to light. Thus the ulterior narrative also poses as a predictive one.[4]

As seers the Rabelaisian and Ariostan narrators seem to usher in a new millennium ruled by princes with messianic genealogies and peopled by heroes whose curiosity typifies Renaissance man. Yet because of his vacillation between didactic and diversional communicative functions, the inspired poet's vision doubles as the baser jongleur's fantasy; and his revelational present is devitalized by equation with the chivalric past of medieval romances.

Apparent contradictions in this hybrid narrative stance are partially explicable in terms of the narrative situation or the storyteller's relationship with his readers or narratees. In order to realize his communication, he must appeal to them on their own terms, exploiting their nostalgia for chivalry and love of play to catch and hold their attention.

4. Cf. Genette, p. 229. Much of the terminology used to analyze the narrative is explained in the chapters "Mode" and "Voix," pp. 183–267.

His deliberate combination of progressive and regressive elements, moreover, plays upon the readers' dual attitude toward the present, upon both their pride in contemporary achievements and their instinctive rejection of actuality's existential uncertainty.

Explicit references to the audience, within the text, enforce this ambiguous reading. Both Rabelais and Ariosto direct their fantasies toward a pointedly literate and leisured ("veu que sommes de sejour" [P.I.171]) community, made up of lords ("chevaleureux champions" [P.prol.167]) and ladies ("donne gentil" [XXIX.2]) who, even as they take credit for cultural and scientific advances, stagnate in an endless round of games and anachronistic privilege. One sees them hunting in the prologue to *Pantagruel* ("allant à chasse" [167]) or engaged in fashionable polemic discussions, intrigues, and poetry readings in the Ariostan exordia, which simulate a court setting. This love of sport is further reflected, within the fiction per se, by the various duels and tournaments which—even when intrinsically tragic in nature— are transformed into *divertissements*.

Be it reflective of Renaissance society or merely a metaphor of the "player" in all potential readers, this dramatized audience or narratee is Pascalian in nature, world-weary, and eager to escape into a land of fantasy. The artist, a product and apparent propagator of establishment values, is prompt to oblige, promising novelty to assuage their restless thirst, feeding their illusions of grandeur with encomium, and soothing their anxieties with his "fines drogues" (G.prol.3) and hypnotic music.

It is as a minstrel and not as a diviner that the poet exerts some of his most potent magic, spiriting readers into a sunny pleasure-dome far removed from existential conflicts. Not only do both narrators speak of literary creation in musical and thus largely nonmeaningful terms, but they employ its materials—sounds and rhythms—to depict life as a dance in their texts. "Je serviray les massons," says Rabelais in the prologue to his *Tiers Livre*, "je mettray bouillir pour les massons, et, le past terminé, au son de ma musette mesureray la musarderie des musars. Ainsi fonda, bastit et édifia Amphion, sonnant de sa lyre, la grande et célèbre cité de Thèbes" (325). If the words "massons" and "mesureray" support the second sentence's contention that art can serve a constructive function in society, so does the automatic association between "musette" and "musarderie" suggest the opposite conclusion: that esthetics have been divorced from ethics and epistemological concerns.

Likewise, Ariosto's comparison of his own task to that of a musician provides a meaningless, purely formal justification for the *Furioso's* constantly changing tonality:

Signor, far mi convien come fa il buono
sonator sopra il suo instrumento arguto
che spesso muta corda, e varia suono,
ricercando ora il grave, ora l'acuto.   (VIII.29)

The *Furioso* itself may be envisioned as a great fugue, which, marked by brilliant flights and brief moments of resolution, engages the restless reader in a diverting poetic "hunt."[5] And with his Dionysian incantations Rabelais propels us even farther away from reality, into a world of pure poetry which is born of unorthodox modulations. In both cases, however, the Platonic connotations of musical references and techniques reinforce the imaginary voyage's idealistic orientation by suggesting a reintegration of esthetics and metaphysics in the harmony of the spheres. Rabelais's reference to Amphion's founding of Thebes ("sonnant de sa lyre") clearly demonstrates his awareness of the supernatural powers that antiquity attributed to music, which was thought by the Greeks to be of divine origin.[6]

Filtering life through a poetic lens, the didactic narrator purports to have extracted a magical "quinte essence," a mythical amalgamation of beauty and truth, which he spreads out before us in spectacular form

5. Further support for this nonliterary explication may be sought in the history of music. See Donald Jay Grout, *A History of Western Music* (New York: Norton, 1960), pp. 153–84. If the baroque fugue has not yet come into existence at the time of Rabelais and Ariosto, the term *fuga* already appears in the fifteenth century, as a referent to passages in strict imitation; and Renaissance innovations in a kindred genre, the canonical motets of Jacob Obrecht and Josquin des Prez, find their literary equivalent in the *Furioso's* contrapuntal construction, as well as in both works' experimental play of fantasy. Like the literary and graphic arts, Renaissance music is just beginning to be accepted as a respected end in itself and no longer serves as the mere handmaiden of "meaningful" lyrics.

Rabelais and Ariosto were, furthermore, undoubtedly familiar with this new brand of music and musician. The two aforementioned composers were both patronized by the Ferrarese rulers, while Rabelais includes Josquin des Prez among a list of contemporary musicians in the *Quart Livre* prologue (531–32).

6. "Greek mythology ascribed to music a divine origin and named as its inventors and earliest practitioners gods and demigods, such as Apollo, Amphion, and Orpheus. In this dim prehistoric world, music had magic powers; people thought it could heal sickness, purify the body and mind, and work miracles in the realm of nature. Similar powers are attributed to music in the Old Testament: we need only recall the story of David curing Saul's madness by playing the harp (I Samuel xvi: 14–23), or of the trumpet blasts and shouting that toppled the walls of Jericho (Joshua vi: 12–20)." Ibid., pp. 4–5.

and announces with great aplomb. Ariosto would lead us back to the "true" life of the past ("Oh gran bontà de' cavallieri antiqui!" [I.22]), while the Gallic doctor teases the reader with hints of a "sustantificque mouelle" (G.prol.5) and "propriétéz occultes" (P.prol. 168). Yet the narrative function and perspective are so unstable that one can even interpret the epistemological voyage in ludic terms. In toying with allegory and symbolism, the poet seems more interested in entertainment than didacticism—an attitude typical of his age. The sixteenth century witnesses a great vogue for epistemological games and dabbling in the occult, both of which constitute a popular pastime among cultivated, humanistic circles. When the contemporary reader is confronted with traditional signifiers—such as colors, landscapes, and personified abstractions—his interpretative skills are challenged and his amusement only enhanced by the "puzzle's" complexity. In fact, both works with their tangled intrigues are enigmas, thus an inexhaustible source ("source vive et vène perpetuelle") of "joyeuseté" and "raillerie" (TL.prol.328).

Despite our efforts to the contrary we cannot reduce Gargantua's livery or Ariosto's portrait of the "iniqua frotta" to a nonliterary signified without ignoring both textual autonomy and artistic intention:

> Croiez-vous en vostre foy qu'oncques Homère, escrivent l'*Illiade* et *Odyssée*, pensast ès allégories lesquelles de luy ont calfreté Plutarche, Heraclides Ponticq, Eustatie, Phornute, et ce que d'iceulx Politian a desrobé? Si le croiez, vous n'approchez ne de pieds ne de mains à mon opinion. (G.prol.5)

In harmony with the sportive propensities of their age the narrators are playing with semiotic convention, parodying their predecessors in the field and creating a purely objective reality which signifies only itself. Beneath Rabelais's arbitrary ("diray en un mot") assertion that "bleu signifie certainement le ciel et choses célestes" (G.X.37) and Ariosto's glib concetti ("son duo negri occhi, anzi duo chiari soli" [VII.12]), this one Petrarchist in flavor, we detect a strong note of irony. In voicing two possible interpretations for both colors (blue as either "ciel" or "fermeté") and the fate's "sembiante" (negative versus positive rapports with essence), the narrators leave only the spectacle itself, described in graphic detail.

Likewise, in his guise of tour guide, the poet seems bent on diverting readers, ushering them into an artificial paradise which, albeit similar in many ways to Renaissance civilization, is larger and more vivid than life. Certainly, the reader draws upon fact to visualize the realms of Thélème, Utopia, and Alcina, enriching these accounts with his knowledge of contemporary court life. Yet within this literary world castles are built not of rocks but of words, which, instead of imitating finite realities, act to impress new and idealized images upon the mind's eye. The inhabitants of Alcina's land, Utopia, and Thélème engage in activities common among the leisured classes of their day: games, hunts, musical soirées, garden walks, prose and poetry readings. Using some similar and some very different techniques, however, both authors effectively transport these kingdoms beyond our mental grasp. In Rabelais their exaggerated specificity and accumulation make the most "mimetic" descriptions virtually impossible to synthesize, while, conversely, Ariosto's blurring of detail with approximations, shadows, muted sounds, rippling movements, and adjectives connoting soft- ness and gentleness generates scenes far more literary than real.[7] This effect is supplemented by nonmimetic verbal processes such as hyperbole, inexpressibility topoi, and the repeated use of *tant* and *sí*. When the narrator says that Alcina has more fish than "non ha stelle il cielo" (VI.39), or that Gargantua's ring is "faict des quatre metaulx ensemble en la plus merveilleuse façon que jamais feut veue" (G.VIII. 30), he sends objects spiraling off toward the ineffable.

By willing his universe autonomous, the poet has set himself up in fanciful competition with God, thereby affirming the audience's hu- manistic illusions of grandeur. No longer an anonymous mouthpiece for the divine Presence, the Renaissance artist rivals his maker with a prolific explosion of *je*'s and *io*'s. The exaggerated relief of this in- trusive, omniscient narrator produces an implicit division between creator and created object, thus regenerating and humanizing the origi- nal heaven-earth hierarchy. By bracketing the unknown in a familar frame of reference, the God-artist metaphor was originally born of a desire to render the unknown intelligible to man.[8] By the sixteenth century, however, the comparison's two terms have been reversed to accord with a more anthropocentric world vision. In assuming an

---

7. In this sixth-canto description of Alcina, for example, Ariosto mentions "*delicati* colli" (20), "*ombrose* ripe e prati *molli*" (20), "aure fresche . . . / che l'alte cime con *mormorii lieti* / fan *tremolar* dei faggi e degli abeti" (24), and castle walls so luminous ("sí risplende" [59]) that they *seem* to be gold ("a me *par oro*" [59]). The italics are mine.

8. Curtius, pp. 544–46.

Olympian stance, the poet acts less to justify the ways of God to man than to affirm man's creative power through metaphysical association with the demiurge.

The mere fact that Rabelais and Ariosto are creative artists is not sufficient to establish their metaphorical relationship to God. What is significant is their dramatization of an analogy which lies forgotten in most finished works of art. By verbally simulating the bard's physical presence, Rabelais and Ariosto manage to unfold an epic in its becoming, in its telling rather than its told; but their compensatory exaggeration and personalization of the narrative ego at the same time detract from the story itself.[9] Longwinded inventories, modulations in style, and narrative interventions all call attention to the creative process, forcing readers to watch a self-conscious artist who delights in his own invention. In Ariosto's parade of British soldiers (X) and in both authors' genealogies, one is made aware that to name, for the Renaissance poet no less than for God, is to create. Within such enumerative passages, words are not left to stagnate in a conventional field of syntactical and semantic structures but are rather reborn in their primitive, material integrity, consubstantial with the referent they denote. Quite obviously, Guaillartlardon and Cocquecygrue (QL.XL.647,650) have no reality apart from their names. Less clearly verbal creations, such as the historical names which both authors incorporate into their encyclopedic enumerations, have likewise been stripped of their real-life referents and regenerated as autonomous appellations; and in the absence of the extratextual signifieds, our attention necessarily alternates between the *name(d)* and the *namer*.

This essay in creative divinity is reinforced by an even more spectacular exercise on the narrator's part in omniscience, omnipotence, and omnipresence. Although all storytellers presumably enjoy a godlike control over their works, this attribute generally goes unnoticed by readers until the artist chooses, as do Rabelais and Ariosto, to exploit it. In order to render explicit this implicit rapport between artist and work, the Gallic and Ferrarese poets position the dramatized narrator, sporadically, in an Olympian relationship to his text. Transcending their characters' mortal myopia, the artists upon occasion give depth to their intrigue with sudden and privileged changes of scene, effected

---

9. Cf. Genette, p. 187: "La quantité d'information et la présence de l'informateur sont en raison inverse, la mimésis se définissant par un maximum d'information et un minimum d'informateur."

by "omniscient" intervention. This is a technique particularly favored by Ariosto. While Alcofribas verbally calls attention to the leap only during the first two books, to illuminate the simultaneous activities of opposing armies (G.XXVIII.88; P.XXVIII.285–86), the Italian poet does so dozens of times, invoking the theatrical principles of variety ("varie fila a varie tele") and order ("che tutte ordire intendo" [II.30]) to justify his shifts.[10]

It is not only God the creative artist but God the master showman as well that Rabelais and Ariosto choose to emulate within their works. Narrative intrusions, the initial division of prologues and exordia from the story, and the constant references to mask and spectacle all encourage one to visualize the fiction as a two-tiered stage, an image similar to the model set up by Rabelais in his Colloquium of the Gods (QL. prol.). There the Olympian deities (we and the narrator) look down on the human beings (characters), casting judgment upon, deriving amusement from, and occasionally intervening in their affairs. On the one hand, this directorial stance espoused by the artist provides readers, who identify with him, a vicarious realization of their aspiration for knowledge and power. Yet on the other hand, the posture's very theatricality reminds us that the omniscience and omnipotence accompanying it are not only limited, and thus faulty, but illusory as well. This articulation of the artist-God analogy in histrionic terms and structures in fact so radically formalizes the original metaphor that its content becomes lost in and negated by the spectacle itself. There emerges an esthetic of mindless entertainment at odds with the inspired poet's message-bearing function. While one may pore long hours over books, searching for abstruse hieroglyphs, the play's immediacy precludes such in-depth analysis and appeals more strongly to the senses than to the intellect.

As carnival minstrels Rabelais and Ariosto balance Olympian theatricality with its nonsignificative twin. It is from this epistemological void that the works' greatest force of reality, and hence greatest illusion, spring. The narrators speak not to some vague and distant reader but to a pointedly live audience, which they seduce with a showman's mixture of respect and informality. Ariosto's opening admission of insanity (I.2), like Rabelais's reference to his "païs de vache"

---

10. The authors are of course exploiting and personalizing romance transitional formulas. See Georges Doutrepont, Les Mises en prose des épopées et des romans chevaleresques du XIVe au XVIe siècle (Liège: Thone, n.d.), pp. 474–76.

(P.prol.169), serves to establish an ambiance of conversational familiarity between narrator and narratee.[11] Notwithstanding this oral style of delivery, moreover, both authors create an optical as well as auditive illusion. Sight imagery and firsthand observations not only strengthen the narrator's role as visionary but also join with eidetic descriptions to heighten the reader's awareness of the text as spectacle and his ability to visualize what he reads.[12] Frequent shifts to the present tense, generous amounts of dialogue, and the repeated use of "ecco" by Ariosto all draw scenes off the page and onto the stage, verbally simulating the play's strong physical relief and immediacy. Ariosto even goes so far as to fabricate verbal curtains ("tele" [II.30]) for his shadow-and-light technique, while Rabelais clothes both his ethics ("la practicque de médicine . . . est . . . un combat et farce jouée à trois personnages" [518]) and his metaphysics ("Mercure reguarde par la trappe des cieulx" [QL.prol.530]) in stage terms.

Ironically, it is the showman's most dazzlingly mimetic scenes and portraits which transport one farthest from reality, since mimesis can only be a linguistic illusion.[13] His accumulation of material detail corresponds, as it does in Ionesco, to an inverse explosion of Beckettian nothingness. The most colorful physical descriptions and portraits, which would be expected to endow characters with a stronger force of reality, are associated with the most illusory figures: Alcina, for instance, who later metamorphoses into an old hag, or the flying pig, who flits on and off stage in purely spectacular fashion. If their graphic depiction renders these abstractions imaginable, it at the same time facilitates our incredulity by endowing them with material but inhuman features which moreover point away from the characters: her breasts are ivory, its ears emerald green, and their teeth similar to topaz and pearls, respectively. Admittedly, the exteriority is explicable in allegorical terms, since both Alcina and Mardigras are symbols of sensuality. It is only fitting that they, unlike Logistilla and the citizens of Ruach, should take on this corporal relief. The dress and physiognomy of nonallegorical figures, likewise, are no longer clues to the individual's character but rather take on the artificial and exaggerated quality of masks and costumes. The elaborate description of Gargantua's livery

11. Apollonio and Fontana, p. 46.
12. On the use of *voir* in Rabelais's prologues, see Floyd Gray, *Rabelais et l'écriture* (Paris: Nizet, 1974), pp. 31–36.
13. Genette, p. 185.

encourages us to visualize not a boy but a gaudy giant. Ariosto pays no less attention than Rabelais to the finery of his figures, cloaking his knights in decorative armor and the ladies in pink, gold, and ivory masks, no more real than sculptures and paintings. Void of all moral and psychological indications, such portraits do little to establish character but rather find their table of reference almost entirely upon the proscenium, in the figures' farcelike actions and stilted language.

Similarly, the manneristic choreography to which they are subjected tends to defuse inherently pathetic or dramatic situations, giving them a comedic form which is the polar opposite of their content. Potentially tragic scenes, such as battles and natural catastrophes, lend themselves quite naturally to a theatrical style of presentation, which Ariosto employs upon occasion to render the characters' suffering more vivid. Encouraging his readers to visualize the African invasion, he compares it to the Venetian attack on Ferrara that they viewed in real life "come in teatro" (XL.2). More frequently, however, the narrators strip duelers of their pathos and transform them into weightless marionettes. In the burlesque fights between Loup Garou and Pantagruel, Frère Jean and the residents of Lerné, or the numerous Ariostan knights, the characters' presumed inner turmoil has diffused outward into a picturesque and often rhythmic flailing of weapons, limbs, and faceless bodies. Moving "quinci e quindi," "di qua e di là" and "à tort et à travers," they generate silhouettes against the backdrop rather than sentiments in the reader. In addition to their stylized movements, actions transformed into meaningless gestures, the characters' language itself, often less expressive than impressive, classifies them as stage creatures. Lovers such as Orlando (VIII.73–78) and Panurge (P.XXI.261) express their sentiments in an affected Petrarchist fashion, while an absurdly ornamental, bookish language clutters their everyday speech.

There is, of course, nothing remarkable in this caricatural stage world, which is conditioned by a variety of cultural factors: by the Renaissance love of pageant, by the ongoing comic and mime tradition which survives the Middle Ages, and by a literary tendency toward archetypal character development that appears stilted to modern readers. What is worth noting, however, is the parallelism between these theatrical figures and their narrator, who, instead of lucidly moderating the spectacle, uses it as a platform for his own weightless words and gestures. Much of the poet's erudition, metaphor, and imagery is functionally superfluous, related less to a logical chain of ideas or extra-textual signifieds than to nonrational associations and purely esthetic considerations. Such momentary lapses in discursive progressions more-over permeate the microcosmic structure, as constant displacements of subject, tone, and style attest to an "entrée en vin."[14]

If, in real life, the Ferrarese politician and Gallic monk are impris-oned within codified speech and behavior patterns, it is here, on stage, that they loosen their repressed tongues and give vent to that mad strain of artistry within each of us. Suddenly the poet can go backward or forward in time, lie if he pleases, or speak merely to hear himself talk, in one of innumerable guises. From out of this newfound freedom emerges a master storyteller, whose main narration branches off into myriad short stories, apparently removed from all semblance of "meaning."[15]

THE KING OF CLOWNS AND HIS MULTIPLE MASKS

To a certain extent, then, the narrative *jeu* is born of the Renais-sance audience's particular exigencies and depends for its success upon a oneness of sentiment between narrator and narratee, upon a common love of diversion and self-aggrandizement. The theatrical medium within which this union is achieved, however, fosters the seeds of dis-cord and narrative duplicity.

Given the fact that he is a stage figure, garbed in a clown's multicol-ored suit and possessed of a forked tongue, the narrator is intrinsically untrustworthy and potentially subversive.[16] No face is really his own but merely a rhetorical instrument through which he achieves a di-dactic or diversional end. Granted, these multiple masks—voyager, madman, philosopher, and poet—fit into the esthetics of variety which he has espoused and provide the audience still another spectacle.

14. "Vous veulx . . . une histoire narrer pour entrer en vin (beuvez doncques)." *Tiers Livre* prologue, p. 320.

15. Cf. P.XXXIV, 312 ("sy pour passe-temps joyeulx les lisez comme passant temps les escripvoys") and Ariosto's letter of 25 October 1515 to the Doge of Venice: "Havendo cum mie longe vigilie e fatiche, per spasso e recreatione de' S.ri e persone di animi gentili e madone, composta una opera in la quale si tratta di cose piacevoli a delectabeli de arme e de amore e desiderando ponerla in luce per solaço e piacere di qualunche vorà e che se delecterà de legerla, et anche cum quello piú beneficio e remuneratione delle fatiche mie duratoli de farla stampire dove meglio a me parerà" (pp. 1466–67).

16. See Jean Starobinski, *Portrait de l'artiste en saltimbanque* (Geneva: Skira, 1970).

The speaker is a jester who dazzles the audience with his many meta-morphoses.

Yet behind this esthetic aim is an ethical goal, expressed in Rabelais's metaphors ("du médicin la face joyeuse . . . resjouist le malade" [519]) and evident in the invective which crops up intermittently in each work. Despite evidence to the contrary, the authors do balance evasion with contrasting moments of confrontation—denunciation of firearms, satire of hypocrites, unsettling comments on basic existential problems. It is only for the reader that they coat the medicine with sugar, promising him a magic looking glass which will glorify his reflected image and transform him into a giant.

It must be remembered that the artist is traditionally an outsider or fringe figure by virtue of his very furor or meditative powers. To be sure, Renaissance artists often appear to ally themselves with the status quo, producing works upon royal commission and praising their princes within. Such is, in fact, the stance which Rabelais and Ariosto initially assume, the one in parodical form under an assumed name and the other because of necessity. But even as they set themselves up as exorcists, minstrels, and magicians—servants, in other words—they are automatically accentuating the reader-writer split. An authorial consciousness of the bystander's or alien's privileged viewpoint is evident even within the fiction, on both an epistemological and satiric level. The overall voyage of cognition revolves around grotto figures such as Melissa and Bacbuc, while it is the objective distance separating Rinaldo and Frère Jan (QL.X) from Scotland and Cheli which allows them to grasp the absurdity of "foreign" customs in those countries.[17] A similar objectivity exists between the narrator and narratee, whose game-loving nature must now be reinterpreted not only as a function of the diversional understanding between them but also in terms of the critical distance that separates him from both narrator and reader. Thus objectified, the dramatized audience becomes revelational instead of diversional. Identifying with the narratee, readers come to see themselves being seen, often in the process of playing ("l'inutil tempo che si perde a giuoco" [XXXIV.75]), and to recognize their own vanity.[18]

17. As an objective bystander Rinaldo interrogates what natives take for granted: "—Una donzella dunque de' morire / perché lasciò sfogar ne l'amorose / sue braccia al suo amator tanto desire?" (IV.63)

18. Cf. Jean Paul Sartre, *Qu'est-ce que la littérature?* Collection Idées (1948; rpt. Paris: Gallimard, 1969), p. 104: "Si la société se voit et surtout si elle se voit *vue,* il y a, par le fait même contestation des valeurs établies et du régime."

In fact, much of the author-audience rapport is constructed around a stylized master-slave relationship, initiated when the narrator refers to himself as an "humble servant."[19] Although this term of self-depreciation is a narrative commonplace, it is also a typically Renaissance form of exhibitionism, which draws attention to the speaker. To hear him talk, he is a mere jongleur who would sell his wares at the Lyon fair . . . or at the Ferrarese court. But the reader knows better: the sixteenth-century artist is no longer a traveling bard or an uncultivated child of the people but an honored figure who might well be termed a prince in his own right. And Rabelais tells us as much:

> Et pour vous donner à entendre de moy qui parle, je cuyde que soye descendu de quelque riche roy ou prince au temps jadis: car oncques ne veistes homme qui eust plus grande affection d'estre roy et riche que moy, affin de faire grand chère, pas ne travailler, poinct ne me soucier, et bien enrichir mes amys et tous gens de bien et de sçavoir. Mais en ce je me réconforte que en l'aultre monde je le seray voyre plus grand que de présent ne l'auseroye soubhaitter. (G.I.7–8)

Any humility is thus little more than a rhetorical vehicle, which allows the poet to affirm his own mastery of the game. Extratextual investigation yields the following unobsequious response, on Ariosto's part, to Cardinal Ippolito d'Este's claim to his services:

> Or, conchiudendo, dico, che, se 'l sacro
> Cardinal comperato avermi stima
> con li suoi doni, non mi è acerbo et acro
> renderli, e tòr la libertà mia prima. (*Satira* I.262–65)

The Ferrarese poet's repeated refusal, in the *Satire*, to assume the servile attitude expected of him finds slightly more subtle expression in the *Orlando furioso*. There and in the Pantagrueline tales, narrative self-abasement is accompanied by simultaneous overinflation of the audience, masters suddenly turned slaves. On a purely poetic level the flattery which works this effect is deceptively flowery, a triumph of form over content: "Erculea prole" (1.3) and the "chevaleureux champions" are not made of flesh and blood but of sounds and rhythms, which bend to the artistic will. Enamored by the sound of his own voice, the poet bombards readers with a stream of "unessentials"—re-

19. See 1.3 ("l'umil servo vostro") and P.prol.169 ("vostre humble esclave").

dundant superlatives and modifiers, such as "*très* illustres et *très* chevaleureux champions, gentilz hommes et aultres, qui voluntiers vous adonnez à *toutes* gentillesses et honnestetéz" (P.prol.167), or "*generosa* Erculea prole / *ornamento* e *splendor* del secol nostro"—which ironically overshadow ostensible signifieds and reflect back on the poet's own ego.[20] Once again, the informer's presence undermines the information.

Reversing his obsequious mask, the "humble esclave" reveals that his true allegiance is to Pantagruel ("lequel j'ay servy à gaiges dès ce que je fuz hors de page jusques à présent" [169]) and insists that the reader also pledge his fealty, at the peril of dire misfortune ("puissiez tomber en soulphre, en feu et en abysme, en cas que vous ne croyez fermement tout ce que je vous racompteray en ceste présente *Chronicque!*" [170]). Thus, no less than Épistémon and Astolfo, readers are lured into a topsy-turvy netherworld, where poets are kings and princes, their pawns.[21] Ariosto's first-canto reference to "Erculea prole," for example, already enigmatically hyperbolic, also calls to mind Seneca's *Hercules Furens* (whence the title *Orlando furioso*) and implicitly integrates Ippolito into the burgeoning list of fools; and when the poet offers words and ink in exchange for Ippolito's services, the implicit nothing-for-nothing equation undermines the entire patronage system.[22] Double entendres and *jeux de mots* serve the brasher Gallic writer equally well, allowing him to mock the respective demigods of sophism and humanism, of ancient and modern civilization. One such victim is Mamotret, a commentator of the Bible and hence pillar of Scholasticism, whom Rabelais transforms into "Marmotretus," author of *De baboinis et cingis, cum commento Dorbellis* (P.VII.196).

The Renaissance "hero" is also affected by this narrative duplicity, his gigantic aspirations made a source of laughter, and his most noteworthy feats depicted in a low and bawdy style. The narrator attaches strings to his wings, making him behave in a clumsy and burlesque manner. To cure their respective "patients," both Astolfo (XXXIX.

20. Italics mine.
21. Cf. I.4 ("vostri alti pensier cedino un poco, / sí che tra lor miei versi abbiano loco") and G.I.7: "Je pense que plusieurs sont aujourd'huy empereurs, roys, ducz, princes et papes en la terre, lesquelz sont descenduz de quelques porteurs de rogatons et de coustretz, comme, au rebours, plusieurs sont gueux de l'hostiaire, souffreteux et misérables, lesquelz sont descenduz de sang et ligne de grandz roys et empereurs, attendu l'admirable transport des règnes et empires."
22. Apollonio and Fontana (p. 47) also find irony in this passage: "Quel ch'io vi debbo, posso di parole / pagare in parte e d'opera d'inchiostro" (I.3). The hypothesis that Ariosto's title is partially inspired by Seneca comes from Rajna, p. 76.

56–67) and Panurge (P.XXX.295) act out a crude and lengthy rite, which adds neither to their dignity nor to that of Orlando and Épistémon.[23] On the other hand, incongruous use of heroic terms such as *cortese* and *courtois*, already rendered comic by their sixteenth-century archaism, serves to splinter both the audience's chivalric ideals and our faith in authorial sincerity.[24] Comic intent is clearly evident when Panurge asks the sibyl's advice "courtoisement" (TL.XVII.388) and when Ariosto insists that his buffoonish infidel is just as "cortese" (I.16) as legendary Christian heroes.

Clearly, the narrator is no less a clown than his marionettes, despite and perhaps because of his masterful guise. His most ambitious efforts, like those of his heroes, constitute a major source of comedy within the work. Setting himself up in competition with God, he is the prototype of Renaissance man, who seeks to conquer the universe and establish his Word as Law. Seen in this light, his inventories, apocalyptic visions, and presumptuous genealogies take shape as an extension of man's existential drive for power. In his hands, however, personified abstractions such as Quaresmeprenant, Silenzio, and Fraude form a mere parody of the allegories he would imitate; and his attempt to create a modern epic, hailed by pretentious invocations and high-flown

---

23. "Adoncq, nectoya très bien de beau vin blanc le col et puis la teste, et y synapisa de pouldre de diamerdis, qu'il portoit tousjours en une de ses fasques; après les oignit de je ne sçay quel oingnement, et les afusta justement, veine contre veine, nerf contre nerf, spondyle contre spondyle, affin qu'il ne feust tortycolly (car telles gens il hayssoit de mort). Ce faict luy fist à l'entour quinze ou seize poincts de agueille affin qu'elle ne tumbast de rechief, puis mist à l'entour un peu d'un unguent qu'il appelloit resuscitatif" (P.XXX.295).

> Lo fa lavar Astolfo sette volte,
> e sette volte sotto acqua l'attuffa;
> sí che dal viso e da le membra stolte
> leva la brutta rugine e la muffa:
> poi con certe erbe, a questo effetto colte,
> la bocca chiuder fa, che soffia e buffa;
> che non volea ch'avesse altro meato
> onde spirar, che per lo naso, il fiato.
>
> Aveasi Astolfo apparecchiato il vaso
> in che il senno d'Orlando era rinchiuso;
> e quello in modo appropinquògli al naso,
> che nel tirar che fece il fiato in suso,
> tutto il votò: Maraviglioso caso!
> che ritornò la mente al primier uso;
> e ne' suoi bei discorsi l'intelletto
> rivenne, piú che mai lucido e netto.   (XXXIX.56–57)

24. Dorothy Gabe Coleman, *Rabelais: A Critical Study in Prose Fiction* (Cambridge: Cambridge University Press, 1971), p. 27.

language, is spoiled by burlesque metaphors and unworthy subject matter. When Pantagruel acts as a harvester, a correspondingly low style suggests that the narrator has descended ("à veoir Pantagruel") from Olympia to the battlefield.[25] Similarly, if Ariosto reascends to "poeticize" Orlando's stance as a frog-gigger who has run six men through with a single lance, his very dignity appears absurd in view of the material and its original burlesque exposition:

> Et uno in quella e poscia un altro messe,
> e un altro e un altro, che sembràr di pasta;
> e fin a sei ve n'infilzò, e li resse
> tutti una lancia. . . .
>
> .   .   .   .
>
> Non altrimente ne l'estrema arena
> veggiàn le rane de canali e fosse
> dal cauto arcier nei fianchi e ne la schiena,
> l'una vicina all'altra, esser percosse.   (IX.68–69)

It is when he appears least authoritative, in fact, that the author wields the most control over the audience, which is implicated in his own dramatization. Feigning humility, he solicits our opinion with questions, engages our sympathy with familiar asides, and takes us off guard with deceptive candor. Bombarding the public with assurances that his tale is true, the author even takes special pains to explain apparent inverisimilitudes, such as Baiardo's heroics ("Signor, non voglio che vi paia strano" [II.20]) and Hurtaly's survival of the flood ("Hurtaly n'estoit dedans l'Arche de Noë . . . car il estoit trop grand; mais il estoit dessus à cheval . . . " [P.I.177]). Their guard lowered by a false sense of security, readers enjoy a feeling of amused superiority over this bumbling artist who, in insisting on his work's veracity, merely reminds one that it is fiction. Only on second glance is it evident that the author's words stand in an ambiguous relationship to his intentions: "si ne le croiez, non foys-je, fist-elle" (P.I.177), says Alcofribas. His far-fetched explanations have in fact ensured our belief and generated a critical audience.

Closer analysis of these affirmations of truth discloses a whole gamut of vacillations on the narrator's part, which produce complementary changes in the audience. We are not only unsure of him but of our-

---

25. "Sembloit un fauscheur qui de sa faulx (c'estoit Loup Garou) abbatoit l'herbe d'un pré (c'estoyent les géans)." (P.XXIX.294).

selves as well. Frequently his protestations of veracity are based not upon authorial omniscience but rather upon his own mortal experience, a technique particularly favored by Rabelais, and upon historical or pseudohistorical sources. Despite the privileged information to which the poet claims access, this descent from Olympia lays him open to attack, not only because of his sudden visibility but also because of the degradation it implies: the poet is inferior to his own Olympian twin, to the authorities on whom he depends, and to the readers against whose skepticism he defends himself. Such intrusive affirmations tend to produce a communication at odds with its purported message. When Ariosto tells readers his tale is true because Turpin says so ("Il buon Turpin, che sa che dice il vero" [XXVI.23]), or when Rabelais cites Pliny to support his account of Gargantua's birth [G.VI. 24]), the audience reacts with a skepticism apparently unwilled by the author.

Although such interpolations are narrative commonplaces, the Ariostan and Rabelaisian storyteller violates their rhetorical neutrality to strengthen his own position. What results is not so much a positive as a polarized figure of speech, charged with negative valence as well. By reason of its compensatory nature the very need to establish authenticity bespeaks a corresponding lack, presumably on the poet's part. Just as the affirmation proves upon closer examination to generate its opposite, however, so does the slave prove once again to be the master of his game. By addressing himself to a dramatized audience or narratee which is critical, knowledgeable, and at least his intellectual equal, the author reminds real-life readers, by force of contrast, of their ignorance and gullibility when it comes to literature. "Un homme de bien, un homme de bon sens, croit tousjours ce qu'on luy dict et qu'il trouve par escript" (G.VI.23), says Rabelais, before announcing that one of his authorities, Pliny, was surely a liar (24). The poet is not, after all, the historian's slave, but rather a critic of those who rely too heavily upon hearsay evidence and pretentious documentation. Similarly, Ariosto cites Turpin as a source in one instance only to doubt his word in a second (XXXIII.85) and condescendingly confirm it in a third (XXX.49).

Gone, clearly, is the reliable but unobtrusive narrator of previous epics, along with the consensus of values that lent historical authenticity to his position. In his place is a storyteller who is neither reliable nor dependably unreliable. He is merely inconsistent, varying his distance, perspective, voice, and function for two principal reasons: to confuse the reader and make us explore with him a variety of structures of knowledge. That his fluctuating, decentralized consciousness should confuse us does not, however, signal a defect in the work. Instead, it accurately reflects the problems and contradictions of a transitional age.[26] For if formerly, in the closed civilization of the Middle Ages, each individual had a fixed place in society, and man a fixed place in the universe, such is no longer the case in the open civilization of the Renaissance.

Insofar as they seek to heighten the reader's awareness of reality's complexity, the authors' didactic success derives largely from this very ability to mystify the audience. Refusing to establish the "rules" in a fashion understandable to both poet and public, they set about to denormalize their fiction through the purposeful negation of narrative logic and unity. We know, first of all, that the author has created his fiction and stands before it as God before the world; and when he includes us in his bird's-eye view of existence, we too feel omniscient. Yet he flaunts his knowledge at one moment only to withhold it from us at the next, reminding us of his ignorance in case we should fail to notice the omission. Albeit consistent with his role as chronicler, the poet's claims not to know if the Proteus legend is true (VIII.58) or whether Gargamelle died during victory celebrations (G.XXXVII.109) are examples of paralepsis scarcely compatible with his Olympian stance.[27] Similarly frustrating for the reader is Ariosto's shadow-and-light technique, which ironically issues from the esthetic principle of variety, espoused for our benefit. Usually, it is when the interest in a given scene is most intense that the narrator changes it, teasing the reader with concealed information and unveiling man's dependence upon divine revelation and whim. Such shifts disorient the reader, granting him a glimpse of multidimensional reality, but defying his one-track mind to grasp its totality.

To a lesser extent, a cat-and-mouse game recurs on a temporal level. Although Ariosto's fragmented narrative creates the impression of

26. Rabelais and Ariosto are in fact wavering between the narrative conventions of the epic and the novel, as defined by Robert Durling: "For if the dominant convention of epic is that its Narrator is a supernaturally inspired man who *transmits* a story received from outside himself, the dominant convention of the novel is that its Narrator (whether Author or character) is a natural man, limited to natural powers, who has (when Author) created the story out of his own experience and observation" (p. 9).

27. Genette, p. 211.

simultaneity, the adjoining frames are not really synchronous but are staggered in time. Consequently, the intersection of different sub-narratives generates some confusion on the part of the readers. Notably, the author does not reveal, in the nineteenth canto, that the fool Angelica encounters is actually Orlando, whom he left suspended in the thirteenth canto. It is only in the twenty-ninth canto that the paladin's own story line completes our understanding of the earlier incident. By withholding this knowledge from readers, the author allows the internal time of each character to develop autonomously. Their physical meeting serves, ironically, to accentuate the psychological distance that separates them.

Although the poet's omniscient and historically posterior relationship to his story would indicate that he knows the future of his characters, it is seldom that he enlightens the reader with insights into it. This effect may be partially explained by the author's choice to inhabit two temporal dimensions—both the present of his own writing and the fictional present of the events he is recounting. Violation of the latter by the former is rare. At the end of *Pantagruel* the poet appears to give a privileged insight into the future of Panurge ("vous verrez comment Panurge fut marié, et cocqu dès le premier moys de ses nopces" [P.XXXIV.311]) and Pantagruel (" . . . comment il espousa la fille du roy de Inde"). Proffered in a tongue-in-cheek manner, this "prophecy" is designed primarily to whet the buying public's appetite and moreover goes unfulfilled. Ariosto's more accurate predictions about his characters generate a similar tension. Ostensibly, they serve to assure indignant ladies that villains like Rodomonte will be punished:

> Donne gentil, per quel ch'a biasmo vostro
> parlò contra il dover, sí offeso sono,
> che sin che col suo mal non gli dimostro
> quanto abbia fatto error, non gli perdono.
> Io farò sí con penna e con inchiostro,
> ch'ognun vedrà che gli era utile e buono
> aver taciuto, e mordersi anco poi
> prima la lingua, che dir mal di voi. (XXIX.2)

Structurally parallel to Orlando's divine punishment (XXXIV.62–66), Ariosto's capricious condemnation of Rodomonte in fact interrogates rather than illuminates the mainsprings of causality and judgment.

Despite his experimentation with omniscience, the narrator varies the modality of his narrative, proffering many judgments from a purely human, unenlightened perspective. Rabelais offers very few evaluations of, or predictions about, his characters, while many of Ariosto's are equivocal. If Alcofribas tells readers that Pantagruel "estoit le meilleur petit et grand bonhomet, que oncques ceigneit espée" (TL.II.335), it is the giant's own words and deeds that prove him wise. Likewise, there is a good deal more showing than telling in Ariosto, who, on the occasions when he does ascribe "moral" qualities to his characters, does so in such unprivileged terms that the modifiers' meanings are neutralized. Words such as *crudele, cortese,* and *generoso,* which are often at odds with the reality they describe, tend in fact to normalize rather than individualize the figures. Related as it is to literary and social codes, this archetypal language is often intended to satisfy our expectations or reflect our own judgment rather than really enlighten the audience. When Ariosto disowns Rodomonte or laments the fate of Proteus's victims ("Oh misere donzelle" [VIII.59]), he playfully hypothesizes the conventional readers' reaction in a melodramatic travesty of the Greek chorus's rhetorical function. Here the technique does not intensify pathos but instead reactivates the readers' objectivity.

Rather than petrify his characters with arbitrary psychological or moral attributes, the artist tends instead to develop them phenomenologically, accentuating speech, actions, and physical attire.[28] This dynamic form of representation, achieved from a human standpoint, produces an effect much more thought-provoking than that of medieval exempla. Despite their figures' marionettelike quality, Rabelais and Ariosto work not to create but to destroy types, allowing contradictory personalities to splinter traditional masks: Angelica is no longer the *donna angelicata*; Panurge, the senseless buffoon; Orlando, the impassible hero; nor Frère Jan, the hypocritical monk.

Nor are the characters totally transparent: not even the narrator claims a complete knowledge of their minds and motives. Certainly, the Ariostan storyteller is privy to a good number of interior and exterior monologues, which enable him to assert that Angelica "ordisce e trama" (I.51) a plot to exploit Sacripante's services and that "nel suo cor l'iniquo conte [Pinabello] / tradir l'incauto giovane [Bradamante] si

28. See Jean Paris, *Rabelais au futur,* p. 141: "Où les classiques définiront les changements de leurs créatures comme des écarts à partir de quelque essence fixe, Rabelais expérimente cette présentation phénoménologique des caractères, dont chaque instant, comme chez Balzac ou Proust, ne met en lumière que telle facette."

pensa" (II.67). Less frequently Rabelais makes use of the same privilege to advance his narrative, telling us, for example, that Pantagruel "voulut . . . essayer son sçavoir" (P.X.213) or that he "feut bien esbahy" (P.XXIV.269). Such inside views are generally brief and serve to supplement words and gestures, which are the readers' greatest source of information. One might indeed venture that the Rabelaisian narrator, at least, is deriving "intentions" and "emotions" from their exteriorization as acts. And in Ariosto, where the technique serves to foreshadow and explain the characters' actions, this interior perspective's true field of reference is no less external. Yet by way of contrast, the omniscient storyteller's rudimentary presence renders his ignorant twin's doubt all the more striking. Ariosto's discourses are permeated with the words *forse* and *parere* as well as either-or constructions ("o che sperasse farlo ritonare / o sdegno avesse udirne biasmo e scorno" [VIII.88]).[29] And while Rabelais also makes use of *sembler* ("Pantagruel sembloit grandement pensif" [TL.XIX.394]), he even goes so far as to have Panurge dispute Alcofribas's character judgment:

—Voire, mais (dis-je) vous vous dampnez comme
une sarpe, et estes larron et sacrilège.
—Ouy bien (dist-il), comme il vous semble;
mais il ne me semble, quand à moy.   (P.XVII.244)

Far from being totally rhetorical, this narrative descent from Olympia is not devoid of extratextual signification but reflects back on the problems of seeming, being, and knowing in a masked society. In assuming this hands-off attitude toward their characters, the narrators defy us to judge our fellowman.

If the narrator's affected ignorance metaphorically captures the reader's relationship with other human beings, it also doubles as a kind of antirhetoric, which explores the possible links between silence, language, and truth. Often, the author's "message" lies not in what he says but in what he does not say, as he forces the audience to read between the lines for an interpretation of the work;[30] and the moderator's equivocal attitude toward discourse is also projected onto his characters.

The taciturnity of Orlando and Pantagruel not only reflects the

29. On the use of *forse*, *parere*, etc., see G. de Blasi, "L'Ariosto e le passioni," *Giornale storico della letteratura italiana* 129 (1952): 330–41.
30. As Glauser notes, "ce maniaque de la parole est aussi un maniaque du silence" (p. 100).

hero's lack of knowledge but points to the existence of an inner self which never really surfaces. Significantly, it is often after his lengthiest soliloquies—such as the Death of Heroes narrative—that the Rabelaisian giant is least communicative: "Pantagruel, ce propous finy, resta en silence et profonde contemplation. Peu de temps après, nous veismes les larmes découller de ses œilz grosses comme œufz de austruche" (QL.XXVIII.619). A thematic link between silence and awe, also present in the *Furioso* ("Stassi d'Amon la sbigottita figlia / tacita e fissa al ragionar di questa" [III.13]), would indicate that Pantagruel is contemplating the vast unknown itself, the mysteries of human existence. Any privileged intuitions which the "sage" might experience are, however, engulfed in the introspective screen, proof that man's profoundest emotions are inexpressible. Orlando's most revealing utterances are in fact his tormented internal monologues, while public discourses—always enigmatically "cortesi"—testify to a profound sense of verbal frustration. If, during his confrontation with Mandricardo, Orlando symbolically removes his helmet ("vo' che mi veggi dentro, come fuore" [XXIII.75]), he does not, however, succeed in casting off his linguistic armor, a set of conventional chivalric formulas which convey much less meaning than his tone ("gridò forte"). Like Pantagruel, whose quiet resistance to the tempest is contrasted to Panurge's passive babbling, the Ariostan paladin resorts not to speech but to action in times of crisis.

This unenlightened method of character portrayal is pursued not only on a psychological level but on a spatial and temporal level as well. Even as they create an elitist fictional world, where historical and geographical roots are of the utmost importance, the authors frequently withhold background material and limit readers to here-and-now judgments. Certainly, Pantagruel's pedigree and Orlando's reputation ostentatiously herald their advent on the scene. These open-book characters are possessed of the most reticent personalities, of an unreadable subconscious, while the apparently extroverted Panurge springs from unknown origins, uncertainly inferred from his appearance in the immediate present:[31]

Un jour Pantagruel . . . rencontra un homme beau de stature et élégant en tous linéamens du corps, mais pitoyablement navré en

31. His "profond souspir" (TL.IX.357), however, suggests unexplored psychological depths.

divers lieux . . . De tant loing que le vit Pantagruel, il dist ès assistans:

"Voyez-vous cest homme qui vient par le chemin du pont Charanton? Par ma foy, il n'est pauvre que par fortune, car je vous asseure que, à sa physionomie, Nature l'a produict de riche et noble lignée, mais les adventures des gens curieulx le ont réduict en telle pénurie et indigence." (P.IX.207)

Instead of rounding out the silhouette with clear-cut, three-dimensional contours, the author chooses to develop the enigma itself, giving it a kaleidoscopic aura of possibility. This spectacular manner of presentation whets rather than satisfies the reader's curiosity, frustrating his desire for positive knowledge through the evocation of an impenetrable unknown.

This narrative refusal to fix figures with a priori definitions stems from a romance tradition,[32] to be sure, but in his introduction of Pinabello upon the scene, Ariosto turns the technique to epistemological purposes. Just as we first see Panurge through Pantagruel's eyes, so is it another character, with restricted vision, who introduces us to the young Count Pinabello. Initiating the characterization with Bradamante's shadowy impressions from afar, the narrator allows the scoundrel to talk his way into the reader's good graces.[33] Omniscient intervention after the soliloquy only serves to reaffirm that human judgment (both ours and Bradamante's) often errs.[34] In the above example the outside-inside narrative progression appears to disparage on-the-spot evaluations, exploiting instead the injustices and illusions it perpetrates. Far from indicating artistic ineptitude, the continued

32. Rajna, p. 88.
33. D'un cavallier la giovane s'accorse;
   d'un cavallier, ch'all'ombra d'un boschetto,
   nel margin verde e bianco e rosso e giallo
   sedea pensoso, tacito e soletto. (II.34–35)
With regard to this unenlightened introduction of characters upon the scene, Apollonio and Fontana note that "in questa ricchezza di chiaroscuro attorno a ogni personaggio che gli fa superare il semplicismo con cui nella narrativa popolare i buoni erano distinti dai cattivi, sta anche la novità e la grandezza dell'Ariosto" (p. 75).
34. Questo era il conte Pinabel, figliuolo
   d'Anselmo d'Altaripa, maganzese;
   che tra sua gente scelerata, solo
   leale esser non volse né cortese,
   ma ne li vizii abominandi e brutti
   non pur gli altri adeguò, ma passò tutti. (II.58)

mise en scène of silhouettelike characters acts as a mirror of life, revealing the necessarily superficial, defective nature of man's judgment. The external criteria such as speech, lineage, clothing, behavior, and reputation upon which man bases his evaluation of others are necessarily imperfect gauges of character. Their value is weakened by the possibility of poor discernment on the viewer's part, deceit on the bearer's part, and the basic inability of external phenomena to express the individual's inner essence. For example, Rabelais's elaborate genealogy satirizes man's emphasis on ancestry in an epoch which deems itself modernistic, while the mystery surrounding Ruggiero's birth, as well as the lapses of veracity in the Utopian and Estense family trees, question the accuracy and value of lineages used to establish a person's "nobility." Despite the importance attached to parentage in the Renaissance, it is generally accepted that an aristocratic birth alone does not constitute true nobility. Likewise, the clothes, reputation, and speech by which men are judged prove to be faulty indicators: Panurge's toga is misinterpreted by Pantagruel, Orlando's *nominanza* relates to his past rather than present identity, and words and clothes are repeatedly connected with deceit in the *Furioso*.

Notwithstanding their limitations, these outer manifestations of inner character are the only guidelines available for the evaluation of one's fellowman, says Count Ludovico da Canossa in the *Courtier*:

> E perchè, com'ho detto, spesso la verità sta occulta, e io non mi vanto aver questa cognizione, non posso laudar se non quella sorte di Corteggiano ch'io più apprezzo, ed approvar quello che mi par simile al vero, secondo il mio poco giudizio. (I.13, pp. 39–40)

A person cannot be judged, on earth at least, by his invisible subconscious or on the basis of good intentions. For in an existential world where doing is being, is man not necessarily what he appears to be— the moment-to-moment sum of his acts? Thus in their largely objective descriptions and character developments, Rabelais and Ariosto not only confront readers with the inadequacy of face-value judgment but also explore the converse hypothesis of form itself as a content, of face value as an absolute in itself.

Not only our attitude toward characters but our entire system of metaphysical and ontological precepts is upended by the narrator's shadow-and-light technique, which represents the workings of a hidden god who reveals or conceals himself at will. One can even detect an evolution of this balance between omniscience and ignorance in Rabelais, whose center of consciousness moves farther and farther away from Olympia and more and more deeply into the maze of man's cloudy, fragmented vision. In the *Tiers Livre* the knowledgeable moderator largely absents himself to give his characters a forum, thus splintering Alcofribas's already polarized perspective into a broken spectrum of partial viewpoints. The *Quart Livre* confusion of an eye-witness *je*, a participatory *nous*, and an objective *ilz* further frustrates the reader's efforts to situate himself in a stable position with regard to the text or to establish a norm for judgment, while the insertion of storytellers-within-the-story completes his decentralization of the speaker's Word.[35] Here, as in Ariosto's secondary narratives, the authoritative "I" is not God but man, whose work is subject to question. When Panurge, the untrustworthy creation of an already untrustworthy author, types Basché as "couraigeux, vertueux, magnanime, chevalereux," or attributes the Chiquanous' arrival to divine will ("comme Dieu le voulut" [QL.XII.572–73]), one must necessarily consider the opposite judgment as an equally reasonable alternative.

Somewhat differently, Ariosto's exposition of Ginevra's misfortunes from several viewpoints or a mixed modality unfolds a labyrinth of see-and-tell, which moves from the monk's hearsay testimony (Ginevra guilty) to Dalinda's repentance (Ginevra innocent) for former lies (Ginevra guilty) to Polinesso's deathbed confession (Ginevra innocent). Yet if the princess's condemnation results from insufficient and partially erroneous testimony, her exoneration is dependent upon a new set of verbal evidence, presumably accurate, but generically weakened by previous lies and allusions. Dalinda's repentance is suspiciously colored with vengeance, while Polinesso's confession is authentically but mysteriously incomplete ("Non finí il tutto, e in mezzo la parola / e la voce e la vita l'abandona" [V.90]).

Far from dominating the narrative, the omniscient speaker seems to represent a largely polemical ideal which accentuates the limitations of normal human power. To drive home the contrast, he has created

35. See Abraham Keller, *The Telling of Tales in Rabelais* (Frankfurt am Main: V. Klostermann, 1963) for a more complete discussion of narrative structure and, particularly, digressions: "In Books I and II he allows his characters to tell only the four anecdotes and two of the stories (Panurge tells them both), for a total of six narrations, whereas he himself tells seven. In Books III and IV, he tells but fifteen (four stories and eleven anecdotes), while the characters tell thirty-seven (eleven stories and twenty-six anecdotes)" (p. 40).

some secondary narrators within the fiction, not only the storytellers but the letter-writers as well. Whereas the Olympian narrator brings disparate points in time and space together, the Utopian kings (G.XXIX, P.VIII, QL.III) and Ruggiero (XXV.86–93) only confirm separation, fragmentation, and mutation in their letters. For the giants and their sons, like the paladin and his lover, are both spatially and temporally divorced, one group belonging to the here-and-now and the other to the then-and-there.

In a sense it is true that the written word acts as a link between the poles, lifting both speaker and listener out of their isolation and suspending them in a realm of mutual intent and understanding. In reality, however, the two attitudes toward the messages are diametrically opposed, if only by virtue of the distance they seek to eradicate. In spite of the liberal attitudes and ideals expressed, the giants' letters to their adolescent sons reaffirm family ties and responsibilities. Gargantua is summoned home for defense of the patrimony, and Pantagruel is urged to study for its continuing glory. In postponing his union ("Voglio quindici dí termine o venti" [91]) with Bradamante, an implicit dedication to the future, Ruggiero excuses himself with evocation of his medieval chivalric duties ("Voglio . . . l'assedio al mio signor levar d'intorno" [90]). This news has moreover become anachronistic in the process of dissemination, as has the *Quart Livre*'s last epistle, which, sent from Utopia to Medamothi, resounds as a distant good-bye.

This temporal fragmentation furthermore parallels a split in the narrator's own mask, which he uses to disorient the reader and provoke a meditation on being and becoming. As God, he inhabits the eternal, a realm where praxis, the act of moving both vertically and horizontally throughout man's apparent pasts and futures, is paradoxically stasis and implies predestination by its very structure. Not content to impose this metaphysical hypothesis as a verity, the poet places the divine Word in the mouths of mortals, dividing it into its component parts and subjecting it to critical scrutiny; thus the scribe and mage meet, one recounting and the other prophesying. Any temporal closure is, however, dependent upon artistic sleight of hand. By virtue of her situation within the Turpin-based chronicle, Melissa tautologically foretells the past, revealing no more about the future than Badebec's midwives when they predict "de l'eage" (P.II.180) for Pantagruel. Unlike many medieval chroniclers, who ignore man for

God in their causal schemas, Ariosto and Rabelais mix with the immutable past an open present, countering chronicle with conversation, Olympian objectivism with participatory subjectivism, and fate with free will.

Such inconsistencies within time sequences may of course be attributed to a kind of antistructure, which purposefully precludes intentionality. Did not Rabelais create "en beuvant," and Ariosto, in intermittent fits of madness ("che 'l poco ingegno ad or ad or mi lima" [I.2])? It is not God's ordered eternity but the idiot's topsy-turvy one, similar in some ways to that of Faulkner's Benjy, which remains with us. What emerges is not so much a sense as senselessness. If the author theoretically recounts examples from the past for our eventual edification, as was the method of medieval moralists, the temporal trio consisting of author, characters, and reader merges into a timeless, defective "us"—a vicious circle which perpetuates human error. In these medieval-knights-made-Renaissance-man, one sees both the classical and modern Ulysses, the reader and the narrator, all joined in a nonsensical cycle of men who search for Godot.

It is not as a sage but as a fool, who neither brackets phenomena with meaning nor sifts them through a judicious eye, that the storyteller offers some of his most penetrating insights into human existence. Whereas medieval artists seek to infuse divine meaning—and Renaissance artists, a human order—into their works, Rabelais and Ariosto often do neither, allowing their battles, netherworld scenes, and enumerations to unfold instead as unmoderated, decentralized spectacles. While there is an element of Olympian objectivity in this stance, which equalizes all terrestrial affairs in their ultimate absurdity, this inability to distinguish between good and bad or between man and object seems to issue from the undifferentiating perspective of madness. The gods' and goddesses' amusement at human tragedy becomes, in the mortal narrator, an aberration. Far from being frightened or horrified by the massacre and mutilation of his fellowman on the battlefield, he demonstrates a primitive fascination with the abstract interplay of shapes and forms that they present. At the same time the fool's amoral bloodthirst serves to illuminate its immoral counterpart in society by awakening readers to their own instinctive sadism. Exploited by modern writers in the *théâtre de la cruauté* and by epic poets of all ages, this capacity for cruelty also appears as an objective theme in both the *Furioso* and the Pantagrueline tales. Ariostan crowds delight in jousts, laughing and jeering ("di ch'altri ne riporta pregio e lode; / muove altri a riso, e gridar dietro s'ode" [XVII.81]) at the new gladiators, while the diversion which Loup Garou promises Utopian troops ("vous aurez vostre passetemps à nous regarder" [P.XXIX.289]) is confused with "les fables de Turpin, les exemples de sainct Nicolas et le conte de la Ciguoingne" (290).

The narrator's madness does not stop at this excess objectivity, however, but merges with the most hallucinatory subjectivism, worthy of a Coleridge, Poe, or Baudelaire. His observations, like those of Céline's Bardamu, are distorted by his own neurotic fantasms, which are in turn provoked by and reflective of a world gone mad. Thus if the dehumanized battle is superficially comical, its ultimate effect is far more disquieting. To cite a more contemporary example, the technique of Ariosto and Rabelais is similar to that of Paolo Uccello, who, in his fascination with perspective, generates an explosion of forms—horses, helmets, weapons—that overpower knights in such paintings as the *Battle of San Romano*. There as in Rabelais and Ariosto, the phenomenological mastery implied by the artist's visual perspective is not accompanied by a mental comprehension of the newly materialized world. Although the objects are no longer divinely ordained symbols, neither have they yet been fully humanized. And in this unstable world of the Renaissance, which stands at the threshold of a new and potentially threatening reality, they take on an oneiric life of their own.

Rabelais's surrealistic Andouille war, with its dehumanized soldiers and concomitant proliferation of matter, provides a capital illustration of this phenomenon. Such is also the effect in Ariosto's tenth-canto parade of soldiers, where emblems, more visually prominent than the soldiers, seem now to possess their possessors. The syntactical dominance of object over man, repetition of *vedi*, crescendo of bizarre emblems, and reduction of men to standards and impersonal numbers all divide the scene between the realms of observation and hallucination. Here and throughout both works, in fact, Rabelais and Ariosto tend to relegate their knights to a shadowy, faceless existence. Thus deprived of their fixed identities, men are metamorphosed by analogy into reptiles, insects, amphibians, and other beasts. In Rabelais's Andouille war, for example, enemy soldiers are visualized as sausages, compared to serpents (QL.XXXVIII.643), and cut down like flies (QL.XLI.651). And while the commonplace animal similitudes represent, on the one hand, a purely rhetorical depreciation of man, they also exteriorize, graphically, the fears of a troubled psyche and an existential vertigo which prefigures that of Sartre's Roquentin.[36]

Part of the foolish narrator's function is obviously satiric, since, as an irresponsible, he can criticize without fear of retribution and, as an outsider, allow society to see itself being seen. Yet the functional disintegration of his personality, another symptom of his madness, prevents him from finding a foothold from which to launch a sustained attack. This lack of crusading spirit in the two works may certainly be attributed to the supremacy of artistic over didactic considerations; but another possible explanation is suggested by the disproportional breadth as opposed to depth of the derision, which extends to most of humanity, and which is dependent upon a split personality for its implementation. Like Erasmus's Stultitia, the narrator steps onto a revolving platform, which allows him to mock warmongers from a pacifist's point of view; navigators, from a meditator's point of view; believers, from a skeptic's point of view, and vice versa. He is two-faced and fickle, eager to change masks, to forsake one side for the other.

Since the technique is Menippean, and directed against all of mankind, the "outsider" must paradoxically be included inside the satiric circle.[37] And ironically, as much as Ariosto deplores the patronage system, he himself is necessarily implicated in its petty politics and must count himself among the lunar courtiers. Similarly, some of Rabelais's most stinging invective, directed against "cagotz," "géants doriphages," and "caphars" (TL.prol.328–29), reflects comically upon his own hypocritical and parasitic condition.

NARCISSUS SPEAKS

Behind the satiric polemics, indeed, lies the artist's dialogue with himself, a dialectical search for that mythical self-knowledge which leads to understanding of the microcosm. Instead of progressing toward unity, a center of consciousness from which he could judge the world,

36. "Et ils sauront que leurs vêtements sont devenus des choses vivantes. Et un autre trouvera qu'il y a quelque chose qui le gratte dans la bouche: et sa langue sera devenue un énorme mille-pattes tout vif, qui tricotera des pattes et lui raclera le palais. Il voudra le cracher, mais le mille-pattes, ce sera une partie de lui-même." *La Nausée* (Paris: Gallimard, 1938), p. 199.

37. See Coleman for further comments on the Lucianic elements in Rabelais, pp. 39–42, 84–109, 111, 118.

however, the narrator continues to waver between the diverse postulations of his own soul—between pragmatism and idealism, nationalism and pacifism; for a pronounced disgust for firearms does not preclude strong verbal support for the Estense (XXV.14) and French (TL. prol.323) military activities. So also do they express contradictory opinions, discursively and symbolically, on such contemporary subjects of debate as religion, art, language, learning, women, and progress. Apparently optimistic passages, including the "Éloge du pantagruelion" and the glowing tributes to Ferrara, reveal the poet to be particularly divided in his attitude toward modernity. Just as encomium is undermined through exaggeration ad absurdum, so is much of the satire devitalized by its rhetorical, gamelike nature. They are opposite sides of the same coin that serve to counterbalance each other and thereby forestall the establishment of a normative morality.

These ambiguities reflect more than the author's desire to confuse his reader. It is the poet's difficulty in taking a position, characteristic of his era, that generates the audience's quandary. The butt of his satire is often his own alter ego, and the public he awakens to consciousness, an extension of himself. Especially in passages where his wit is turned against the court or its rulers, Ariosto is largely speaking to another self, since only initiates will capture the full flavor of his necessarily subtle humor. It is to the *Satire* that one looks for a more direct expression of the writer's likes and dislikes. Although Rabelais's early work, presented as it is under a pseudonym at the fair, would appear to be less restricted by social considerations than that of Ariosto, one might well venture that the "key" to much of his discourse is accessible only to a reader sharing the author's vast and varied education. Such a fully appreciative public obviously can exist only in the poet's own mind. The explicit reader or game-oriented narratee is no less an embodiment of the writer than this implicit one, however. The vapid dilettantes to whom he openly addresses himself reflect his own inability to leave the comfortable world of make-believe for a definite political, social, or intellectual commitment.

It is not only in the content but in the structure as well that one sees evidence of a psyche divided against itself. The narrator's Dionysian furor is held firmly in leash by its Apollonian counterpart—and lyricism, by ironic twists.[38] Posing as a kind of demigod, the poet seeks the Ideal, a truth he can communicate to the masses in an act of

---

38. "Le Rabelais créateur est observé par le Rabelais critique." Glauser, p. 37.

generosity. The epic's earthly orientation and values, which prefigure those of the modern era, are, however, at odds with this revelational goal, which is still conditioned in Rabelais and Ariosto by the preceding era's transcendent standards. Also, the heavenly Unity that the poet seeks is ill reconcilable with the multiple, ambiguous reality with which he must reckon. The fragmented structure and antithetical language reflect the resulting tension and moreover testify to the idealistic poet's failure. Limited like us to tunnel vision, he only creates the illusion of phenomenological mastery, feigning temporal and spatial mobility within a fictitious medium; and even this simulation is defective, since the artist's mortal limitations prevent him from grasping more than one concept at a time. Thus, if anti-Aristotelian forms are part of a game to frustrate the reader, they are also expressive of the author's own vertigo before a fragmented reality. Amorphous encyclopedism and unmoderated dialogue, from this standpoint, signal the triumph of chaos over the author's rational efforts to organize and integrate what he perceives.

Even if it were accessible to man, the godhead's perspective would not be complete but would rather be paradoxically partial in its very perfection. Just as Dante seems inspired in his *Inferno* by human failings, so does there emerge in Rabelais and Ariosto a love of man's "instabil mente" (XXIX.1), of man in his baseness as well as his moments of greatness. And no less than that of his characters, so does the narrator's own stature vary, in terms of his height, his size, and the power he wields. Thus we witness, particularly in Alcofribas's gastroworld voyage, a narrative descent from pinnacle to abyss, a repeated up-down movement which reflects the corollary of man's desire to play God. It is a new variation upon the classical and Christian myth of God-become-man. This reversal of roles between creator and created is expressed in Rabelais's slavery to Pantagruel and in Ariosto's choice at times to follow rather than lead his characters ("*seguitiamo* Angelica che fugge" [I.32]).[39] Both of these phenomena are examples of au-

39. The italics are mine. See also:

> Di questo altrove io vo' rendervi conto;
> ch'ad un gran duca è forza ch'io riguardi,
> il qual mi grida, e di lontano accenna,
> e priega ch'io nol lasci ne la penna.

> Gli è tempo ch'io ritorni ove lascai
> l'aventuroso Astolfo d'Inghilterra.   (XV.9–10)

thorial metalepse[40] and constitute a rhetorical recognition of the reversible master-slave rapport which exists between the author and his
personae. Once objectified, the originally dependent character takes on
a self-consciousness of his own and an independence with regard to his
maker, who, as an abstract mediator, in turn finds himself dependent
upon his characters for the telling of the story. This rapport also reveals
a new twist in the writer-reader relationship. While the audience appears to be unessential in the writing, it becomes essential in the reading
of a text. The narrator's paradoxical slavery to his characters and his
public is given metaphysical overtones by the divine analogy: just as
the text reaches completion only through the objectified personae and
upon contact with an audience, so is God affirmed only in human
consciousness.

In addition to these different narrative guises through which the
artist essays his capabilities, failings, and affinities, he also projects
himself into the intrafictional characters, who at times seem mere
mouthpieces for the author. In Rinaldo's refusal to drink from the
chalice of truth (XLIII.6–8), we seem to hear the artist's own desire for
mediocrity and liberty, a preoccupation which recurs throughout his
Satire. A similar ideological identification between Rabelais and
Utopian royalty is, moreover, supplemented by biographical affinities
manifested during the Picrocholine War, a conflict inspired by the
artist's own childhood memories.[41] One probable source of this episode
is a property dispute between the artist's father and a neighbor, who
serve as prototypes for Grandgousier and the King of Lerné, respectively. The anti-Machiavellian kind of government favored by Grandgousier not only resembles that espoused by the narrator at the beginning of the *Tiers Livre* (I), but the calm, deliberate style in which
he (XXIX) and Gallet (XXXI) expound their views on war rings with a
conviction seldom present in the Pantagrueline tales.

Biographical interpretations such as these, however, oversimplify
the complex artistic mechanism. Given the works' fictional nature and
multiplicity of characters, the mere notion of a single authorial spokesman rings false. Undoubtedly, the "good sense" of Pantagruel and
Rinaldo represents a possible alternative to the contrasting follies of
Panurge and Orlando, but narrative sympathies appear equally divided

40. Genette, pp. 243–46.
41. Boulenger, introduction, p. xvi.

between the two poles. In his self-styled role of "wise fool," the creator himself exhibits both rational and irrational tendencies, which help account for inconsistencies in style and changes in point of view. Ariosto admits an affinity with Orlando at the very beginning of his work (1.2), while the exaggerated highs and lows, hopes and fears, of Panurge parallel the dramatized narrator's vacillations much more closely than does the steadiness of Pantagruel, who appears instead to embody the backstage artist's calm equilibrium.

From a psychological standpoint, textual fragmentation and multiple heroes may be interpreted as a cathartic expression of the artist's possible selves. Panurge's social nonconformism, dreams of absolute happiness, and verbal exuberance are all reinforced by the narrator himself. In view of both authors' stifling life as public servants, it is tempting to read a certain revolutionary edification into Orlando's and Panurge's transgressions of social norms. The one first appears in rags and later dons a long robe, while the other goes nude. Financially, they move from the realm of the exploited to that of the exploiters: Panurge steals more than he contributes to the church (P.XVII.243–44), while Orlando tries to trade his dead horse, which he praises as being otherwise undefective, for a shepherd's horse plus some additional compensation (XXX.5–7).

Far from being limited to major characters, the list of alter egos is enormous. The dying poet Raminagrobis, the *negromante* with his magic book, and Astolfo the "metamorphoser" are all projections of the creative artist, for example. Characteristically, the miraculous powers attributed to each figure are set into critical perspective by the comicality of their portrayal. More significant than the nature of their individual virtualities, furthermore, is their loosely bipolar disposition. The nonproductive pedantry and rituals of Rabelais's theologians balance Frère Jan's earthier religion, just as Isabella's chaste but suicidal devotion is offset by the Scottish priests' condemnation of their country's rigid morality (IV.59). Trusted mages such as Melissa and Bacbuc find antipodes in the sibyl and Atlante, while aggressors like Picrochole and Mandricardo meet conciliators in Gargantua and Orlando. In this balancing of positive and negative forces, one encounters not only the principle of variety upon which cosmic harmony is based but the inner conflict of the human soul as well.

Far from being naive expressions of the artist's subconscious, characters serve an epistemological and ethical function not too different from that of psychological allegory. Contrasting figures, like personified vices and virtues, are exteriorized players in an interior debate, conflicting instincts and interests that have been dramatized in typically Renaissance Socratic form. Rabelais and Ariosto fail to resolve the differences of these polarized figures in a consolidated heroic ideal or moral norm. Instead, each character checks his opposite's ascendance, while the narrator, who also undergoes cell division, varies in his attitude toward the figures: he may be approving or disapproving, both or neither. The only self-knowledge that emerges from this introspection is a recognition of man's schizophrenia, which ironically fulfills the apocalyptical promise of Pantagruel's "Know thyself." As a microcosm of the macrocosm the individual's personality mirrors the universe's disjointed form. The Rabelaisian and Ariostan version of Narcissus's pool is a multifaceted, refracted image which, in contrast to the unifying medieval *specula*, reflects the disorder of man's mind and his world.

Also mirrored in this fictional universe is the reader, who is induced by the narrator to participate in his self-analysis. Direct address serves, first of all, to dramatize the *vous* and *voi* no less than the *je* and *io*, while occasional use of the first person plural further implicates readers in the fiction. On one level, we are convoked as judges. Far from allowing us to follow the story passively, the narrator directs his moralizing reflections at us, particularly in the prologues and exordia; poses questions to us, both explicitly and implicitly; and reacts to our reactions. Yet the readers' judgments are far from objective. The questions are leading and our responses, to a large extent controlled by the narrator, even in their ambiguity. Nor does the reader maintain a disinterested attitude toward characters. The liberal use of lively monologues and conversations as character-building devices strengthens reader-identification with the figures, as does their depiction by a frequently sympathetic narrator. Instead of judging Panurge and the Ariostan paladins as a total outsider might, condemning their departures from the "camin dritto," the public is indoctrinated to their points of view by the author's own mobile and infectious humor. Since they are extensions of himself, there is doubtless an element of apology or confession in this process: in the characters' *superbia*, an admission that Ariosto does not totally adhere to *mediocritas*; in Panurge's knavery, an admission of the Gallic monk's own irreverence. The created audience minimizes these transgressions by sympathizing with both the characters and the narrator and, in so doing, assumes a share in their blame.

On a didactic level our participation in the author's narcissism leads to self-evaluation as well, slyly imposed by a narrator "judge-penitent." A microcosmic projection of the macrocosm, this fictional mirror not only reflects the author's ego but captures our image as well— and not always in its most admirable light. The portrayal of Panurge and Ariostan knights by a sympathetic narrator, who shares the characters' perspectives, induces readers to participate in their follies as well as their feats. This participatory storyteller makes us accomplices in his characters' wrongdoings and errors of judgment, forcing us to recognize similar virtualities in ourselves. An objective look at the errors by a second speaker, however—the judicious narrator or his fictional spokesman—provokes critical evaluation on the other side of understanding. Ariosto interrupts Ruggiero's idyllic vision of Alcina with a reminder of Astolfo's warning to Ruggiero (VII.16–17), a picture of the anxiety he is causing Bradamante (33–37), and Melissa's reflections upon his infidelity (40–42). And while Alcofribas takes Panurge to task only briefly and half-heartedly in the *Pantagruel* (XVII), a more serious Pantagruel does so throughout the *Tiers* and *Quart Livres*.

This dual perspective is at work even in the characterization of some antagonists. While the negative actions of Rodomonte and Picrochole toward the protagonists generate a primarily hostile audience reaction, the reader also relates to them against his will. This effect is achieved by the creation of types with which one must identify intellectually and who, in Ariosto at least, are often sufficiently individualized to produce public sympathy. Despite the judicious narrator's running condemnation of the Saracen warrior, his participatory twin's detailed accounts of and interest in Rodomonte's heroics bespeak both admiration of the knight's courage and sympathy for his aberrations. Furthermore, his extraordinary behavior can be reduced to ordinary passions, love and a sense of military honor, which are shared by author and readers alike. While Rabelais's less realistic characterization of Picrochole establishes no comparable bonds of empathy between readers and the villain, our negative reaction to his delusions of grandeur, which distort his judgment and render him susceptible to flattery, is turned reflexive by an objective bystander's axiomatic commentary: like all men, according to Echephron, the King of Lerné has a tendency to count his chickens before they are hatched.[42] This invocation of a common denominator not only implicates readers in the antagonist's transgressions but also tempers our ultimate judgment with understanding. Closer analysis reveals that Picrochole is not so much a villain as a victim of his own obsessive ambition, dramatized by his advisors in the thirty-third chapter of *Gargantua*.

Not merely allegorical extensions of a fragmented self, the characters are contradictory and multidimensional people, involved in an introspective odyssey of their own. Like the author and narrator, they too confront a looking glass, which splinters them into all their virtualities: for Astolfo and Épistémon, this image is the netherworld; for Panurge and Pantagruel, the *Tiers Livre* fools and *Quart Livre* islands; for Ariostan knights, the different allegorical castles. The effect is vaguely reminiscent of that used by Van Eyck in his *Giovanni Arnolfini and His Bride*. There, a mirror behind the couple captures both their reflection in the foreground and, in the background, that of two spectators who share our perspective. Similarly, the fictional mirrors reflect not just the protagonist but the narrator who is watching him behind the scenes, the world that forms a backdrop behind the artist, and the reader that regards the text. What results is not the differentiated portrait of individuals that one sees in the painting but a kaleidoscopic composite of different types that is at once Everyman and Nobody, the One and the Many, Self and the Other. Together, they form the ambiguous face of Folly.

This mirror technique is by no means new to fictional narrative, especially that concerned with epistemological problems. Medieval poets and moralists, narcissistic meditators and mages all make use of the reflected image. Unlike Rabelais and Ariosto, however, they employ the device to transcend mortal caducity and ignorance. In the eyes of the *donna angelicata,* enamored bards caught glimpses of God, moving up the Great mirror-Chain of Being, while the young "thinker" seeks reunion with the original androgyne, as well as an enlightened view of reality.

Although their goals are similar, Rabelais and Ariosto do not arrive

42. "Là présent estoit un vieux gentilhomme, esprouvé en divers hazars et vray routier de guerre, nommé Echephron, lequel, ouyant ces propos, dist:

"J'ay grand peur que toute ceste entreprise sera semblable à la farce du pot au lait, duquel un cordouannier se faisait riche par resverie; puis, le pot cassé, n'eut de quoy disner" (G.XXXIII.101).

at this stable Unity. Certainly, the narrator is searching for the One point of view, just as Orlando and Panurge seek to reconcile the contradictory pulls on their psyche—the paradox of Beauty and Truth—in a single *cogito*. Yet, as seen earlier, this introspective voyage through the looking glass is not a unifying but a disruptive agent, which proliferates from the backstage artist's One to the narrator's Many to the fiction's More to the netherworld's Infinity. The movement is inescapable, an implosion which splinters ideals and values again and again, playing havoc with the anticipated Platonic progressions. As he attempts to transcend the vaulted cell of man's existence, the poet is met by an opaque wall, and his mirror of truth, refracted and turned reflexive by the contact. Like Humpty Dumpty, the demigod has fallen from his pedestal; and in his place rises the eternal, tragicomic clown.

IV. TIME AND ART

As Renaissance civilization becomes more anthropocentric, man's attitude toward time undergoes a concurrent humanization. No longer seen as a mere degeneration of the past or as a defective model of eternity, the present assumes a conceptual supremacy made manifest in a contemporary flood of epicurean thought and its accompanying cry of *carpe diem*. Out of this blossoming of the current moment, there emerges a complementary and yet paradoxically divisive glorification of the future on earth, as well as a renewed appreciation for antiquity's original humanism.

As man's center of values shifts from heaven to earth, however, the ensuing importance attached to duration renders flux all the more vertiginous. To combat this inevitable dissolution of mortal existence, artists of the period strive to glorify and eternalize it, creating figures and scenes which are in many ways more vivid than life itself. Tormented by the same anxieties and ambitions as their contemporaries, however, Rabelais and Ariosto objectify them, transforming their creative duel with temporality into a reflexive literary motif, into a critical look at the movement of history, at man in time and time in man, and at the value of art as a transcendental force.

FROM JANUS'S POINT OF VIEW

An intense awareness of time's many dimensions is already evident in the narrators' opening comments, which are launched from a pivotal platform somewhere in the paradoxically timeless present of literature. Turning their gaze, within these introductory pages, alternatively backward and forward, into history and futurity, the authors initiate a temporal tension which persists throughout all the opus. Janus, in other words, is already at work. Beginning his *Gargantua* with references to Socrates and Homer, Rabelais traverses contemporaneity to arrive at a vision of his own work-to-come: "Car en icelle bien aultre goust trou*verez* et doctrine plus absconce, laquelle vous révé*lera* de très haultz sacremens et mystères horrificques, tant en ce qui concerne nostre religion que aussi l'estat politicq et vie oeconomicque" (G.prol.5). The same progressive pattern may be observed in the *Pantagruel*, where the *Chronicques Gargantuines*, anterior in time to the writer's present, are projected forward into posterity:

> Et à la mienne volunté que chascun laissast sa propre besoigne, ne se souciast de son mestier et mist ses affaires propres en oubly, pour y vacquer entièrement sans que son esperit feust de ailleurs distraict ny empesché, *jusques à ce que* l'on les tînt par cueur, *affin que,* si d'adventure l'art de l'imprimerie cessoit ou en cas que tous livres périssent, *on temps advenir* un chascun les peust bien au net *enseigner à ses enfans,* et à ses *successeurs* et *survivens* bailler comme de main en main, ainsy que une religieuse caballe.
>
> (prol. 167)

The Ariostan tense sequence reveals a similar temporal vacillation, a juxtaposition of the speaker's immediate *io canto* with the remote subject matter (*che furo al tempo*) and an equally remote realization of his word before the audience:

> Voi *sentirete* fra i piú degni eroi,
> che nominar con laude m'*apparecchio,*
> ricordar quel Ruggier, che *fu* di voi
> e de' vostri avi illustri il ceppo vecchio.
> L'alto valore e' chiari gesti suoi
> vi *farò* udir, se voi mi *date* orecchio.   (I.4)[1]

When taken out of context, this initial sequence of tenses appears to be no more than a given, often unvoiced, of the communicative and creative process. The writer borrows in order to build, even as he anticipates his own work's eternity. Yet this purely literary "time," which normally has little to do with its physical and historical counterparts, is also related by its intratextual context to the Renaissance theme of

---

1. The italics are mine, both here and in the two preceding quotations.

temporality. Specifically, Ariosto's predominant use of the present and future tenses in this stanza of the exordium corresponds, stylistically, to the myth of man-progressing. Within this "open" set of tenses, which belong to the discursive rather than narrative mode, the past is of interest only as a function of the present and future.[2] On the one hand, then, what Ruggiero "fu" is a metaphor for what his offspring, the Estensi, *are*. On the other hand, however, use of the *passato remoto* in the exordium also anticipates the past tenses, past time, and pastime of the narration to follow, which clash sharply, on a stylistic level at least, with Ariosto's theme of progress. Within this retrogressive modality, what Ruggiero "fu" has nothing to do with man-progressing but becomes a value in itself. By virtue of its remoteness in time it provides an escape from the anxieties of actuality. Thus, the "once upon a time" of narration enters into a tension with the here-and-now of discourse.

Temporal conflict is seen not only in the opposition between discursive and narrative tenses but also in the imagery, vocabulary, and discussions related to time; and there are many of these. For proof of this one need only review Ariosto's opening exordium and the prologue to *Pantagruel*. The one uses such varied temporal expressions as *furo al tempo* (1), *ad or ad or* (2), *gran tempo . . . / fu* (5), *immortal trofei*, (5), and *tosto si pentí* (6). Similarly, one finds in the other such locutions as *avez maintesfoys passé vostre temps, mémoire sempiternelle, oubly, cessoit, on temps advenir, successeurs*, and *survivens* (167). Here, as throughout both works, time is used as a referent to both destruction and construction; passage and eternity; past, present, and future. In the kaleidoscopic spectrum of meaning produced by the ensuing dialectic, one sees reflected not just the Renaissance artist's rather commonplace preoccupation with fame and fortune, invention and imitation, but also the schizophrenic symptoms of an age in temporal ferment and the eternal crisis of man before death and mutation.

The fiction is not self-contained as an autonomous pastime, then, but is also situated in time, depending for its realization upon a set of extratextual associations which are both historical and contemporary. It is essential that one link the knights' magnificent odysseys and the narrators' messianic genealogies to the Renaissance's progressive no-

2. The theory of narrative and discursive tenses is taken from Émile Benveniste, *Problèmes de linquistique générale* (Paris: Gallimard, 1966), pp. 237–50; and Harald Weinrich, *Tempus* (Stuttgart: Kohlhammer, 1964).

tions about time. Lest the reader miss this metaphorical connection, the narrator provides it to him discursively, making him relate the past narration to present phenomena. "Jamais je ne me assubjectis à heures: les heures sont faictez pour l'homme" (G.XLI.121),[3] says Frère Jean, voicing that change in attitude which also produces Gargantua's positive historical vision: "Je voy les brigans, les boureaulx, les avanturiers, les palefreniers de maintenant, plus doctes que les docteurs et prescheurs de mon temps" (P.VIII.205). Hyperbolizing this progression in his melioristic genealogy, Ariosto goes so far as to hypothesize a return to the Golden Age:

> Quindi terran lo scettro i signor giusti,
> che, come il savio Augusto e Numa fenno,
> sotto il benigno e buon governo loro
> ritorneran la prima età d'oro. (III.18)

Within the fictional framework, one sees this millennial hope projected into the idealistic expectations of the heroes, the utopian depictions of Thélème and Ferrara, and the paradisiac quest.

On the one hand, this predominantly positive thrust toward the future accords with a humanistic vision of time, in which passage is less expressive of divine will than of man's self-propelled becoming: "Ce n'est plus Dieu de l'extérieur qui impose la vie à la création, mais c'est cette création qui contient en elle la force créatrice."[4] Apparently, it is both the individual's own inventive use of the instant and his purely biological regenerative powers which help him forge human destiny. Frequent alternation of the narrative past tense with the historical present, imperfect, present participle, and infinitive support this hypothesis by restoring movement, openness, duration, and becoming to the predetermined world of history or narration.[5]

---

3. Cf. P. XV.237 ("toutes choses ont esté inventees en temps") and TL.XL.473 ("le temps est père de vérité"). See also CL.XLVII.889: "car par temps ont esté et par temps seront toutes choses latentes inventées, et c'est la cause pourquoy les antiens ont appelé Saturne, le Temps, père de Vérité, et Vérité fille eut Temps."

4. Jacques Ehrmann, "La Temporalité dans l'oeuvre de Rabelais," *French Review* 37 (1963): 190.

5. For example: "Lors Gymnaste, *voyant* son advantaige, *descend* de cheval, *desguaigne* son espée et à grands coups *chargea* sus les plus huppés, et les *ruoit* à grands monceaulx blesséz, navréz et meutriz, sans que nul luy resistast, *pensans* que ce feust un diable affamé, tant par les merveilleux voltigemens qu'il avoit faict que par les propos que luy avoit tenu Tripet en *l'appelant pauvre diable*; sinon que Tripet en trahison luy voulut *fendre* la cervelle de son espée lansquenette; mais il *estoit* bien armé et de cestuy coup ne sentit que le chargement, et, soubdain se

Textual evidence of this newfound attitude toward time may be found not only in explicit references to progress but also in the literal and physical voyages, which are implicitly temporal as well as spatial. Great importance is attached, in the course of these journeys, to generative and nutritive cycles, which depend upon passage for their realization and which thus root the odysseys in temporality. When Gargantua and Astolfo interrupt their epistemological explorations to "soy entretenir et nourrir" (G.XXIII.75) and to satisfy nature "col cibo, cosí col riposo" (XXXIV.61), they are not so much repairing past wear and tear on their bodies as fortifying themselves for the future. This banquet imagery and the marriage theme as well are both positive symbols of cycle, the negative connotations of which are represented by death. By subordinating the latter to the former and capturing this circular movement in its upswing, Rabelais and Ariosto emphasize the creative potential of temporality over its destructive and degenerate side. The spatial progression which accompanies the characters' growth also represents a blossoming in time. Moves to the sky in Ariosto and to the sea in Rabelais symbolize not just the literal voyages of discovery but also the temporal developmental process which allows man to "agrémenter son être même," "s'intégrer dans un mouvement universel," and "révéler son authentique devenir et conquérir une immortalité personnelle."[6]

Running counter to this seemingly spontaneous blossoming of man through time, however, is a persistent deterministic strain which is not just biological. Even the search for a marriage partner, which appears on the one hand to represent a mature and independent decision by the characters to accept their temporal responsibilities, seems from another perspective to be divinely controlled. Panurge suspects that the success

---

tournant, lancea un estoc volant audict Tripet, et, cependent que icelluy se couvroit en hault, luy tailla d'un coup l'estomach, le colon et la moytié du foye, dont tomba par terre, et, tombant, rendit plus de quatre potées de souppes et l'âme meslée parmy les souppes" (G.XXXV.106). Also:

> Mentre costei conforta il Saracino,
> ecco col corno e con la tasca al fianco,
> galoppando venir sopra un ronzino
> un messaggier che parea afflitto e stanco;
> che come a Sacripante fu vicino,
> gli domandò se con un scudo bianco
> e con un bianco pennoncello in testa
> vide un guerrier passar per la foresta.   (I.68)

6. Ehrmann, p. 190.

or failure of his marriage is foreordained, while Ariosto more blatantly declares that the union of Bradamante and Ruggiero is fated. The temporal coexists uneasily with the "other" of time, which is controlled not by man (characters) but by God (narrator). Only under these circumstances can prophecies exist. Moreover, the temporal structure of the works also supports this hypothesis; for just as the historical present restores life and decision making to history, so does the past tense of narration work the opposite effect upon discourse. Although Melissa's prophecy is recounted in the present and future tenses of commentary, its narrative framework reminds readers that this literary "future" is actually their historical past and present. Since Bradamante's priviness to eternity assures her that humankind will progress, of course, this determinism is not necessarily at odds with a melioristic historical vision; but it does have some negative implications for the unenlightened likes of Panurge.

Inherent in the quest for lost paradise is the notion that man is a fallen creature, who, according to some theorists, continues to descend through time. Although this doctrine is totally out of step with the optimism of many humanists, its first part at least is a cornerstone of Christian theology which will be rearticulated in the Renaissance as a corollary of pessimistic Protestant thought. References to both original sin and predestination, which reflect this "other side of the Renaissance," may be found in the works of each author and loom as a shadow over apparently positive progressions. Every forward step is a potential descent, historically illustrated by the regressive invention of gunpowder. Anticipation of this inevitable fall increases the tension in each of the characters' acts and confrontations by injecting an unknown, inhuman factor into them. "Estoit-ce icy que de périr nous estoit prædestiné?" (QL.XIX.596) cries Panurge during the storm, vocalizing a universal fear which is particularly intense during the Renaissance:

> L'être déchu ne se sent vivre que d'instant en instant et par miracle. Chaque instant qui lui est accordé est inévitablement un instant de chute. Dieu semble moins prolonger continuellement l'existence humaine, que suspendre de moment en moment un acte de vengeance et d'annihilation.[7]

In this post-Edenic world where human progress is paradoxical regression, redemption must be sought in a future which is past, in a forward

7. Georges Poulet, *Études sur le temps humain* (Paris: Plon, 1949), p. xiii.

which is backward. The quest for lost paradise is thus necessarily a journey through the looking glass.

A similar ambiguity colors implied authorial attitudes toward specific historical movements and moments, most notably the transition from Middle Ages to Renaissance. There is, on the one hand, a tendency on the part of both narrators to emphasize and even celebrate the rupture which separates the "then" from the "now," often by describing one age in terms of light and the other in terms of darkness. Like many of his contemporaries, Rabelais employs this Renaissance topos to characterize the rebirth of humane studies, which have once again been illuminated after a period of obscurity ("la lumiére . . . a esté . . . rendue ès lettres" [G.VIII.204]). Ariosto also uses light-related imagery to describe the splendor of Renaissance Ferrara but gives the theme a more distinctly Italian development in his thirty-third and thirty-fourth cantos by linking the Ethiopian "Dark Ages" with peninsular politics. Since Senapo is condemned to blindness for the humanistic sin of *superbia*, it is true, one at first surmises that the Harpies which starve him are a figure of medieval intellectual stagnation and oppression. At the beginning of the thirty-fourth canto, however, Ariosto identifies them with the foreign dominators of Italy, suggesting that the Renaissance will not be complete until the Old Empire has regained some measure of unity and Italy has been liberated from her foreign oppressors.

Bondage is another figure that both authors use to dramatize the break between a closed past and the open present. The chains which sacrificially bind the sleeping Angelica, like those which link Pantagruel to his cradle, derive from an "empia lege antica" (VIII.58), an institutional monster which would stifle the free blossoming of natural beauty and human curiosity; and symbolically, it is the contemporary hero, the globe-circling Ruggiero and thirst-ridden Utopians, who triumphantly shatter the bonds. Similarly it is Astolfo, also on the hippogriff, who brings freedom to Ethiopa; and the Estensi, light to Ferrara.

Linked, as one might expect, to the period's apparently progressive rupture with the past is an underlying malaise which manifests itself in images and metaphors. Openness becomes a negative virtue of the Renaissance. In order to capture the break's full pathos, each author transcribes it in terms of generational division, emphasizing chasms between father and son, old self and new self, or, most strikingly, between mother and child. Both Rabelais and Ariosto use the example of Ceres, whose grief for Proserpina produced a famine on earth, to express poetically the cataclysmic effect of this rupture: her distress is comparable to that of Orlando, who has become estranged from Angelica and the ideas of his past (XII.1–2), or to that which Gargantua would experience if Pantagruel should marry without his consent (TL. XLVIII.497). In the second instance the childless mother is clearly the structural equivalent of father figures such as Gargantua, the Duke of Amone, and Atlante. Her grief merely adds emotional depth to their conservative position.

Just as the progenitor exercises a restraining yet loving influence upon the child's free growth, calling him to defend the homeland, forbidding his marriage, or determining his religious affiliation, so does Ariosto's metaphorical mother beast resist invasion of her sacred domain (XVIII.14–15). Not only possessive, she is also portrayed as the figure itself of love (I.53), who is herself injured, like Ceres (XII.1–2), by the loss of a child. And her demise, though inevitable, is lamentable, a source of both freedom and insecurity to her survivors. Gargantua sheds tears over his wife's death even as he rejoices at Pantagruel's birth, while Ariosto's orphaned animals sorrowfully flee the scene of their mother's massacre:

> Qual pargoletta o damma o capriuola,
> che tra le fronde del natio boschetto
> alla madre veduta abbia la gola
> stringer dal pardo, o aprirle 'l fianco o 'l petto,
> di selva in selva dal crudel s'invola. (I.34)

Here the lost child's groping uncertainty and disorientation are intensified by the present tense, infinitives, and the subjunctive mood, as well as by the loose "o . . . o . . ." construction. If such images emphasize rupture and discontinuity, however, genealogies work the opposite effect. The vertigo of rupture is forestalled by the reassuring lineages which integrate Renaissance man into a continuous chain of classical and medieval heroes.

Despite the ostentatiously future-oriented thrust of each work, one still notes a certain affinity to medieval ideals and conventions in both narrators and characters. Ariosto is more vocal, if equivocally so, in expression of this attitude, to the extent that his entire opus has been viewed as a statement of nostalgia for chivalric times. The *Furioso's* very opening, that retreat to "le donne, i cavallier, l'arme, gli amori . . . che furo al tempo che passaro i Mori / d'Africa il mare" (I.1), carries with it a storybook, once-upon-a-time flavor which is supported by reference to the "gran bontà de' cavallieri antiqui" (I.22) and by the opposition of modern cruelty to medieval *cortesia* and *gentillezza* (XI. 26–27).[8] Similar leanings on Rabelais's part must be sought not in the storyteller's comments but in the feudal magnanimity of Gargantua to the defeated inhabitants of Lerné (G.L.143), in his regret at the corruption of honorable wars by greed (G.XLVI.134), or in Gargantua's exhortation that his son learn "la chevalerie et les armes" (P.VIII.206) to defend the family domain. These father figures serve as last bastions of a crumbling poetic ethos, based on godliness, family responsibility, and personal integrity, which is rapidly giving way to a ruthless new world where morals are compromised for conquest.

This is not to say that Rabelais and Ariosto are reactionaries. The age of knighthood is not so much an absolute value as a polemic base from which to criticize, negatively and positively, departures from and continuations of this tradition. Far from representing a realistic appraisal of medieval life, both authors' praise of the medieval knight's goodness, generosity, and honor is intended primarily as a derogatory reflection on the present: on an age in which the pillaging of conquered territory is commonplace, in which one-to-one combat escalates into large-scale massacres, and in which crusades against the infidels have been replaced by war among Christians. What both authors regret is not the Middle Ages, which certainly saw its share of these abuses, but rather those selected "medieval" morals which coincide with, or can be made to coincide with, those of Christian humanism. To attribute these Renaissance morals to recent as well as remote history is to strengthen their value as universals. Even though Rabelais and Ariosto intend their forefathers' ideals—or what they choose to call their forefathers' ideals—to serve as examples and accusations to their peers, they never suggest that these values are exclusively or inclusively medieval. By citing Julius Caesar (145) and Charles V (143) as additional practitioners of the generosity Gargantua has inherited from his ancestors, Rabelais suggests that this humane treatment of subjects and prisoners is a governmental principle that transcends time. Thus,

8. In this instance Ariosto is idealizing medieval warriors, referring to them as "cavallieri" and "signori" (27) of great "onore," "valore" and "virtù" (26), so as to accentuate the modern cannon's cruelty ('il piú crudele' [27]).

history ceases to be an escape mechanism and instead becomes a subject of discourse.

Just as Rabelais and Ariosto lament the decline of certain medieval beliefs and practices in contemporary society, so do they mock those which linger anachronistically, without phenomenological justification.[9] Both within and without the fiction, courtly forms and values either survive or are revived as ideals and game elements, which coexist with incongruous socioeconomic realities: the idealized lady lives on, poetically, alongside the much more worldly and liberated Renaissance woman; a quixotic desire for honor, alongside the pragmatic politics of Machiavelli; and diversional recreational jousts, alongside artillery-powered massacres on the battlefield. This is not to say that such discrepancies between belief and behavior, appearance and reality, did not already exist in the Middle Ages or that they do not continue, for that matter, in modern-day society. During the Renaissance, however, increased tension between the ideal and the real is triggered in part by a revaluation of the latter over the former. If, during the Middle Ages, behavior tends to be judged by abstract standards, the opposite occurs more and more in the Renaissance. During this period the impossibly high standards of Christian chivalry are submitted to the test of experience and modified or discarded accordingly.

One sees evidence of this new mentality in Rabelais and Ariosto, who constantly mock the old rules of the game. Courtly etiquette, chivalric idealism, and theological dogmatism all become the butt of their satire, in a confrontation of the ideal and the real: in other words, "once upon a time" is demythified. Pantagruel's lies to a departing enemy prisoner (P. XXVIII.284–85), the Ariostan narrator's defense of Machiavellian deceit (IV.1), and the demise of Ruggiero's scrupulous resistance to magic tactics (VII.79,VIII.1–10) all involve an implicit choice between purity and pragmatism, the one attached to actuality and the other to an anachronistic ideal. Option of the latter, which entails the sacrifice of purity to efficacity in a valuing of ends over means, produces a mixed response in the reader: both regret for corrupted ideals and admiration for the more realistic values that are replacing them.

Much of the irony in the two works derives from both the conflict between different medieval codes and their confrontation with and in-

9. Ricardo Quinones rightly notes that the Renaissance was both "arrière-garde" and "avant-garde," "vigorously traditionalist and learnedly vital." *The Renaissance Discovery of Time* (Cambridge, Mass.: Harvard University Press, 1972), p. 118.

fection by the modern world's increasingly practical values. Even Gargantua's generosity is political in motivation, while the Ariostan knights' "gran bontà"—a decision not to fight but to search for Angelica—derives from their own self-interest. If these rational, common-sense tactics modify chivalry in a positive fashion, so do alternative behavior patterns represent negative variations upon other knightly characteristics. A continuation of the Ariostan fight would actually be much more in keeping with the medieval warrior's crusading spirit and do-or-die sense of honor than the flight that actually occurs: here the fool in love of romance wins out over the epic warrior's fury. Rabelais is no less complex. Articulation of the Picrocholian conflict in terms of baseless "oultraige," reference to the King of Lerné as a "chevaleureux prince" (XXXIII.97), and the crusade flavor of some of his ambitions all suggest that his folly is a mutant combination of exaggerated chivalric values and Renaissance "thirst." Certainly, then, what one first perceives as temporal dialectics in Rabelais and Ariosto cannot be classified as a mere quarrel between Ancients and Moderns but emerges as a reflection of the Renaissance in its hybridity, in its simultaneous continuity and iconoclasm. Also outlined within this history of the times is timelessness itself—the eternal conflict between the means and extremes of human behavior—as all eras merge in the eternal present of the fiction.

Renaissance man's attitude toward Greek and Roman antiquity is purportedly more positive than his attitude toward the recent past. Many humanists have a tendency to deify classical heroes individually and en masse, proposing their concepts and behavior as models for contemporaneity. One anticipates that the overwhelming majority of these examples will be affirmative. Not unexpectedly, both authors admire certain qualities of the Caesars. If Rabelais compares Julius Caesar's justice to that of Gargantua, so does Ariosto use his military prowess (XV.33) and Augustus's wisdom (III.18) as a yardstick by which to measure the accomplishments of his own princes. As we have seen, numerous other such heroes are mentioned in a comparable context, while others still serve largely as ornaments, the mere presence of which supposedly adds merit to the text. Nonetheless, one must recall that the heroes of Rabelais and Ariosto are not exclusively classical. They both refer to medieval and contemporary giants, such as Charlemagne, Charles V, and Renaissance explorers, in an equally approving manner. Time after time, moreover, Rabelais mocks the ancients, whose feats are often deemed inferior by both authors to those of their own characters.

They also cite negative as well as positive examples from antiquity, such as the ancient tyrants Marius and Sylla to whom Ariosto compares certain of his contemporaries (XVII.1) and the classical conquerors that Grandgousier criticizes for invading other kingdoms:

> Le temps n'est plus d'ainsi conquester les royaulmes avecques dommaige de son prochain frère christian. Ceste imitation des anciens Hercules, Alexandres, Hannibalz, Scipions, Césars et aultres telz est contraire à la profession de l'Évangile, par laquelle nous est commandé guarder, saulver, régir et administrer chascun ses pays et terres, non hostilement envahir les aultres, et ce que les Sarazins et Barbares jadis appelloient prouesses, maintenant nous appellons briguanderies et méchansetéz. (XLVI.133)

This denunciation of ancient conquerors and their contemporary emulators by Grandgousier, the spokesman of medieval Christianity, serves to counterbalance the more apparently humanistic attitudes of Gargantua and Alcofribas. Also significant is the fact that Rabelais, unlike Ariosto, is not criticizing the accepted villains of history but rather the heroes eulogized by historians and poets. The Ferrarese poet does admit, however, that Aeneas and Achilles may not have been quite so heroic, nor Nero so villainous, as their chroniclers would have us believe:

> Non sí pietoso Enea, né forte Achille
> fu, come è fama, né sí fiero Ettorre;
> e ne son stati e mille e mille e mille
> che lor si puon con verità anteporre:
>
> . . . .
> Non fu sí santo né benigno Augusto
> come la tuba di Virgilio suona . . .
>
> . . . .
> Nessun sapria se Neron fosse ingiusto,
> né sua fama saria forse men buona,
> avesse avuto e terra e ciel nimici,
> se gli scrittor sapea tenersi amici. (XXXV.25–26)

Once again, the mythic past is demystified.

At the other end of the temporal spectrum, the Renaissance's highly idealized future is no less exempt from dialectic degradation. While

Rabelais and Ariosto both give voice to a melioristic view of history, they counter this hypothesis with its opposite. In their works there occurs a meeting of humanistic ascent and unredeemed descent, a temporalization of the Great Chain of Being in both negative and positive directions:[10] while the world may be getting better, it may also be getting worse. What is involved here is a dual world view, the vision of a civilization on the upswing and one which merely continues the Fall. This ambiguous attitude toward the future is evident in the protagonists' words and actions. Even as they visualize utopia in the future, the protagonists counter this forward thrust with a paradoxical inertia, at once seeking and fleeing that ill-defined "novelty" which connotes both paradise and hell. Panurge is optimistic about his fate only from a distance, cringing in fear at each forward step in his *Quart Livre* exploration of a monstrous new world. Equally implicit in Rinaldo's rejection of his temptor's potion is the possibility that the future will not be better but worse than the past: "Potria poco giovare e nuocer molto; / che 'l tentar qualche volta Idio disdegna" (XLIII.7).

Rinaldo's use of the sporadic "qualche volta" instead of a unilateral "sempre" in the above passage supports neither a descending nor an ascending historical pattern but rather an alternating combination of both. Precedence for this may be sought in poetry's traditional Wheel of Fortune, reflected in Ariosto's Fortuna and in Rabelais's discourse on generational reversals which initiates *Gargantua*:

> Je pense que plusieurs sont aujourd'huy empereurs, roys, ducz, princes et papes en la terre, lesquelz sont descenduz de quelques porteurs de rogatons et de coustretz, comme, au rebours, plusieurs sont gueux de l'hostiaire, souffreteux et misérables, lesquelz sont descenduz de sang et ligne de grandz roys et empereurs.   (I.7)

And if one pursues this circuit a step further in time, it is clear that human conditions will once again reverse themselves, in that "aultre monde" which may or may not be the afterlife (8).

For this reason, time has traditionally been thought of as an instrument of justice which serves, in accordance with Ariosto's "pro bono malum," as a consolation to the long-suffering and as an admonition to the rich and powerful. It is flux itself which comforts Gargamelle

---

10. In his *The Great Chain of Being* (Cambridge, Mass.: Harvard University Press, 1936), Arthur O. Lovejoy employs this term in relation to the eighteenth century.

upon the birth of Gargantua ("la douleur . . . seroit briefve" [G.VI.22]), while Ariosto advises one not to "disperarsi per Fortuna avversa, / che sempre la sua ruota in giro versa" (XLV.4). Far from demonstrating that all things work together toward the best possible end, however, Rabelais and Ariosto have set in motion a wheel which revolves incessantly, moving not only from bad to good but back again as well: "Si vede . . . che 'l ben va dietro al male, e 'l male al bene" (XLV.4).

Within this metaphorical model of the world the only constant is inconstance, which acts, in a sense, to make time stand still, obliterating generational differences and creating a kind of historical relativism. Far from being limited to a specifically Renaissance context, then, anthropological images such as the parent-child rupture contain within them both the individual's transition from innocence to experience and each age's equivocal rapport with its neighbors, past, present, and future. Like Beckett's Clov, Ariosto and Rabelais seem to affirm that "quelque chose suit son cours," or, like Winnie, that "jamais rien ne change."[11]

THE EXISTENTIAL EXPERIENCE

Renaissance humanism aims to wrest time from fortune's hold and harness its dynamism for constructive rather than destructive purposes. On a socioeconomic level, this change is directed by a rising bourgeoisie, who reject the aristocracy's idle pastime and fixed clerical hours in favor of a productive instant, which, when judiciously employed, ostensibly serves as a building block for further accomplishment.[12] Of such a tenor is Gargantua's new educational regimen, so intense that it accomplishes in two years more than the sophists could do in fifty-three years, ten months, and two days. Now each day becomes an ever-varying challenge to his creativity and commonsense, his personal pride and social commitment. Nor is the program devoid of purpose, as was that earlier period of meaningless activity, but is rather directed toward long-range goals, attested to by numerous clauses of intent and utilitarian considerations: "On apportoit des chartes, non *pour* jouer, mais *pour* y apprendre mille petites gentillesses et inventions

11. Samuel Beckett, *Fin de partie* (Paris: Minuit, 1957), p. 29; and *Oh les beaux jours!* (Paris: Minuit, 1963), p. 61.
12. Quinones, pp. 3–27.

nouvelles. . . . Et, *pour* se exercer le thorax et pulmon, crioit comme tous les diables. . . . Et, *pour* gualentir les nerfz, on luy avoit faict deux grosses saulmones de plomb" (G.XXIII.71–74).[13] No longer a slave to the intransigeant monk's schedule, the child is free to seize each day and humanize it, using his own native intelligence to establish the what, where, and when.

In this rose-colored world of nascent humanism, man's freedom before the instant has not yet become a source of anguish, a phenomenon which confronts one more forcibly in the *Tiers* and *Quart Livres* and throughout the *Furioso*. Perpetually faced with existential opportunities, with decisions that will be their making or breaking, characters feel the full weight of their future within the present, realizing that time—like one of Ariosto's wild horses—must be mounted at the right moment in the right manner. For on one hand all things have their "season": Gargantua will perform great feats "en son temps" (G.III.13) and Sacripante's "rose" (I.42) must be plucked when it first blooms. Such is the rationale behind Bridoye's defense of the dilatory judiciary process:

> Je consydère que le temps meurist toutes choses; par temps toutes choses viennent en évidence; le temps est père de vérité . . . C'est pourquoy, comme vous aultres, Messieurs, je sursoye, délaye et diffère le jugement, affin que le procès, bien ventilé, grabelé et débatu, vieigne par succession de temps à sa maturité.
>
> (TL.XL.472–73)

Nevertheless, the exaggeration of this watchful passivity, like the excessive length of Bridoye's speech, shows just how easily this commonplace "ripeness" turns into needless delay. In waiting for time to turn his way, the prudent Sacripante lost Angelica to suitors who precipitated the propitious moment and seized the rose as a bud. Profiting from their experience, the Saracen thus determines to "pigliar . . . il tempo buono" (I.57), taking advantage of Angelica's apparent dependence upon him. Sharing the narrator's overview, however, readers are aware that the Saracen is instead being used by time, in the figure of Angelica, whose own judicious deliberation ("di quella aventura il fine *attende*" [I.39]) is now contrasted to Sacripante's gullible precipi-

---

13. "Car telles choses *servent* à discipline militaire . . . Car (disoit Gymnaste) telz saulx sont *inutiles* et *de nul bien* en guerre . . . Car tant en prenoit que luy estoit de *besoing* à soy entretenir et nourrir" (G.XXIII.72–75). The italics are mine.

tousness.[14] The short-term duration of his happiness, even as it accords with the concept of *carpe diem*, reflects the rising and ascending motion of time, a wave which, like Montaigne's "cheze d'or" (III.6), cannot be ridden indefinitely;[15] for "en son temps" refers not only to the positive future but to the regretted past as well, to a Grandgousier that was (G.III.12).

In the abandon to a hedonistic *carpe diem*, there is a certain limited victory to be gained over the demon time, which is a function of the imagination. An instant of pleasure, fully lived, tips the quantitative scales of eternity with its qualitative force:

> There is a Moment in each Day that Satan cannot find
> Nor can his Watch Fiends find it, but the Industrious find
> This Moment & it multiply. And when it once is found
> It renovates every Moment of the Day if rightly placed.[16]

In Rabelais and Ariosto, however, these are less moments in time than moments out of time—utopias, paradises, *locus amoenus* scenes—which belong at once to the mystic past, the eternal present, and the prophetic future. Flux ceases in the Ariostan knights' sojourns by the water's edge and in Rabelais's pastoral scenes. There one encounters the perpetual spring of peace and hope, reflective of man's innermost desires: Ariosto tells us that "duo chiari rivi," in the "boschetto" where Angelica hides from her pursuers, "sempre l'erbe vi fan tenere e nuove" (I.35). A similar phenomenon is evident on a larger scale in paradisiac domains such as Alcina or Logistilla, where greenery does not die but renews itself perpetually, thus conjuring up the Fountain of Youth. Inhabitants of these gardens do not grow old but remain anachronistically young ("di fiorita etade" [VII.10]), as do the adolescent residents of Thélème.

Far from being limited to a few paradisiac scenes, this psychological distortion of time occurs upon a much larger scale, on the macrocosmic as well as microcosmic levels of the text. Although melioristic currents, historical references, and the encomium of contemporaneity all lead one to believe that the two sagas are firmly rooted in time, the fictional medium in which these elements are contained suggests the opposite conclusion: no matter how timely its subject matter, the literary ex-

14. Italics mine.
15. "Des coches," bk. III, ch. vi (II, 349).
16. William Blake, "Milton," *Poetry and Prose of William Blake*, ed. David Erdman (New York: Doubleday, 1965), p. 135.

perience is necessarily a moment out of time. In Rabelais and Ariosto it is in part this very effort to generate an impression of contemporaneity, immediacy, and historical presence which conjures up its other. For the Renaissance here-and-now is no more present than that of Montaigne and Pascal.[17] Man in time, according to them, is paradoxically out of time as well. Incapable of either grasping or confronting the present, we inevitably turn our gaze backward and forward or engage in other diversionary activities. So also is the Renaissance a Janus head, whose present is its past and its future.

Just as the utopistic elements in Rabelais and Ariosto constitute a clearly atemporal, escape-oriented fantasy, so do the poets rarefy and fantasize upon historical facts within a purely literary instant. The past which allows readers an outlet from their immediate frustrations is not, at least at first glance, a problematic moment of flux, anguish, and indecision. Instead, it is peopled with shining figures and exciting events which have been extracted from the humdrum of life, dramatized, and transformed into mere artistic images. What Augustus and Nero have become is not what they were, says Ariosto (XXXV.26). Myth, legend, and history have removed the story of their becoming from time, giving them a coherent literary identity which was not theirs originally. Not limited to historically documented figures like Augustus and Nero, this stylized look backward also encompasses mythological and literary figures such as Hector and Aeneas, already one step removed from time and its ravages. Instead of returning these heroes to temporal mutation and allowing them to develop as characters within the fictional world, Rabelais and Ariosto have a tendency to evoke them as names and types. Whatever their effective function, be it satiric, encomiastic, or authoritative, discursive references to the ancients have an affective result totally separate from their semantic value. The authorities that Panurge cites at the beginning of the *Tiers Livre* to justify his eccentric clothes and behavior, for example, constitute temporal if not thematic digressions. Here and throughout both

---

17. "Nous ne sommes jamais chez nous; nous sommes toujours au-delà; la crainte, le désir, l'espérance nous élancent vers l'avenir, et nous dérobent le sentiment et la considération de ce qui est, pour nous amuser à ce qui sera, voire quand nous ne serons plus." *Essais*, bk. I, ch. iii (I, II).

"Nous ne nous tenons jamais au temps présent. Nous anticipons l'avenir comme trop lent à venir, comme pour hâter son cours; ou nous rappelons le passé, pour l'arrêter comme trop prompt." *Pensées*, no. 172, p. 119. In her *Montaigne et le problème du temps* (Paris: Nizet, 1972), Françoise Joukovsky traces this "nonexistent present" back to Saint Augustine's *Confessions*, X (pp. 34–35).

works, the names work their own magic, attracting us like glittering gems toward an exotic lost paradise which—as it encompasses past, present, and idealized future—in truth never was.

Along with this poeticized, escape-oriented history, however, there is another past represented within both works, one which recalls readers to actuality by posing ethical problems. In addition to their picturesque evocations, certain names also conjure up behavioral models, whose actions provide answers to situational crises common to all periods of history. Diogenes' barrel rolling (TL.prol.) constitutes a viable *modus vivendi* for Rabelais; and Alexandrian charity (TL.I.332), a reasonable means of governing. While both authors remark negative as well as positive patterns of behavior in the ancients, Ariosto, like Montaigne, points out that the same "reasonable" course of action may produce different results in different situations. While Sobrino suggests that Agramante turn to his friends and relatives for military support, Ariosto interjects that Hannibal's poorly chosen allies in fact became his conquerors (XL.41). Caesar's courage and prudence, he says, do not by themselves guarantee a ruler's success; without the fortune of Alexander, they are worthless (XXVI.47). Rabelais's and Ariosto's limited development of these behavioral examples, which are so common in the Renaissance as a whole, does not indicate an indifference to ethical problems. Instead, it may be attributed to a basic mistrust of historical sources and to a certain skepticism about the value of these case histories, which reveal no absolute truths about the human condition. They are situational rather than revelational.

While the moral counsel to be drawn from historical examples is purely mortal, depending as it does upon a fallible mediator and one's own limited powers of reason, Rabelais and Ariosto are both intrigued by the possibility of direct, immediate, and irrational contact with the past. To hear the dead speak as well as act, to know the workings of their minds and profit from their experience, is a dream as old as man and one which, in its realization, would constitute a victory over the forces of temporal oblivion. This, ostensibly, is the function of Melissa's and Astolfo's netherworld visits, of Épistémon's voyage to hell, and of Panurge's attempt, during the *Tiers Livre*, to penetrate the occult. Such descents into the lower regions express man's traditional belief that life does continue after death, in an eternal realm where all mysteries are at last made clear. By sharing the inhabitants' a posteriori insights into problematic situations and by knowing how individual judgments relate to the final one, characters hope to smooth their own life journeys. They are not content merely to see the fate of those who lived before them but also seek, within this eternal order, the outcome of their own actions. Panurge would base his present choice ("Me doibs-je marier?") on a knowledge of the future ("Seray-je coqü? Seray-je heureux?"), while the revelation that her descendants will include Renaissance princes encourages Bradamante to persevere in her love for the itinerant Ruggiero.

This proposed penetration of past and future represents the ultimate realization of man's becoming, a total transgression of chronological barriers, and an expansion of his being to the limits of its potential. Because it involves an exteriorization of inner virtualities, this external movement doubles as a looking-glass plunge into man's own psyche which is itself a potential mirror of the cosmos. Borrowing from the theories of Hermes Trismegistus, Panurge hypothesizes that all eternity exists intact within his dreams, beneath the surface of chronological existence. While man's temporal body sleeps, his soul is awakened to a higher level of reality.[18]

> En ceste façon nostre âme, lorsque le corps dort et que la concoction est de tous endroictz parachevée, rien plus n'y estant nécessaire jusques au réveil, s'esbat et reveoit sa patrie, qui est le ciel.
>
> De là receoit participation insigne de sa prime et divine origine, et en contemplation de ceste infinie et intellectuale sphære, le centre de laquelle est en chascun lieu de l'univers, la circonférence poinct (c'est Dieu scelon la doctrine de Hermès Trismegistus), à laquelle rien ne advient, rien ne passe, rien ne déchet, tous temps sont præsens, note non seulement les choses passées en mouvemens inférieurs, mais aussi les futures, et, les raportent à son corps, et par les sens et organes d'icelluy les exposant aux amis, est dicte vaticinatrice et prophète.   (TL.XIII.371–72)

Although the revelation that Panurge seeks is personal in nature, it is clear that the internal abyss he envisions is not a mere Proustian network of affective associations from the past but rather a place of potential contact with God. Like the downward voyages of Bradamante and Astolfo, descent into this netherworld of consciousness promises a transcendent, atemporal perspective.

18. Cf. *Corpus Hermeticum*, ed. A. D. Nock, trans. A.-J. Festugière (Paris: Société d'Édition "Les Belles Lettres," 1945), Treatise X (I, 113–36).

If visions of the afterworld are taken by the characters to be super-natural, they are viewed by the more critical reader as a finite product of the poet's own introspective journey. It is neither God's eternity nor a universal past which the poet finds within him but a purely personal time, limited in its scope to the sum of his education, experience, and imagination. Despite his claim to prophetic powers, the poet can thus do no more than project a mortal image onto the page. The dead and unborn souls seen by Bradamante and Épistémon are for the poet only mute names gleaned from history books, who will not reveal their im-mortal secrets. Even when the figures speak, as do Lidia and the gastro-world characters, their revelations are mere human testimonies, which mirror man's own faults and ignorance. In his very negation of tran-scendence, however, the poet consummates an appropriately humanis-tic Orphic journey: within his own defective psyche he finds an eternity of human virtualities, which come to life in his fiction. As one man among many, who all live and die, the poet can empathize with those who lived before him, intuiting the universals if not the particulars of their existence. The mock epics are consecrated to a study of these constants, the most notable of which is inconstancy itself. By men-tioning historical characters in contradictory, though not necessarily veracious, contexts, Rabelais and Ariosto grasp "truths" about them that transcend biography and fact. To subject heroes such as Alexander and Caesar to their own changing fantasies is to return them, poetically at least, to temporal flux and the world of becoming.

The authors' subjectification of the past serves to remind readers that all history is distorted, given the fact that man can only make educated guesses about periods in which he has not lived. Not only history but all elements of time—passage and eternity, present and future—are necessarily subjectified by the individual. From this standpoint, flux and mutation may be viewed not only as externally induced phenomena but also as reflections of man's unstable mind, which, even in the pres-ence of eternity, could not perfectly grasp its totality. Universal change is perhaps no more than an image of one's own vacillating desires and perpetually metamorphosing train of thought. Narrative reference to man's "inferma e instabil mente" (XXIX.1) in Ariosto is not just a passing illusion but a generative force of the entire poem, just as it is in Rabelais. Characters change passions and personalities just as readily as they cast off old garments, a fact to which the Ferrarese artist calls

our attention by stylistically accentuating temporal chasms in his discourse: he speaks of Orlando as a "uom che sí saggio *era stimato prima*"
(I.2) and "che *gran tempo* inamorato / *fu* de la bella Angelica" (5).[19]
This inconstancy finds physical representation in the erratic thoughts
and actions of characters, who perpetually vacillate between duty and
desire, memory and forgetfulness, illusion and reality.

Nor does this temporal discontinuity necessarily span a long period
of time, but rather occurs from instant to instant, as one may observe
by studying the characters' discourse: "en vos propositions tant y a
de si et de mais," says Pantagruel to Panurge, "que je n'y sçaurois
rien fonder ne rien résouldre" (TL.X.361). It is ironically appropriate
that the fool, Rabelais's most mutable figure, should be most interested
in eternity. Like his Ariostan counterparts, Panurge also dons new
masks across time, playing the hero and villain, coward and conqueror,
scholar and fool in rapid succession. More than most characters, he is
the figure of passage itself. Glimmers of understanding pass before
him only to yield in the face of new intuitions, as absolute truth and his
own eternal essence diffuse into thin air. He cannot remember but only
creates, and by eating "son bled en herbe" (TL.II.334), he consumes
his future in the present. The latter is subsequently engulfed by the
former during Panurge's *Tiers Livre* attempts to foresee his life to
come.

A further manifestation of this interior instability is the shifting
landscape itself, which reflects the fickleness of both man and fortune.
On one hand, the fantastic voyage and its various ports of call reflect
the characters' transformational change of attitudes and outlooks. Alcina appears when a figure is disposed toward love and disappears
when he is not. Similarly, the entire *Tiers Livre* and its different
characters may be viewed as extensions of Panurge's own changing in-
clinations, which orient themselves now toward literature, now toward
the occult, now toward the establishment. Since the author is no less
flighty than his creations, it may further be surmised that his own mutating fancy underlies each work's fragmented construction. Like his
characters, the Rabelaisian and Ariostan narrator changes style, subject matter, and his own identity right and left, anticipating Montaigne's
mercurial self-portrait. Ariosto candidly admits to this obvious incon-
sistency, confessing that he experiences lucidity only by intervals

19. Italics mine.

(XXIV.3). Upon occasion, however, he shifts the burden of his limited attention span onto the readers by insisting that his varied discourse is tailored to suit their fluctuating interests.

Given the inevitability of change in nature, mere recognition of this fact constitutes a potential center of gravity for man, in the same way that recognizing the impossibility of *scientia* is actually a knowledge in itself. While the Ariostan and Rabelaisian characters may lack verisimilitude, their constant metamorphoses give them both a psychological and existential authenticity which is not gratuitous. Whereas successive personality transformations seem to be naive expressions of the individual figure's subconscious, they represent for the author a deliberate analysis and acceptance of his own inconstancy. The conflicts between different characters at any given moment add depth to the diachronic study by revealing synchronic inconsistencies as well.

It is the knowledge of his fickleness, coupled with that of fortune, which enables the poet to at once adapt himself to and even mentally transcend the linear processes of temporal passage. Although both epics necessarily follow a skeletal chronological sequence, it is the poet's own interior time, the pace of which is totally different from that of nature, which dominates the works. They are filled with atemporal digressions and frequent references to the past, which, together with dialogues and expansive descriptions, effectively distort the uniform flow of phenomenological time. More importantly, utopian and *locus amoenus* scenes exteriorize subjective moments of man's fluid interior time. Although these expanded instants may have no objective relationship with passage, they are no less real from a psychological standpoint than chronology. Despite the growth cycles that structure both works and the changes which separate beginning from end, most of the action takes place in a hybrid world of fantasy outside any single dimension of time. It is the poet's own netherworld, an outward projection of that internal abyss where past, present, and future live together not only as facts but as desires, perceptions, and possibilities. While this imaginative manipulation of flux does serve an evasive, diversional function, it also constitutes a conscious redemption of time in its multidimensionality, as an affective as well as objective measure.

Memory is recognized by Rabelais and Ariosto as a relative mental function rather than as a technique of total photographic recall. It is moreover a theme that they, like many of their contemporaries, exploit. Characters in general do not remember things as they were. Forgetfulness, indeed, fits in well with Ariosto's theme of human instability and is mentioned in various contexts: Ruggiero "né piú memoria avea del suo signore / né de la donna sua, né del suo onore" (VII.40), while Angelica forgets Sacripante's past services to her (I.80). Scenes and events, people and places which characters do recall are moreover transformed, made into objects of creative elaboration. If "out of sight, out of mind" characterizes Ruggiero's attitude toward Bradamante, Angelica's appeal to her various suitors is intensified by her absence. She becomes Sacripante's regretted "rosa" and Orlando's "bel fior" (VIII. 78), both grossly idealized. Even Pantagruel's "propre et näifve" memory of his father is rarefied, "escripte, voyre certes insculpée at engravée on postérieur ventricule" (QL.IV.549), while Panurge's recollections blossom into tall tales, miniatures of the author's creative process.

It is this, the mind's paradoxical ability both to retain and to change, which, once recognized, constitutes a means of coping with external mutation and the vicissitudes of fortune. Such is one basis of Rabelais's Pantagruelisme, that "gayeté d'esprit conficte en mespris des choses fortuites" (QL.prol.523), which, as it integrates each new experience into its undulating depths, always regenerates an inexhaustible source of hope and consolation.

Parallel to man's quest for a personal grasp of time, to be achieved within his own psyche, however, is the problematic desire for exterior dominion over flux, to perpetuate one's own subjective "moment" indefinitely, both in the minds of others and upon the face of civilization. One potential method of reconciling a well-lived instant and a durable eternity is the heroic act, which, born as a personal and creative expression of liberty during a given situation, leaves such a mark (be it physical or spiritual) on society that it takes on mythic relief in retrospect. To have actively participated in mankind's struggle against oblivion and implacable destiny, first of all, is already a kind of immortality in death for the ardent humanist, who sees his own contributions integrated into a Platonic spiral, or, as Malraux says, "incrustée(s) comme les inscriptions des empires primitifs dans les gorges des fleuves."[20] Far from being content with a nameless eternity, however, Renaissance man desires to be remembered as an entity as well as a part, as a hero whose fame survives him and whose name, words, and deeds last on as a monument to his existence.

20. *La Condition humaine,* in *Romans* (Paris: Bibliothèque de la Pléiade, 1947), p. 432.

To secure this personal and permanent seat in the annals of history is, of course, problematic and accounts in part for the Renaissance's particular fascination with the ancients, who by some strange magic live on even centuries after their deaths. When paladins dispute over Hector's armor, when Panurge seeks communication with Vergil, and when Rabelaisian and Ariostan knights seem to model their behavior after classical heroes, they are in fact striving for a similar long-lasting fame. Far from placing their trust in fickle fortune and human memory for immortality, characters would like to guarantee the timelessness of their acts by creating a concrete shrine, physical evidence of their passage upon earth. Just as the Romans left triumphal stone arches upon sites of victory or conquest, so would Pantagruel and Panurge build "un trophée en mémoire de leur prouesse" (P.XXVII.280). A close relationship between monuments and tombs, an equally important Renaissance mania, is, however, established by both authors, who suggest that such constructions honor death and not life. The contrast between Rodomonte's marble memorial and the breathing Isabella, between statues and Panurge's "pierres vives: ce sont hommes" (TL.VI. 349), shows how existence is deformed and petrified in its very immortalization. An alternative form of self-perpetuation is biological procreation, whence the importance of marriage in both works. Children, says Gargantua, are Platonic mirrors of their parents (G.VIII. 202–03).

That conventional monuments and fame itself are also corroded by time and subjected to fortune is of course a commonplace of Renaissance literature, which finds both graphic and discursive expression in the works of Rabelais and Ariosto. Already a sham because of its burlesque justification and general setting, Pantagruel's trophy makes a mockery of the overused "mémoire éternelle," suggesting that such fame is not necessarily a function of merit. The monument is further denigrated by Panurge's culinary imitation of it, as the traditional tree upon which armor hangs becomes a stick laden with meat and symbolic cooking utensils, a Gargantuan shish kabob which finds "eternity" in the biological cycles of nature. An Ariostan counterpart to this antimonument may be found in the trophy to Orlando which Zerbino erects (ironically, after the paladin's breakdown instead of his death) in an attempt to preserve the hero-that-was and combat the inevitable disintegration of his forces. Predictably, however, the "spoglie" of Orlando, strung like those of Pantagruel upon a tree, become the spoils of

Mandricardo, and his fame, the glory of another (XXIV.57–59).

It is not impossible that a hero's prowesses, once obliterated by time, may once again be "remembered." Ariosto discourses at length about the self-reversing pattern of fame, using the varying fortune of ancient dignitaries as an illustration of this theory (XXXV). This circularity of fortunes is a generating force of the Pantagrueline tales, on both a thematic and structural level. Just as kingdoms rise and fall, implies the artist, so do their principals often lie forgotten until a poet or historian excavates them. Accordingly, Rabelais claims that the "antiquité et généallogie" of Gargantua were found written on the bark of an elm tree and entombed in a meadow near Chinon (G.I.8). After many years of oblivion and even physical decay, the book is resurrected by a narrator-scribe, whose own work will undoubtedly be buried and unearthed in its turn.

THE ARTISTIC EXPERIMENT

Of all man's weapons against time, art exerts the strongest and most lasting impression. Is it not the artist who, at least, to a certain extent, determines the long-range fortune of momentary heroics, even as he accomplishes for himself the ultimate humanistic act? The notion that art and particularly the written word can provide a continuing link between civilizations is implicit in the Renaissance's frequent identification of artists with archaeology, a dual function that Rabelais and Ariosto playfully assume in their role as scribes. The poet not only creates masterpieces but excavates and preserves them as well. It is owing to the efforts of writers, says Ariosto, that the fame of painters is often preserved:

> Timagora, Parrasio, Polignoto,
> Protogene, Timante, Apollodoro,
> Apelle, piú di tutti questi noto,
> e Zeusi, e gli altri ch'a quei tempi fôro;
> di quai la fama (mal grado di Cloto,
> che spinse i corpi e dipoi l'opre loro)
> sempre starà, fin che si legga e scriva,
> mercé degli scrittori, al mondo viva.   (XXXIII.1)

That art can serve as a medium for just that sort of generous but heroic engagement sought by warriors is a possibility that Rabelais and

Ariosto, like their twentieth-century counterparts, explore. Rabelais chooses, in his prologue to the *Tiers Livre*, not to lift arms but rather to "roll" his pen in defense of his homeland, while Ariosto's incorporation of political and philosophical discussions into his superficially diversional narrative would appear to indicate that he has a similar expectation for his own work. This thesis is supported intratextually by the characters' own instinctive supplementation of heroics with inscriptions and epigrams. The monument that Zerbino constructs from Orlando's armor is inscribed with "breve carme," while Panurge and Pantagruel complete their "beau trophée" in commemoration of the Dispodian war by writing victory poems (XXIV.57; P.XXVII).

As such analogies between the writer and his characters suggest, Ariosto and Rabelais are engaged in both literature and metaliterature, creating even while they analyze that process. Parallel to the poet who narrates, we have seen, are intrafictional artists that he studies and who hold both a mythic and mystical role in the story. They include the Ariostan magicians, who often use books to produce spells, and a more differentiated series of occult figures in Rabelais: the sibyl, Raminagrobis, and Bacbuc would all initiate Panurge into the eternal mysteries by use of the written word. The importance of the artist in this apocalyptic scheme may be explained in historical terms. If all men yearn to move freely through past and future, the poet reputedly comes closer than most to accomplishing this goal, not only through the literary resurrection and perpetuation of masterpieces but also by virtue of that divine furor which traditionally places him in direct contact with atemporal realms. This Orphic conception of poetry is the underlying premise in such varied episodes as Panurge's epistemologically oriented consultation with the dying poet and Astolfo's accompaniment through the netherworld by Saint John the Evangelist.

In a sense the book-bearing English paladin and certainly the innovative Panurge may be viewed as would-be artists, whose communion with mages will serve as preparation for creative acts of their own. Astolfo will turn branches into ships and stones into horses, while Panurge supplements his previous poetic efforts, in the *Quart Livre*, by proposing to write a testament and throw it out to sea. Even as they purposely exploit the oracular associations attached to art, Rabelais and Ariosto realize these expectations in parodical rather than revelational form. Astolfo's metamorphoses are a burlesque variation on Ovid's tale of Deucalion and Pyrrha, while Panurge's victory poem is

vulgar and his proposed testament, ludicrously inadequate to the situation. These two artist figures, together with their occult mentors,
are also counted among the works' most comical, unheroic characters.
Thus the mock epic's general irreverence toward absolutes in no way
spares art but rather decrees from the very beginning its own failure
as a unilateral solution to the human condition.

Instead, each romance is an essay in and upon art, a test from within
the medium itself of its epistemological and esthetic limits. Just as he
projects himself into the fiction, the artist also mirrors within the work
its own reflected image, whose dissected virtualities are allowed to
blossom independently: sound is transformed into music, movement
into dance, design into painting, and form into sculpture. To a certain
extent, one may interpret this intratextual art, particularly that depicted at the courts of Thélème and Alcina, as a mimetic tribute to
contemporary culture and man's inventive direction of nature toward
his own utilization and pleasure. Alcina and Thélème, for example,
are centers of artistic ferment which seem inspired by any number
of Italianate Renaissance courts. There sweet music is turned to a diverting secular end. Fashionable lute or madrigal performances take on
Olympian, almost decadent overtones and blend with the music of the
spheres:

> A quella mensa citare, arpe e lire,
> e diversi altri dilettevol suoni
> faceano intorno l'aria tintinire
> d'armonia dolce e di concenti buoni.
> Non vi mancava chi, cantando, dire
> d'amor sapesse gaudii e passïoni,
> o con invenzioni e poesie
> rappresentasse grate fantasie.   (VII.19)

Like many graphic and plastic masterpieces of the Renaissance, the
art depicted in these two epic romances tends to glorify the human
body and thus renew man's appreciation for material as well as spiritual existence. In matters of dress the inhabitants of Thélème and
Alcina's court rival nature in the variety of their costumes, changing
them according to daily ("due e tre volte il dí mutano veste" [VII.31])
or seasonal ("les robes, selon la saison" [G.LVI.157]) cycles. So richly
ornate is their clothing, or particularly in the Italian's descriptions of
women, so revealing, that characters seem painted or sculpted onto the

pages. Alcina's gold, pink, and ivory beauty, which is common to Petrarchist poetry and contemporary paintings, rivals both nature and art:

> Di persona era tanto ben formata,
> quanto me' finger san pittori industri;
> con bionda chioma lunga et annodata:
> oro non è che più risplenda e lustri. (VII.11)

Works of art, on the other hand, seem to move and breathe. Rabelais's Three Graces are animated by the water which flows from body openings (LV.154–55); Ariosto's bronze door figures "sembrano spirar, muovere il volto" (XLII. 74); and one of the latter poet's fountains captures eight noble ladies in motion, as they support the ceiling with one hand and hold an overflowing cornucopia in the other (XLII.79–80).

That this intrafictional art serves more than a mimetic function is indicated by its place within the work's quest structure, where it often promises mystical insight into the unknown. Traditionally, artists entwine allegorical lures with the esthetics of a work, as Botticelli did in his *Primavera*.[21] No less than their counterparts in that tableau, the Three Graces of Rabelais and Ariosto seem related to concepts outside themselves, to the harmonious millennial vision in which they appear. Whatever three concepts one associates with them—be it intelligence, strength, and sensibility or beauty, chastity, and pleasure —the trio finally moves as one, united productively by symbolic horns of plenty (G. LV. 154) or, in the following Ariostan description, by the birth of a prince whom Jove and Mercury, Venus and Mars all watch over:

> Quivi le Grazie in abito giocondo
> una regina aiutavano al parto:
> sí bello infante n'apparia, che 'l mondo
> non ebbe un tal dal secol primo al quarto.
> Vedeasi Iove, e Mercurio facondo,
> Venere e Marte, che l'aveano sparto
> a man piene e spargean d'eterei fiori,
> di dolce ambrosia e di celesti odori. (XLVI.85)

Located near the end of their respective books, the figures may be viewed as emblems for the entire work, symbols of that utopian con-

21. See Edgar Wind, *Pagan Mysteries of the Renaissance* (New York: Norton, 1968), pp. 113–27.

cord into which Logistilla and Alcina, action and meditation, Christians and pagans have merged.

Far from being mimetic expressions of "the way things are" or the mere exteriorization of abstract concepts, many works of art in Rabelais and Ariosto purportedly contain occult properties which issue from the craftsman's transcendental furor for comprehension by a very limited élite. Imbuing his pavilion with those same prophetic powers which Rabelais claims for his own works, Ariosto has rendered its visionary designs so hermetic that only initiates such as Bradamante can understand the apparently diversional images and inscriptions on it:

> Le donne e i cavallier mirano fisi,
> senza trarne construtto, le figure;
> perché non hanno appresso che gli avvisi
> che tutte quelle sien cose future.
> Prendon piacere a riguardare i visi
> belli e ben fatti, e legger le scritture.
> Sol Bradamante da Melissa instrutta
> gode tra sé; che sa l'istoria tutta.   (XLVI.98)[22]

Inasmuch as it sets forth a bird's-eye view of history, this art work is comparable to the immense and numerous canvases bought by Gymnaste at Medamothi, which depict in great detail the entire "vie et gestes de Achilles" (QL.II.543–44). In this same scene, Rabelais stretches the apocalyptical expectations of art to their limits by hypothesizing a picture which does not merely anticipate the future, as did Ariosto's pavilion, but which instead expresses the ineffable itself: Épistémon's painting captures the Ideas of Plato and the Atoms of Epicurus, while Rhizotome's tableau represents the invisible Echo.[23]

22. See Rajna, pp. 376–88, for the sources of this scene. Inspired by both Vergil's prophetic shield (*Aeneid*, VIII.626–728) and the historical *padiglioni* of medieval romances, this graphic depicting the future is a topos of epic literature. It has been expanded by Ariosto into four episodes (XXVI.29–53, XXXIII.1–58, XLII.73–96, XLVI.77–98), rearticulated within the context of Renaissance esthetics, and fleshed out with detailed descriptions. Notably, art has become the content as well as form of some prophecies, which not only pay implicit tribute to Titian, Raphael, and Michelangelo (XXXIII.2), but also explicitly portray "poeti" (XLVI. 92) such as Bembo (XLII.86). On a less positive note, however, Ariosto laments the extinction of this apocalyptical art in modern times (XXXIII.5).

23. As Michel Beaujour remarks in his *Le Jeu de Rabelais* (Paris: l'Herne, 1969), there is doubtless an element of satire in these impossible paintings: "Les limites de la peinture éclatent avec évidence lorsqu'il s'agit enfin de représenter les 'Idées de Platon' et les 'Atomes de Epicurus'" (p. 133).

What both writers envisage is an art so perfect and so total that it rivals or even betters the original creation, uniting the concrete with the abstract, passage with eternity, and the human with the divine.[24] Successful completion of this project would make of the artist a kind of Pygmalion, who, in his desire to create a second self more perfect than the first, bestows upon his statue the breath of life and achieves through her his own immortality.[25] Endowed with the durability and superhuman relief which belongs only to stone ("ce seroit bien leur meilleur estre ainsi après leur vie en pierres dures et marbrines convertiz que retourner en terre et pourriture" [QL.prol.530]), the female figures in Ariosto's gold and white fountain not only appear to move but are supported by male carvings who open their mouths to speak as well, perhaps to utter the words inscribed below them (XLII.83–95). Rabelais places this dream of total representation in a more purely poetic context during the account of the "parolles gelées," syllables which are more than mute words on the page or invisible sounds. Not only acting as a primitive sound track, which enables Utopians to hear voices and noises from the past, the words also possess visual, motile, and tactile properties; they range in color from azure to gold, sound like neighs and music, are cold and then warm, stable and then dynamic. Their message is at once temporal and atemporal, terrestrial and, according to Pantagruel, potentially celestial as well. He sees in them, among other things, a possible emanation from Petronius's "manoir de la Vérité," which contains "les Parolles, les Idées, les Exemplaires et protraictz de toutes choses passées et futures" (QL.LV. 691).

The esthetic and epistemological ideal projected into the works moreover mirrors the experimental thrust of the epic romances themselves. Their structure, style, and content reveal an effort on the author's part to produce a living organism no less expressive and communicative than the one he hypothesizes on a fictional level. Ariosto and Rabelais do not simply tell a story but rather conjure up impressions in the reader's mind, evoking a vivid array of sounds, colors,

24. Such preoccupations are by no means exclusively poetic but may be witnessed in the writings of contemporary theorists, who were often practicing artists. Michelangelo, for example, seeks a balance between naturalism and idealism, a reconciliation which becomes increasingly difficult with passing time. For a general discussion of this subject in a nonliterary context, see Anthony Blunt, *Artistic Theory in Italy 1450–1600* (1940; rpt. Oxford: Oxford University Press, 1974).

25. Such is also the goal of Montaigne in his *Essais*.

forms, and movements which distinguish their works from much conventional narrative. They appeal not just to the intellect but to the
senses as well, begging the reader to see ("Voyez-cy" [TL.prol.328])
and hear what they have written. Their eidetic imagery further engages
our vision in the story; their sonorous poetry, our hearing; and their
rhythmical discourse and variety of verbs, our motility. Logically, this
creation of extralinguistic effects through language will improve upon
the defective and partial communications of purely semantic structures, capturing life instead in its multidimensionality, in its materiality as well as its spirituality.

Concomitantly, the poet's discovery of the power and potential of
words suggests a return of language to its original apocalyptical value.
Several elements in each work appear to indicate that the poetry is a
code for some higher meaning. Among these are each author's contention that his work is prophetic, his use of allegorical forms, Rabelais's mention of "symboles Pythagoricques" (G.prol.5), his characters'
search for some transcendent *mot*, Ariosto's termination of his book
with a cryptic *motto*, and the mystical nature of his intrafictional art.
Yet their exploitation of words for nonmeaningful purposes, along
with the *libro*'s flesh-and-blood content[26] and the physicality of the
"parolles gelées," signals the genesis of a revelation which is sensuality
as well as sense. In this regard Rabelais and Ariosto stand between the
medieval and nineteenth-century symbolists. Their text is not a divinely inspired code but a vast metaphor of human experience, a symbolic network born of the poet's own epistemological intuition, which
—like the "parolles gelées"—has been frozen for indeterminate time
on white pages and which depends upon "acte des amoureux" (QL.
LVI.693) to revitalize it.

Very important in this context is the notion of metamorphosis, which
dominates the relational structure between author, work, and reader.
The first of these transformations is marked by a movement from life's
fluidity to the hard purity of art, which survives its creator. Thus
Rabelais would reduce existence to a magic "quinte essence," that
mysterious and miraculous alchemical substance associated with "la
sustantificque mouelle" and the hermetic symbol, while Aristo chisels
his crude raw material in the manner of a sculptor, giving it form and

---

26. Trassene un libro, e mostrò grande effetto;
    che legger non finí la prima faccia,
    ch'uscir fa un spirto in forma di valletto.   (II.15)

beauty (III.3). The stone artifacts such as tombs, exotic gems, statues, and building blocks that recur throughout each work suggest themselves as figures of both creation in general and of Rabelais's and Ariosto's specific endeavors. Despite the fluid, haphazard appearance of their epic romances, both writers deliberately reworked their manuscripts at great length, and the extreme density of their poetry attests to its rocklike refinement.

If one fails on first reading to grasp the works' sophistication and notes only the seemingly haphazard spontaneity, this too corresponds to authorial intent and constitutes a second metamorphosis. Life is reintroduced into art by the audience, which conjures up living, moving forms from inanimate words in the text. Thus when Astolfo changes tree limbs into armed ships and stones into horses, the transformation is complete only in our imagination. The inanimate rocks and branches are words, which we turn into boats, men, and animals. Likewise, the *Quart Livre*'s squabbling academicians (prol.) find their second existence not on the immobile page but rather in the reader's own mind. The men's repetrification before one's very eyes further reminds readers that what one sees has indeed already happened in the writing of the text: Rabelais himself has petrified Ramus and Galland by making them words in his prologue.

The success of this transformational process depends upon the presence of a sympathetic audience, who will be able, on one hand, to function as a kind of paramour to the poet and help him give birth to his progeny. Significant in this context is the author's particular solicitation of lovers and bon vivants, who will mold their thoughts to his own. Before concluding that the works' appeal is elitist or hermetic in nature, an attitude supported by Rabelais's rejection of unsympathetic readers, one should note that the artist's creation is double, that the public helps realize the work and is metamorphosed in the process. Just as the book is his child, so are the readers his children, who perpetuate him in their memory, in their reformulation of his thought. In this sense, we are Panurge's "pierres vives," Gargantua's "image visible" (P.VIII.203), and Bradamante's and Ruggiero's descendants. The very dialectics of the poet's narrative technique—shifts from past to present tense, insertion of vivid dialogue, eyewitness accounts—capture this desire to create a bond of immediacy across the centuries between himself and the reader. Temporal anomalies, such as Ariosto's suspension of one instant to develop it spatially or Rabelais's exaggeration of Gargantuan chronology (G.XIV.47–48), would eternally affirm the artist's dominion over passage and duration, reimposing his internal time within the psyche of another.

Even as they explore the redemptive potential of art, both authors demonstrate a keen awareness of its limits, which are again partially explicable in terms of the reversible master-slave relationship which exists between writers and readers. Just as the poet hopes to create poem and readers in his own image, so do the latter, reciprocally, re-create and thus deform the poet. Time is always on the side of the living, who inevitably impose upon old works new values and inter-pretations. Certainly both authors provide ample testimony to this fact in their own stylized interpolations from the ancients and from medieval narrative, such as Ariosto's transformation of the Roland legend or Rabelais's reframing of allusions to the golden bough (TL. XVII.388). The fear that their works may suffer a similar fate is also reflected intermittently, in Panurge's trauma before the bandits of Anti-Parnasse (QL.LXVI.723–25) and Ariosto's almost obsessional references to theft, displacement, and the ravishing of beauty.

As if in anticipation of their own works' becoming, the poets have generated an open, fragmented structure, which—filled as it is with enigmas and paradoxes—seems to encourage ever-changing interpre-tations, thus welcoming the future. With each new reader, the work is not merely perpetuated but recreated, as old and new join in that pro-ductive mutation called growth. Thus temporalized, the writer-reader relationship is in keeping with the Renaissance's generally progressive attitude toward time and parallels the past-present structure in two metaphors for generational change: broken chains and the parent-child rupture. Their unfinished dialectical structures remove the texts from the shackles of authoritative, preordained readings, while enigmas and ambiguities encourage the reader-child to develop interpretive inde-pendence.

More threatening to the artist than this mere flux of interpretations is the transmutation of literary values, which leads not to deformation but to that same oblivion which obliterates heroes and erodes stone monuments. Included in the ruins of the Macræons are forgotten and illegible hieroglyphs and inscriptions (QL.XXV.610–11), while Ariosto's comparable Rocca di Tristano (XXXII), with its constant displacement of esthetic values, chains art to the vacillating Wheel of Fortune.

The vanity of poetry, indicated by its inclusion in Ariosto's netherworld ("e di poeti ancor ve n'era molto" [XXXIV.85]) and by Rabelais's merging of "en vin" and "en vain" (TL.prol.319), derives both from its probable impermanence and from its inadequacy as a response to the human condition. Creation can become, quite easily, a waste of time, a degradation of the instant into idle pastime. Should not Panurge, as Frère Jan suggests, strive to protect himself against the tempest and save his life—or pray and save his soul—rather than write a testament, which will probably sink anyway? (QL.XIX.595).

The problem is one of functionality, here broached from the artist's point of view and elsewhere developed in relationship to public edification. This latter question forms the basis for a vast polemic discussion between those who believe that art must be utilitarian in nature and those who contend that a purely esthetic end is equally justifiable. As if in agreement with this cult of gratuitous form Rabelais defends the artist's right to paint whatever he chooses (P.V.187), while Ariosto affirms that beauty is a truth unto itself: "O vero o falso ch'all'occhio risponda, / non è cosa piú bella o piú gioconda" (VI.71). Yet at the same time, Épistémon's monk affirms his own preference for serviceable kitchens over the most beautiful architectural monuments at Florence (QL.XI.568–69); and Bradamante is advised to feast stomach first and eyes later ("Meglio fia che voi / pasciate prima il ventre, e gli occhi poi" [XXXII.96]). Here and throughout their works, the authors counterbalance man's efforts to transcend with a strong current of earthy pragmatism, a realization that the only sure continuity is found in natural life-and-death cycles.

There is at the same time a kind of functionality, albeit often negative, inherent in the word "art," which denotes that rational and sometimes deceptive process by which man takes control of his environment and seeks earthly success. It has already been seen, in this context, how different characters and the narrator himself divert language from its communicative ideal, using rhetoric in an attempt to manipulate both the actions and the opinions of their audience. With his lies Polinesso convinces listeners of Ginevra's transgressions (V), while Panurge and the Écolier Limousin would impress others with their erudition (P.IX, VI). This basic contamination of art with deceit is given further, large-scale development within the symbolic realms of Alcina and Messere Gaster, both advocates of art in opposition to nature. "Con semplici parole e puri incanti" (VI.38), the fate induces voyagers to forsake the trials of life to join her in a land of sheer illusion. Similarly, the *Quart Livre* Engastrimythes practice ventriloquism, a dramatic rebuttal of Pantagruel's "parle-tu naturellement" (P.VI.193), while the Gastrolâtres hide beneath artificial costumes and customs: "Je vous asceure qu'en la vesture de ces Gastrolâtres coquillons ne veismes moins de diversité et desguisement" (QL.LVIII.699).

Far from being merely nonfunctional, the fine arts may also be criticized as mimetic and moral falsehoods, which, in rechanneling and improving upon nature, deform it and transport both artist and audience to an artificial paradise. Such is the argument which orthodox ecclesiastics, following the footsteps of their medieval predecessors, would launch against humanistic art, holding that it turns man away from God.[27] From this standpoint, secular poets are often called liars, the Devil's own workmen.[28] In diverting the traditional allegorical expectations of their own burlesque works, however, Rabelais and Ariosto satirically suggest that transcendental art—particularly that steeped in religious symbolism, such as the *Quart Livre*'s images of God—is potentially the biggest sham of all, precisely because of the immense gap which separates available means from purported ends.

Both the ultimate lie and the ultimate truth, art finds its meaning, finally, in paradox itself, a form which Rabelais and Ariosto exploit with great verve. Their apparent failure to produce a great epic masterpiece in fact realizes an intention, reflects an intuition, and hence

27. Tracing its roots back to Plato's *Republic* X, this critique of poetry finds a strong proponent in Agrippa of Nettesheim, who labels it "ars non in aliud inventa, nisi ut lascivientibus rythmis, syllabaribus numeris, ac ponderibus, nominumque inanstrepitu, stultorum hominum aures demulceat, ac fabularum oblectamentis, mendaciorumque centonibus decipiat animos." Henrici Cornelii Agrippa ab Nettesheym, *De incertitude & inanitate scientarum* ([Cologne? 1539?]), n. pag. In his *Defence of Poesy* (London: Macmillan, 1919), Sir Philip Sidney will give this cogent summary of his contemporaries' objections to the art and its practitioners: "Now, then, go we to the most important imputations laid to the poor poets; for ought I can yet learn they are these.

"First, that there being many other more fruitful knowledges, a man might better spend his time in them than in this.

"Secondly, that it is the mother of lies.

"Thirdly, that it is the nurse of abuse, infecting us with many pestilent desires, with a siren's sweetness drawing the mind to the serpent's tail of sinful fancies. . . . And, lastly and chiefly, they cry out with an open mouth, as if they had overshot Robin Hood, that Plato banished them out of his Commonwealth. Truly this is much, if there be much truth in it" (p. 32).

28. This attitude toward art is of course much more prevalent toward the end of the century and is given codified expression by the Council of Trent and Counter-Reformers: "From this dictation of ecclesiastical authorities to artists we see that art had, in the most literal sense, returned to its medieval position and had become once more the handmaid of religion." Blunt, p. 131.

constitutes their greatest success. Instead of resisting passage, the works are the figure of time itself. Even as they lend themselves to constant reinterpretation, so do the artists stress the importance of biological continuity, constructing their works around a cycle of flux and regeneration. Similarly, their attempt to hypothesize and develop an apocalyptical art, totally expressive and totally communicative, is consummated in the transmission of an antimessage, one of ambiguity and nescience. And ironically, the very enrichment of the literary phrase with different perspectives—those of both mobile narrator and mixed-media artist—clarifies only in complicating our perception and answers only by posing new questions.

V. FOLLY

In many respects the Rabelaisian and Ariostan brand of folly would appear to have evolved one hundred and eighty degrees from its traditional value, serving no longer as a figure of *indignitas hominis* but rather as a symbol of humanistic creativity and optimism.[1] In the *Orlando furioso* and Pantagrueline tales the fool has moved to stage center, there merging with the hero, and serves in many ways as the standard-bearer of contemporary culture.[2] The ebullience of such extravagant figures as Panurge and Astolfo signals the *joie de vivre* of a

1. According to Robert Klein, however, the Renaissance fool is still a "figure de l'*indignitas hominis*, obsédante pour les contemporains exacts de ceux qui avaient fait de la *dignitas hominis* la pierre angulaire de leur philosophie." "Le Thème du fou et l'ironie humaniste," *Umanesimo e ermeneutica*, *Archivio di Filosofia*, no. 3 (1963); rpt. in *La Forme et l'intelligible*, Bibliothèque des sciences humaines (Paris: Gallimard, 1970), p. 433. Throughout this study the terms "folly" and "madness" must be understood as imperfect referents to a concept which no longer exists and which can no longer be approximated in a single word. The pathological connotations of such terms as *furore, pazzia, follia,* and *folie* in Rabelais and Ariosto are closer in meaning to madness than to folly, which no longer means insanity in English. Yet absent in "madness" are the negative moral connotations of folly which are so necessary to an understanding of the theme's mechanism in the *Orlando furioso* and Pantagrueline tales. Renaissance *furore, pazzia, follia,* and *folie* are actually a cross between madness and folly, then, which unites their combined meanings of insanity, frenzy, furor, imprudence, unreason, rage, sin, and error within a single conceptual structure.

2. As Michel Foucault rightly notes, the fool has already moved to stage center in many farces and *soties* of the late Middle Ages: "Il n'est plus simplement, dans les marges, la silhouette ridicule et familière: il prend place au centre du théâtre, comme le détenteur de la vérité—jouant ici le rôle complémentaire et inverse de celui qui est joué par la folie dans les contes et les satires." *Histoire de la folie à l'âge classique* (1961; rpt. Paris: Gallimard, 1972), p. 24. In this context, see also Joël Lefebvre, *Les Fols et la folie: Étude sur les genres du comique et la création littéraire en Allemagne pendant la Renaissance* (Paris: C. Klincksieck, 1968), p. 18.

new era, while the humanistic voyage is born of their inane, impossible dreams. As if to strengthen this apparent *encomium moriae*, the Rabelaisian and Ariostan narrators also assume the madman's mask, thereby making folly the mode as well as matter of their discourse. Following in the footsteps of Erasmus's Stultitia, they have given literary form to the lively feast of fools, in apparent rejection of the more pensive dance of death. Not only are many of their characters classified as fools but they also delight in verbal variations on the theme of folly. Pantagruel and Panurge modify the word *fol* in over two hundred ways, while Ariosto bombards the readers with more than twenty different terms that relate to madness or folly, in a veritable linguistic "feast."[3]

Further analysis of the motif, however, reveals that it is neither totally positive in directionality nor perfectly synonymous with either High Renaissance hedonism or heroism. Although folly, by the beginning of the sixteenth century, has come to enjoy many affirmative associations, it still retains the old biblical overtones of vice and vanity.[4] Rabelais frequently links *fol* with *diable*, moreover relating folly to the "fall" of Antiphysie (QL.XXXII.629), while Ariosto describes Orlando's folly

---

3. For example: "furore" (1.2), "furioso" (XXIX.40), "matto" (1.2), "irrazionale" (XXI.35), "folle" (I.6), "follia" (XXIII.133), "rabbia" (II.5), "sciocco" (XV.84), "sciochezza" (V.37), "furia" (XI.1), "pazzo" (XII.41), "pazzia" (XII.41), "insensati" (XII.34), "insania" (XXIV.1), "forsennato" (XXIV.4), "uscito di sé stesso" (XII.86), "fuor d'ogni ragion" (XX.41), "poco saggio" (XV.4), "fuor di me" (XXX.4), and "senza senno" (XXXI.45). Obviously, it can be argued that each term corresponds to a different form of "folly," which is indeed a multiple phenomenon. While the adjective "folle" appears figuratively in such expressions as "folle ardir la guancia" (I.6), for example, the substantives "folle" and "follia" are restricted in use to Orlando's literal insanity, which is a combination of *rabbia, furore, pazzia*, etc. *Follia* thus becomes the cumulative, crescendo expression of all these "follies," which are found individually not only in Orlando but also in animals (XIX.7), natural phenomena (II.28), and warriors (XVI.85). But the author's general tendency to use the same term to describe different characters and phenomena, and conversely, different words in similar or identical contexts, indicate that each "folly" is envisioned by him as part of a single concept. *Furore*, for example, is not limited to divine frenzy (III.1) but also refers to bestial rage in men and animals (XIX.7). At times, moreover, the choice of synonyms is dictated by esthetic exigencies such as rhyme and "varietà." Also, for an analysis of Rabelais's "fol éloge de la folie," see Rigolot, *Les Langages de Rabelais*, pp. 162–72.

4. For a comprehensive account of folly's changing faces during the Middle Ages and Renaissance, see Barbara Swain, *Fools and Folly during the Middle Ages and Renaissance* (New York: Columbia University Press, 1932). Specifically, she notes that the fool served temporarily, during Erasmus's lifetime, as a symbol of both man's weakness and his strength, as "one of those elastic terms binding together a number of specific meanings, all different, yet all similar in their reference to a common basic image" (p. 2). For a review of folly's biblical use and meanings, see Lefebvre, pp. 16–17.

as *errore* (XXXIV.66; XXXIX.58,60).[5] It is this historic multidimensionality, and not a single one of the concept's faces, which Rabelais and Ariosto seize upon, using its contradictions as a vehicle to express their own conscience-taking process. For them, folly is still unreason, but alongside the negative kind which impedes rational progress is a creative furor (*furore* [III.1] and *fureur* [TL.XLV.489]) which works the opposite effect. To such an extent is folly itself and its contrary, indeed, that it even comes to be associated with reason: positively, as the intellective furor, and negatively, as the vanity or folly of trying to know.

This exploration of the ambiguous relationship between wisdom and folly is rich in epistemological implications and consubstantial with the countervoyage structure. Because of its perfect alterity, madness provides a potential and peculiarly Renaissance response to the traditional search for wise "otherness." By positing this goal in two contradictory poles, each of which gives back the other's image, Rabelais and Ariosto have "resolved" their quest in the domain of pure paradox. In their ascending voyage toward truth they have reflected its mirror opposite—the fool's descending, irrational odyssey which hypothesizes an inverse wisdom.

Traces of this voyage through the looking glass of madness manifest themselves and will be analyzed at three principal levels of the narrative. The humanists' ordered landscape, first of all, its forms and its symbols, have been infected with those perverted ones traditionally associated with folly. Out of this perversion of the setting there emerges both an esthetic of the grotesque, which runs counter to the mainstream of Renaissance art, and a sense of metaphysical vertigo, an intuition that "all is folly." A parallel doubling of foolish wisdom and wise folly is evident in the disposition and realization of characters. By varying their fictional center of consciousness, the authors allow readers to see in mad "otherness" a caricature of their own supposed sanity. This constant mutation of subject-object rapports pulverizes all fixed notion of normality and precipitates in the audience an awakening of the consciousness. It is from the vantage of a third dementia, creative and conceptual in nature, that the authors transcend contradictions—not in the unity of a single artistic furor but rather through the espousal of madness (and hence multiplicity) as the ultimate cognitive structure.

5. Petrarch's "giovenile errore" (I.3) has been transformed by Ariosto into "giovenil furori" (I.1).

ON THE OTHER SIDE OF REASON

*Ab*normality, sense*less*ness, *d*erangement—such are the terms which are generally used, in English, to define (or rather *not* define) folly, relegating it to a realm of negative relativity, amorphous otherness. In Rabelais and Ariosto, equivalent negations would be *poco saggio* (XV.4), *insensati* (XII.34), *insania* (XXIV.1), *irrazionale* (XXI. 35), *insenséz* (QL.XXXII.629), *écerveléz* (629), and *desguarniz de bon jugement et sens commun* (629). Assumed in this negative definition is a precise conceptual norm, which, as one emerges from the Middle Ages, is based upon the restrictive structure of medieval society, sophistic logic, and Christian dogma. All that deviates from this mean or that is alien to the culture's exclusive framework is classified by default as folly. Accordingly, one notes that fools and foolish behavior in Rabelais and Ariosto are characterized, upon occasion, in terms of exclusion and exteriority: *fuor d'ogni ragion* (XX.41), *forsennato* (XXIV.4), *uscito di sé stesso* (XII.86), *hors les metes de raison* (G. XXXI.93), *hors soy* (TL.XXXI.442), and *contre raison* (P.XXVIII. 284). In medieval moral treatises, similarly, the term *fool* is reserved for the outsider, for offenders against the code, and is used as a synonym for erring man.[6] That this labeling should occur more frequently during the fifteenth century in ever-varying contexts signals a crisis in the code itself, a simultaneous breakdown in the old set of values and a compensatory effort on the part of moralists to solidify and stabilize the system. Such is the intended function of Brant's *Ship of Fools*, a list of contemporary follies so long that it encompasses all mankind. Among these aberrations are excessive intellectual and physical appetites which, though long condemned by the Church, are now so prevalent that even Brant counts himself among the offenders. Humanistic curiosity exacerbates this natural breakdown of traditional norms by opening the old circle of wisdom up to new facts and philosophies. Although undertaken in the name of reason, penetration of the barrier between rationality and madness triggers a reverse influx of otherness into sane sameness. It is this double movement that one sees in Rabelais and Ariosto.

On the one hand, Renaissance man's growing commerce with folly reflects not so much a devaluation as a revaluation of reason, a renewal

6. Swain, p. 10.

of the cognitive processes. Inherent in Renaissance syncretism is the notion that superficial oppositions can be reconciled, integrated through revelation or rationality into a single *cogito*. This, apparently, is the hope that Rabelais and Ariosto espouse. Many apparent follies that occur during their voyages of discovery seem sublimated in rational, progressive figures: the Picrocholian War, in the Abbaye de Thélème; Panurge's *Tiers Livre* vagaries, in the futuristic "Éloge du pantagruelion"; Ruggiero's infidelity to Bradamante, in their founding of the Estense dynasty; Alcina, in Logistilla; and Orlando's madness, in his subsequent defense of France. Yet on the other hand, it would be inaccurate to suggest that folly does not hold its own or even dominate parts of the narrative.

Unlike their Thomistic ancestors and Cartesian successors, Rabelais and Ariosto do not exclude folly from their discourse nor circumscribe it within the walls of reason.[7] Instead, they involve it in active dialogue with its opposite, unfolding the quest for knowledge in both negative and positive directions. Esthetically, one witnesses a countervoyage, not the conquest of folly by controlled lucidity but the invasion of the latter by the former. Parallels for this dual perspective may be found in the graphic arts. The rediscovery of perspective, mastery of objects in space, and glorification of man that characterize much Renaissance art are counterbalanced, in other tableaux, by chaotic, hallucinatory explosions of inhuman forms. Rabelais and Ariosto, similarly, do not allow their epistemologically oriented themes and forms to achieve a perfect end but rather infect them with the very chaos they would seek to

7. Since Rabelais and Ariosto enclose the panegyric of reason within a fantastical, anti-Aristotelian structure, one might well argue that the opposite is true: that rationality, during the Renaissance, has been subjected to the rule of madness. Yet in Rabelais and Ariosto the rejection of rational discourse is an act of reason; and the apparent nonsense, a sense in itself. As Jacques Derrida indicates, in fact, the writer who would evoke madness has already betrayed it, since folly and the written word are mutually exclusive: "Le langage étant la rupture même avec la folie, il est encore plus conforme à son essence et à sa vocation, il rompt encore mieux avec elle s'il se mesure plus librement à elle et s'en approche davantage: jusqu'à n'en être plus séparé que par la 'feuille transparente' dont parle Joyce, par soi-même, car cette diaphanéité n'est rien d'autre que le langage, le sens, la possibilité, et la discrétion *élémentaire* d'un rien qui neutralise tout." "Cogito et histoire de la folie," *Revue de Métaphysique et de Morale*, nos. 3–4(1964); rpt. in *L'Écriture et la différence* (Paris: Seuil, 1967), pp. 84–85. By virtue of its dialectical structure, however, the Renaissance praise of folly comes closer than most genres to "ce point de contradiction intime qui est le propre de la connaissance pure du cogito." Klein, pp. 449.

tame. Allegory fragments into the grotesque; water and wood symbolism equates truth with folly; and the "conquered" landscape is metamorphosed into a menacing jungle. Doubling as an image of the unknown and as the mirror of an ordered universe, this artistic limbo shatters man's scientific pretensions, undermines his basic ontological premises, and restores ambiguity—doubt, ignorance, and madness itself—to his secure, one-dimensional viewpoint.

Allegory, first of all, normally serves to communicate a system of knowledge, an integrated statement on universal verities. Not only do Rabelais's and Ariosto's personified abstractions defy all rational attempts at schematic interpretation; they also transport the reader into a deformed, phantasmal universe, reminiscent of that evoked in the paintings of Bosch and Breughel.[8] There one finds projected upon the canvas not only the mind's oneiric caverns, given over to irrationality, but also that physical reality of which it is perhaps the reflection, that monstrous, uncontrollable world which lies beyond the Gates of Hercules and beyond the rational structures which are erected as a protection against the unknown.

Important in this imaginary landscape is the animal form, which has traditionally been used to allegorize human follies. In Rabelais and Ariosto animals are first introduced onto the scene implicitly as figures of speech. Protagonists are described in bestial terms when they behave with total abandon, allowing instinct to overrule reason. Sacripante and Rinaldo duel with the "rabbia" of "can mordenti" (II.5), while the young, medieval Gargantua eats with his father's dogs ("Les petitz chiens de son père mangeoit en son escuelle; luy de mesmes mangeoit avecques eux" [G.XI.38]) and cries like a cow ("il se print à plorer comme une vache" [XV.50]) upon meeting Eudémon.[9] In these instances animals are not so much an allegorization of human vices as the general illustration of a more philosophical concept: the affinity

8. In Renaissance painting, Foucault sees "la tragique folie du monde." *Hist. de la folie*, p. 380.

9. In Jean Drouyn's translation of Josse Bade's *Stultiferae naves*, entitled *La Nef des folles, selon les cinq sens de la nature* (Paris: Marnef, n.d.), a gluttonous fool is condemned for eating like a horse as follows: "Comme le cheval quant il veoit son adveine il commence a vannir et s'en esjouyt: puis il la mangust immoderement" (n.pag.). This traditional association between bestiality and madness is further reflected in the asses' ears of the foolscap. In the *Orlando furioso*, the words "bestia" and "bestiale" are quite often used in connection with folly. Mad Roland is described as a "bestia" (XXIX.66) for his appearance and behavior, while the Moor encountered by Anselmo is characterized as "persona . . . bestiale e matta" (XLIII.139).

of man with—or more dramatically, our inhabitation by—the lower, irrational species.[10]

This inner, figurative bestiality finds external representation in the "literal" animals and monsters of the fiction that actually interact with characters—both as physical realities in the geographical voyage and as symbols in the allegorical odyssey. At first glance Rabelais's monstrous Shrovetide and pig-god, like Ariosto's sixth-canto animal army, appear to fall into the second category: the names Quaresmeprenant and Mardigras both elicit figurative interpretations, while the bellicose *torma* appears in a patently allegorical context, at the beginning of Ruggiero's journey to Erifilla, Logistilla, and Alcina. Yet while the various animals mentioned by Ariosto in his description of the herd do have specific symbolic connotations, these meanings are overshadowed by the beasts' grotesque appearances. Here, as well as in Rabelais's *Quart Livre*, symbols of unreason are not given rational exposition by a lucid narrator but are rather liberated in all their senselessness by a demented storyteller.

Far from restricting the figures to their fixed allegorical identity, the poets give independent life to their forms, which modulate and fragment unstably into other things. The Ariostan beasts are not normal animals, possessed of their own interior unity and logic, but monsters which defy definition: they may have the trunk of a man, the face of a monkey, and goatlike feet. Similarly, Quaresmeprenant and the flying hog are so anomalous that they can only be described comparatively, in terms of what they are not. The monstrous demigiant's tongue is like a harp; his beard like a lantern; his chin like a mushroom; and his hair like a scrubbing-brush. The pig, in its turn, has wings like a windmill, eyes like a carbuncle, and feet like those of geese. What emerges is not meaning but madness, a general impression of otherness, deformity, and irrationality that is thematically enforced by such figures as the "monstruosa orca" (VIII.58), the "dispietato mostro"

10. Foucault notes the difference between medieval and Renaissance animal images: "Dans la pensée du Moyen Age, les légions des animaux nommées une fois pour toutes par Adam, portaient symboliquement les valeurs de l'humanité. Mais au début de la Renaissance, les rapports avec l'animalité se renversent; la bête se libère; elle échappe au monde de la légende et de l'illustration morale par renversement, c'est l'animal, maintenant, qui va guetter l'homme, s'emparer de lui et le révéler à sa propre vérité . . . L'animalité a échappé à la domestication par les valeurs et les symboles humains; et si c'est elle maintenant qui fascine l'homme par son désordre, sa fureur, sa richesse de monstrueuses impossibilités, c'est elle qui dévoile la sombre rage, la folie infertile qui est au coeur des hommes." *Hist. de la folie*, p. 31.

Caligorante (XV.51), the "monstrueux physétère" (XXXIII.629), and Gaster's "effigie monstrueuse" of Maschecroutte (LIX.700).

Developed in implicit opposition to the encomium of blossoming humanism, this monster motif calls attention to the inhumanity of man and the unnaturalness of nature. Both are variations upon the world-upside-down topos which, because of its reversal, corresponds perfectly with folly. The two themes have already been joined in the Middle Ages, for example, in Nigel Wireker's *Mirror of Fools*.[11] While Rabelais's and Ariosto's rhetorical development of the world-upside-down topic stems from both Menippean and medieval satiric tradition, its grotesque graphic representation throughout the text anticipates d'Aubigné's more cataclysmic version of the "monde à l'envers."[12] Like their baroque successors, Rabelais and Ariosto use the structure not so much to satirize abstract vices and petty weaknesses as to reflect, impressionistically, the era's military and social upheavals. Thus relegated to the other side of the looking glass, the atrocities committed by despots and barbarians of the day are revealed to be aberrant monstrosities. Turning kings into tyrants and heroes into fools, protagonists into animals and antagonists into monsters, Rabelais and Ariosto already suggest that man is no longer a man.

More important than this satire against contemporary "folz et insenséz" (QL.XXXII.629) are the metaphysical implications of their perversion. In his *Quart Livre* myth of Physis and Antiphysie Rabelais attributes the birth and procreation of monsters to the original fall. According to him, these monsters were first engendered by Antiphysie, the corruptness of nature. Her role in Rabelais's rendition of the myth, borrowed from Calcagninus, is parallel to that of Eve, the biblical corruptress of man whom Josse Bade calls the "mère de toutes folies." Her sins of *superbia* and *concupiscientia*, evident in her physical and intellectual appetite for the apple, are shared by the Rabelaisian and Ariostan characters. Thus their voyage through the looking glass—in search, moveover, of a symbolic lady—parallels the fall of man.

That this descent is perhaps an historical, continuous process is suggested by inverted evolutionary patterns in the voyage's figurative landscape. Alcina moves from paradisiac innocence (VI.21–22) to decadence (VII.19–30) to hideous old age (VII.72–73). Even more dra-

11. Curtius, pp. 94–98.
12. "Misères," *Les Tragiques*, line 235, in *Œuvres*, ed. Henri Weber (Paris: Bibliothèque de la Pléiade, 1969), p. 26.

matically in Rabelais, the infant giants with their creative thirst find perverse realization in the rapacity of Quaresmeprenant ("un grand avalleur de poys gris" [QL.XXIX.620]) and the physétère ("il nous avallera tous . . . comme pillules" [QL.XXXIII.630]). Ironically, the moral corruption involved here—symbolic of civilization's march toward the final debacle—is at once parallel to an inverted enlightenment. The grotesque netherworld, like Dante's inferno, is a mirror of truth, which reveals to man his own deformity.[13]

If on the one hand these grotesque figures allegorize man's follies, they also reflect his fears about the world around him. While the swallowing mouths of Quaresmeprenant and the *orca* ("di lor carne l'orca monstruosa / . . . si notrica" [VIII.58]) represent the obsessions of an inhuman society ("da . . . inumana gente era abitata" [X.93]) given over to irrational and unnatural practices, they, the "physétère," and Caligorante ("molti ne squarta e vivo alcun ne 'ngoia" [XV.43]) also symbolize a devouring universe. The whales' aquatic environment moreover helps define their threat as flux, metamorphosis, and illusion, all of which thwart man's efforts to comprehend his world literally and figuratively. Indeed, the internal *rabbia* and *furore* of characters find external reflection in the frenzied winds and fluctuating waters: "Il Vento . . . / sollevò il mar intorno, e con tal rabbia, / che gli mandò a bagnar sino alla gabbia" (II.28).

Beyond the city walls there lies a wilderness stocked with monsters which are, by definition, deviations from the norm. In this sense, they are the figure of physical and metaphysical unreason, which at once threatens and is threatened by rational Renaissance explorers. As the only corporal creature endowed with a mind, man should logically control his environment. Indeed, it is in part the hero's reason which enables him to name, define, and prepare an appropriate plan of attack against the monster. Ruggiero uses the hippogriff, which Logistilla tamed for him, to kill the *orca*, while Rabelaisian and Ariostan characters generally reason together about the beasts before confronting them. Yet their definitions of these monsters are by and large out of keeping with known natural laws: Quaresmeprenant is defined as the other of reason and nature, while Orrilo and the hippogriff are genetic and physical impossibilities.[14] Logically, the "rational" response to this

---

13. See Lefebvre, pp. 80–85.
14. The hippogriff is a cross between a griffin and a mare, while Orillo was born of an elf and a fate ("d'un folletto nacque e d'una fata" [XV.66]).

world upside-down is irrational. Orlando's entry into the whale's mouth to affix an anchor there, the Utopians' choice to fight the Andouilles with cooks, and Astolfo's depilation of Orrilo's scalp are all deviations, albeit resourceful, from heroic and rational behavioral norms.[15] Thus, although beasts in this perverted landscape are the face of external disorder, which challenges humankind's integrative powers, they also reflect and exteriorize man's own latent irrationality.

A second recurrent figure of this environmental perversion is the tree, which—linked to both wisdom and folly by virtue of its Edenic heritage—is normally a graphic model of cosmic harmony and balance. To master the tree and its hermetic secrets through emulation or utilization would represent an apocalyptical step in man's rational coming of age. During the *Quart Livre* storm does not the vertical arboreal stance represent an ideal of fortitude and wisdom?[16] And does the forest not also provide the raw material which, wisely utilized to build boats, tools, and monuments, serves as a source of protection and cultural advance?[17]

Even as they sustain the reader's awareness of wood's positive potential, however, Rabelais and Ariosto do not cease to remind him, by deformation of expected patterns, that the tree of knowledge is double, providing in its duplicity the wood for both *Narrenschiff* and Magel-

15. In Ariosto one manifestation of this departure from "rational" norms is the use of magical tactics and weapons, some ironically provided by Logistilla, to combat environmental irrationality. On the relationship between magic and madness in the *Furioso*, see Giulio Ferroni: "La magia è nel *Furioso* una delle matrici fondamentali della pazzia: non soltanto perché nella famosa rassegna delle follie umane di XXXIV, 85 si accenna anche alle 'magiche sciocchezze,' ma soprattutto perché attraverso di essa passa quella creazione d'imagini fittizie ed illusorie che costringono gli uomini a perdere coscienza di sé."

16. "Pantagruel, préalablement avoir imploré l'ayde du grand Dieu Servateur et faicte oraison publicque en fervente dévotion, par l'advis du pilot tenoit l'arbre fort et ferme" (QL.XIX.594).

17. The transformation of trees or plants into ships becomes a figure of all humanistic accomplishments in both the "Éloge du pantagruelion" and in Astolfo's metamorphoses. In the first example, hemp is depicted as a kind of supertree ("roys de boys" [TL.LI.506]), which, once mastered by man, will render boats fire-resistant, navigable, and unsinkable. The branches cast into the sea by Astolfo, secondly, "diventaro navi / di differenti qualitadi, et tante / quante raccolte fur da varie piante" (XXXIX.27). As far as monuments are concerned, moreover, both Zerbino and Pantagruel follow the traditional custom of stringing armor over a tree, the one to celebrate Orlando's prowesses and the other to commemorate his army's victory over the Dipsodes. The Ariostan paladin "tutte raguna l'arme, / e ne fa come un bel trofeo su 'n pino" (XXIV.57), while his Rabelaisian counterparts "dressèrent un grand boys" upon which they hang arms and armor (P.XXVII.280).

lan's vessels, for both defensive and offensive weapons, for trophies and monuments which return man's heroics to the oblivion of cycle and flux.[18] Since both Orlando's breakdown and the myth of Antiphysie are variations on man's original folly and exclusion from the Garden of Eden, it is natural that both episodes should involve arboreal imagery. Looking for shelter within the trees, it is upon their bark ("in quella scorza" [XXIII.103]) that the hero of Roncesvaux reads the truth of his own alienation, just as the tree, acting once again as devil's advocate, provides that false analogy which allows Antiphysie to corrupt and madden mankind.[19]

Out of tune with the universe which he thinks to exploit, the would-be hero is transformed into a fool or court jester. For him the tree becomes a clown's baton, an unwieldy instrument with which he flails blindly and ludicrously about, in a buffoonish attempt to control both nature and knowledge. The tree-armed Rabelaisian hero, it is true, seems at first to symbolize superhuman power, notwithstanding the stance's burlesque comicality. It is with an uprooted "arbre de sainct-Martin" (G.XXXVI.107) that Gargantua attacks an enemy fortress, as if to illustrate, graphically, the strength of enlightened man. This very force is rendered equivocal by Ariosto, who tells us that the crazed paladin "rami e ceppi e tronchi . . . / non cessò di gettar ne le bell'onde" (XXIII.131) in a grandiose but futile gesture of vengeance against natural impassivity. The mark which the paladin makes upon the landscape is negated by the labyrinthine forest's eternity. And a similar contrast may be drawn between the humanistic plains of *Gargantua* ("mais feust tout le pays réduict en campaigne" [XVI.53]) and their temporal realization in the jungles of Macræon: "Et par la forest umbrageuse et déserte, descouvrit plusieurs vieulx temples ruinéz" (QL.XXV.610).

18. "Autre symbole du savoir, l'arbre (l'arbre interdit, l'arbre de l'immortalité promise et du péché), jadis au coeur du Paradis terrestre, a été déraciné et forme maintenant le mât du navire des fous tel qu'on peut le voir sur la gravure qui illustre les *Stultiferae naviculae* de Josse Bade; c'est lui, sans doute, qui se balance au-dessus de la *Nef des fous* de Bosch." *Hist. de la folie*, p. 32. On the tree's symbolic value, see also Jacques Bonnet, *Les Symboles traditionnels de la sagesse* (Roanne: Horvath, 1971), pp. 97–113, 131–44.

19. "Avoir les pieds en l'air, la teste en bas, estoit imitation du Créateur de l'Univers, veu que les cheveulx sont en l'homme comme racines, les jambes comme rameaux, car les arbres plus commodément sont en terre fichées sus leurs racines que ne seroient sus leurs rameaux, par ceste démonstration alléguant que trop mieulx, plus aptement estoient ses enfans comme une arbre droicte, que ceulx de Physis, lesquelz estoient comme une arbre renversée" (QL.XXXII.628).

Fallen trees eventually give way to new growth, transforming the hero who felled them into a marionette of the gods and his acts into meaningless gestures.

Structurally related to arboreal imagery, within the broader category of folly, is the aquatic theme, equally epistemological in its promise and equivocal in its development. That vast ocean which man would navigate, a corollary of the labyrinthine forest, tends to liquefy the brain when interiorized as a thirst-quenching fluid. Not original to Rabelais and Ariosto, this association of water and madness or folly is steeped in tradition. It harks back to the medieval notion of the mortal soul as a rudderless craft, set adrift in a sea of follies, and looks forward to Ophelia and the Lorelei. Clearly, this recurring analogy or metaphor finds its inspiration in the unstable, fluid character of dementia, which tends to manifest itself as "un élément obscur et aquatique, sombre désordre, chaos mouvant, germe et mort de toutes choses, qui s'oppose à la stabilité lumineuse et adulte de l'esprit."[20]

In Rabelais and Ariosto this "chaos mouvant" is at once an interior and an exterior phenomenon, both psychological and metaphysical in nature. The link between water and wine is, first of all, implicit in both works. Rabelais exploits the theme of drunkenness in his prologues and throughout the fiction, while, in both works, the voyage is accompanied by inebriate hallucinations, flux, and discontinuity of ideas, as if its magic waters had been swallowed or interiorized. The very element which promises apocalypse effects a total confusion between fantasy and reality. Indeed, many of the most surrealistic episodes—the *Quart Livre* mirages, Alcina's illusions, and Astolfo's miraculous metamorphoses—are explicitly aquatic.[21] As an imperfect mirror, which sends back images distorted by its own constant motion, that liquid which permeates the fiction counterbalances Logistilla's clairvoyance. It is instead a fictional realization of the Pauline "through a glass darkly" and by this virtue acquires epistemological significance. Man is condemned to see life and his own psyche through the rippling waters of Narcissus's pool, in which objective reality and his own madness merge.

When one considers the figurative, and often literal, alienation of the fool from society along with the *Narrenschiff* icon, the theme is brought into even clearer focus. During the Middle Ages and Renaissance cer-

20. *Hist. de la folie*, p. 23.
21. These episodes all take place at sea, either on the water or during one of the stopovers. Moreover, Alcina is compared to a fisherman (VI.37–38) and Astolfo transforms leaves and branches into ships (XXXIX.26–27).

tain fools were exiled outside the city walls, others were interned within the gates themselves, and others still were apparently cast out into boats on the river.[22] However frequent or infrequent this last practice may have been, the association between fool and voyager is ensured by the likes of Brant, Bosch, and Bade, who, in uniting the theme of folly with the voyage of life, quite naturally relegate their erring characters to boats. Given this preexistent union of the two figures, it is easy to imagine how Rabelais and Ariosto in turn should come to equate the humanistic voyage with that of the ship of fools, and life within the walls with the wandering aquatic existence beyond.

Madness, in other words, has been interiorized, familiarized, made rule rather than exception in a fictitious universe which ironically parallels our own. Whereas the medieval idiot was an outsider, the Renaissance's voyager-fool is at once the Other and Everyman, different from readers only in the intensity of his experience and the paradoxical clarity of his perspective.[23] No longer protected by those social and mental structures which create man's "normal" illusion of permanence and order, he comes face to face with the relativity of values and customs, the discontinuity of ideas, people, and phenomena.

Within the duration of their voyage, away from the security of *terra firma*, hero-fools experience the fragmentation of their stable humanistic universe through space and thus, implicitly, through time as well. It is as if their world had exploded into islands, which defy both physical and mental integration. From Utopia, France, or Ferrara—within the closed walls of "normality"—man is exposed only to the unified image of his own idiosyncracies and prejudices, a function of custom. It is from the outside, in a world given over to flux and division, that he discovers the relative-absolute truth of existence. During the course of this netherworld journey different religions and regents—Alcina and Logistilla, Quaresmeprenant and Mardigras—pass before his dumbfounded eyes; soldiers metamorphose into sausages; castles disappear and disintegrate. In this mutating parade Rabelais and Ariosto have portrayed the rise and fall of men, civilizations, and philosophies; and in the insular structures they have captured the incoherence of natural phenomena, the inability of both fools and wise men—each one an island unto himself—to synthesize it.

22. *Hist. de la folie*, pp. 18–24.
23. "Le monde entier est fou," says Klein, "et le fou a pour nom *Chascun, Elckerlijk, Everyman, Jedermann*" (p. 437).

OF WISE MEN AND FOOLS

If from an Olympian viewpoint all men are fools, such is not the case within society. There rational order has been imposed upon chaos, and folly made exception to the "reasonable" rule. The duality of this perspective—which balances the intrasocial, partitive definition of madness against its universal, extrasocial double—is particularly important in the area of character development and to the understanding of the demented figures around whom the works revolve. Not only comic devices, used to titillate our sane superiority, these fools also serve now to satirize, now parody, those established dementias which frequently pass for "normality."

One psychotic symptom which Rabelais and Ariosto exploit to great effect is the outward projection of an inner passion, a rechanneling of the universe which is common among paranoiacs and monomaniacs, and which, in extreme cases, results in the total blocking out of objective reality. Most obviously afflicted with this disorder, among the characters, are Panurge and Orlando, who, given the disparity of their literary origins, seem too diverse to justify comparison. While Ariosto's paladin descends from a long line of romantic fools, overwhelmed by ill-fated passion, his Rabelaisian counterpart arises, apparently, from the farcical tradition of buffoons and court jesters.[24] Yet, upon closer analysis, one realizes that the latter's ancestry is decidedly mixed and that, by virtue of his marital inquiry, the clown doubles as fool in love. It is this mania, a fixation upon the ideal lady, a metaphorical truth and happiness, which the paladins allow to rule their existence and which, indeed, gives form to much of the authors' fictitious universe. If such recurring figures as devouring monsters, trees, and water must have issued, initially, from the creator's psyche, they have been regenerated on a fictional level and made to coincide with the characters' own fears, presumptions, and passions.

The labyrinth motif, for example, is not only central to the landscape's metaphysical symbolism but also, on a psychological level, traditionally corresponds with the fool's twisted mental structure.[25]

24. Bonaventura Zumbini discusses several of mad Roland's ancestors, such as Yvain, Lancelot, and particularly Tristan, in his "La follia di Orlando," *Studi di letteratura italiana,* 2d ed. (Florence: Le Monnier, 1906), pp. 303–58.

25. In her *Les Fous et la folie en Espagne 1500–1650* (Paris: Centre de Recherches Hispaniques, 1972), Martine Bigeard notes (pp. 37–39) the occurrence of this motif in Spanish works involving madness.

Panurge's inner "lacs de perplexité" (XXXVII.461) are exteriorized in his *Tiers Livre* consultations, which, like the "vani sentieri" (XII.11) followed by Orlando both inside and outside Atlante's castle, take on the convoluted form of a maze. Theirs are not just random wanderings, the result of simple confusion, but misdirected ones precipitated by false inner leads which have been projected outward. Panurge imagines that each authority holds the answer to his marital dilemma, while Orlando's vagaries are all motivated by the image of Angelica, which, after first appearing in a dream (VIII), leads him to Ebuda and Olimpia (IX.14–15), into Atlante's castle (XII.6), and into the grotto where Isabella is held prisoner (XII.86–91). Like the room in Atlante's castle, these paths or corridors reflect, and thereby appear to contain, "che quella cosa sia, / che piú ciascun per sé brama e desia" (XII.20).

This hallucinatory edifice further resembles a labyrinth not only because of its circuitousness but also because of its basic closure. Both Orlando and Panurge forsake war, or the external world of public life, for love, which is private and subjective: the first fool leaves Charlemagne to pursue Angelica, while the second casts aside his military armor to signify his readiness to marry. And while the different paths and corridors may lead away from rather than toward this goal, they are not exits from but merely detours within the maze. When conversation strays, during the interview with Rondibilis, from Panurge's obsessive "me doibs-je marier?" he directs the discourse back to the object of his fixation: "Retournons à nos moutons" (XXXIV.453), he interjects. Orlando, similarly, is frustrated by the digressions into external reality which infect his subjective journey, begrudging every moment away from Angelica:

> né un'ora senza lei viver gli giova;
> che s'in Ibernia mette il piede, teme
> di non dar tempo a qualche cosa nuova,
> sí ch'abbia poi da dir invano: —Ahi lasso!
> ch'al venir mio non affrettai piú il passo.   (IX.92)

Lashing out pitilessly at his foes, he impatiently completes his public duties and then doggedly resumes his pursuit of Angelica. So complete is his entrapment in the "amorose reti" (I.12) that, ironically, when he at last attempts to extricate himself and rejoin Charlemagne, he cannot do so:[26] just as the vision of Angelica lures him away from reality, so does it thwart his return.

From this hall of mirrors Orlando and Panurge are attempting to construct not a prison but a pleasure-dome, which, like that of Coleridge's Kubla Khan, would exclude life as it is and enclose life as it should be—a totally reflexive image. Thus their outward quest paradoxically doubles as a retreat into the self, an imposition of inner desire upon exterior reality. When Orlando hears Angelica's voice and sees her face (XII.20), he is merely generating his madness like a mirage, an artificial paradise which replaces defective fact.[27] Their dementia is not, of course, totally impervious to objective reality but nonetheless fights to expel all impressions which conflict with its integrity. When Orlando discovers Angelica's name entwined with that of Medoro upon trees and stones, he attempts first to reconcile this new knowledge with his mania ("pensa come / possa esser che non sia la cosa vera" [XXIII. 114]) and, secondly, to destroy the offending source of data ("Tagliò lo scritte e 'l sasso, e sin al cielo / a volo alzar fe' le minute schegge" [XXIII.130]).[28] Panurge's similar rejection of unfavorable omens, during the *Tiers Livre* colloquium, is attributed by Pantagruel to self-love ("philautie"), a symptom of madness which is an integral part of man's instinct for self-preservation.

In their maniacal structuring of existence and in their propensity for self-delusion, Orlando and Panurge are not alone. All men bracket phenomena with personal meaning, create pleasure-domes, and have their own characteristic obsessions. The verity of this analogy is attested, on an extratextual level, in the artificiality of our own beliefs and behaviors, or by the critical juxtaposition of different life styles within the romance. For the inhabitants of Cheli and Scotland ("dirò che fu ingiusto o che fu matto / chi fece prima li statuti rei" [IV.65]), laws and custom have become an obsession; for Rodomonte, it is jealousy ("rabbia detta gelosia" [XXXI.1]) and honor; for Picrochole, Mandricardo, and the Dipsodes, it is conquest; and for the *Tiers Livre* consultants, their profession ("un tas de folz philosophes et médicins" [XXXIII.

26. These "amorose reti" are in fact a topos of Renaissance love poetry. The originality of Ariosto is to have incorporated these *lacci* of love, along with the Petrarchan poets' *bosche* and *smarrimento*, into the theme of folly, by developing their labyrinthine potential.

27. *Hist. de la folie*, p. 36; Bigeard, p. 29.

28. The psychological and scientific verity of Orlando's madness is attested by Enrico Nencioni in "Le tre pazzie: Orlando, King Lear, Don Chisciotte," *Saggi critici di letteratura italiana* (Florence, 1898), pp. 143–75.

309]). One of the authors' most revealing satirical devices, in fact, is this confrontation of wise and foolish fools. In the *Tiers Livre*, Panurge's meeting with the doctor Rondibilis and the judge Bridoye reveals that professionalism, no less than romanticism, can be compulsive, and that the fanatical sophist, no less than the madman, often deforms reality to fit his own world views.

On one hand, passions such as the above may be adjudged positive in value, since they enable man to cope with life's tragedies and with phenomenological chaos. In this sense, a certain degree of dementia is not only inevitable but necessary for the sustenance of life and, paradoxically, of sanity itself. "The fact is," writes Erasmus, "that the more ways a man is deluded, the happier he is, if Folly is any judge."[29] If delusion is more pleasant than lucidity, it furthermore acts as a constructive force within society. Panurge's dream preexists the voyages of discovery, while the "false" paradise sequence symbolizes that inspiration necessary to real-world city building. And if folly cannot change the essential verities of existence, it nonetheless serves to enrich man's experience therein:

> From this source arise all those memorable exploits of doughty heroes which are extolled by the pens of so many eloquent men. The same foolishness gave rise to cities, by it empires are maintained, along with magistracy, religion, policy, and courts; nor is human life in general anything but a kind of fool's game (35). . . .

> If a person were to try stripping the disguises from actions while they play a scene upon the stage, showing to the audience their real looks and the faces they were born with, would not such a one spoil the whole play? . . . Destroy the illusion and any play is ruined . . . All things are presented by shadows; yet this play is put on in no other way.   (37)[30]

29. Cf. *Stultitiae laus* (The Hague: M. Nijhoff, 1898), p. 72; "Verum hoc quisque felicior, quo pluribus desipit modis, Stultitia judice, modo in eo genere insaniae maneat." The English translation is by Hoyt Hopewell Hudson, *The Praise of Folly* (Princeton, N.J.: Princeton University Press, 1941), p. 53.

30. "Atqui hoc fonte nata sunt fortium Heroum facinora, quae tot eloquentium virorum litteris in coelum tolluntur. Haec stultitia parit civitates, hac constant imperia, magistratus, religio, consilia, judicia, nec aliud omnino est vita humana, quam stultitiae lusus quidam [45] . . . Si quis histrionibus in scena fabulam agentibus personas detrahere conetur, ac spectatoribus veras nativasque facies ostendere, nonne is fabulam omnem perverterit, dignusque habeatur, quem omnes e theatro velut lymphatum saxis ejiciant? . . . Verum eum errorem tollere,

On the other hand, folly is no less consuming, within the individual or collectivity, than the devouring universe it mirrors. In the lunar netherworld, for example, one finds Christian prayers, the crowns of monarchs, social masks, castles, and cities—all restrictive physical and mental structures which, even as they consumed the energies and interests of their prisoners, were themselves, in turn, consumed by time. On an individual level, furthermore, these dementias resemble Racine's monstrous passions, which destroy both the madman and those with whom he comes in contact. Despite their moments of brutality—Panurge's sadistic involvement with the Turks and Dindenault or, more clearly, Orlando's crescendo of massacres—these two exemplary fools are less homicidal than self-destructive. For an example of the murderous fool, one must turn to Picrochole, Mandricardo, or Rodomonte, mad warriors who allow ambition or honor to snuff out their respect for human life.

Parallel to the passions' exaltation, in Panurge and Orlando, however, is a simultaneous disintegration of the ego, characteristic of both pathological and literary mental illness. Just as King Lear and Père Goriot sacrifice their belongings to an obsessive fatherly love, so one observes a similar self-destruction in Panurge's loss of property (TL.II) and the breakup of Orlando's armor (XXIII.133), both physical manifestations of an interior fragmentation. In conjunction with the exteriorization of values and aspirations, which are projected onto an imaginary lady, there arises a complementary alienation of the self, a division of the psyche which Orlando reveals when he calls Angelica "cor mio" (VIII.73).[31]

This coupling of monomania with schizophrenia does not destroy the characters' integrity but rather increases their efficacy as polemical and didactic devices, complicating their relationship to "normal" people and allowing them to stultify a variety of social and literary types: romantic, chivalric, and sophistic fools. Acting as linguistic and be-

---

est fabulam omnem perturbare [48] . . . Adumbrata quidem omnia, sed haec fabula non aliter agitur [49]."

31. This alienation of the lover's heart or soul from his body to that of his lady is again a topos of Renaissance love poetry. In his *Rime*, Petrarch as well insists that "il mio cor . . . per lei lasciar mi volle" (CCXLIII.5, p. 317) and that he is divided from himself ("sì da me stesso diviso" [CCXCII.3, p. 378]). This alienation, says Martine Bigeard, is an identifying characteristic of the fool in love. She notes that Calisto, in the *Celestina*, will go so far as to say he *is* Melibea (p. 104). See also the *Orlando furioso*, XL.41: "sempre ha riputato pazzo espresso / chi più si fida in altri ch'in sé stesso."

havioral travesties of the first species, Panurge and Orlando at the same time use the stance to interrogate the military establishment, which declares war sane and love irrational: "che non è in somma amor, se non insania, / a guidizio de' savi universale" (XXIV.1), asks Ariosto with a subversive qualification.

Just as the amorous vagaries of the Ariostan knights constitute an upward alienation of the self toward the ideal, so the conflict from which they are fleeing represents a downward alienation, a degradation of man into that bestial madness so aptly termed *furore* and *rabbia*. In a similar vein Panurge insists that his heroic master is mad to fight Loup Garou (P.XXIX.293), and he himself refuses to don the harness of war—an act which Pantagruel decries for its lack of conformity to common usage: "Chascun abonde en son sens, mesmement en choses foraines, externes et indifférentes, lesquelles de soy ne sont bonnes ne maulvaises. . . . Seulement me desplaist la nouveaulté et mespris du commun usaige" (TL.VII.352).

What frequently distinguishes normality from abnormality, both within this fiction and within civilized society, is the degree to which each personal folly coincides with that of the culture as a whole. Indeed, many acceptable behavior patterns are merely socialized manias.[32] Thanks to their schizophrenic versatility, however, Panurge and Orlando interrogate not only from without but from within the system as well, wearing "wise" masks in order to contaminate them with folly.

Each paladin is well versed in a variety of exotic languages (P.IX; IX.5), while the Gallic buffoon—using his philosophic conundrums and pretentious citations to exalt his own ego and exploit his milieu—ofttimes parodies the traditional sophist.[33] As the conquerer wields his sword, so the knave and the usurper wields his wit, claiming a hero's stage center and devitalizing letters like so many weak opponents, as he manipulates their form and content to suit his purposes. At Panurge's hands, during the "Éloge des debteurs," Plato is misinterpreted,

---

32. See Ronald D. Laing, *The Politics of Experience* (1967; rpt. New York: Ballantine Books, 1974), pp. 27–28: "There are forms of alienation that are relatively strange to statistically 'normal' forms of alienation. The 'normally' alienated person, by reason of the fact that he acts more or less like everyone else, is taken to be sane. Other forms of alienation that are out of step with the prevailing state of alienation are those that are labeled by the 'normal' majority as bad or mad."

33. See Bigeard's discussion of "la folie intellectuelle," pp. 82, 149–50; Gérard Defaux, *Pantagruel et les sophistes: Contribution à l'histoire de l'humanisme chrétien au XVIe siècle* (The Hague: M. Nijhoff, 1973), pp. 165–97; Ernesto Grasso, "La mania ingegnosa" in *L'Umanesimo e la follia* (Rome: Abete, 1971), pp. 107–26.

scholastic procedures turned comic, and learning in general abused. This diabolic irreverence with which the clown pursues his ends, rather in the manner of Molière's Don Juan, further reminds one that truth is a forbidden fruit of Satanic allure. And this notion is mirrored not only by Orlando's confrontation with the figurative trees but also by the revelation that his madness stems from divine retribution: "Sappi che 'l vostro Orlando, perché torse / dal camin dritto le commesse insegne, / è punito da Dio" (XXXIV.62). All questions of sin aside, it is an unparalleled act of folly for man to pit his intellect against the universal mysteries. The devout Christian knows that knowledge on earth is illusion, while the skeptic finds truth only in the lack of knowledge.

Even as they parody those who profess to "know," Orlando and Panurge are at the same time breaking away from "ignorant learnedness" (as opposed to "learned ignorance") and seeking a truth outside the bounds of reason, civilization, and culture. The realm of apparel provides a means to such ends. The fool is a traditional nonconformist who sports either excessively garish raiment, such as Panurge's second costume with its "longue braguette" (P.XV.237), or, more frequently, austere and even beggarly garb, exemplified by Panurge's original rags (P.IX), his ultimate toga (TL.VII), and Orlando's nudity after his breakdown.[34] This sartorial simplification, in conjunction with the previously mentioned breakup of armor and kingdom, corresponds to that mental and cultural regression so typical of many dementias. Time is turned backward for the fools, who revert not only to childhood but also to a more primitive moment in the evolution of man.[35] Thus Panurge's toga, a relic of Roman times, merely exteriorizes a mental return toward the past, which culminates in Saturnian simplicity:

> Ainsi ne pourveut nature à la perpétuité de l'humain genre, ains créa l'home nud, tendre, fragile, sans armes ne offensives, ne défensives, en estat d'innocence et premier aage d'or, comme animant,

34. See Paolo Valesio, "The Language of Madness in the Renaissance," *Yearbook of Italian Studies* 1 (1971), 201–06, for a discussion of traditional iconic representations of the fool or madman.

35. "La maladie mentale se situe dans l'évolution, comme une perturbation de son cours, par son aspect régressif, elle fait apparaître des conduites infantiles ou des formes archaïques de la personnalité." Foucault, *Maladie mentale et psychologie* (Paris: Presses Universitaires de France, 1972), p. 95. In this context, Carlo Ossola quite rightly notes the connection between the theme of folly and the lost paradise motif during the Renaissance, in his "Métaphore et inventaire de la folie," *Folie et déraison à la Renaissance* (Brussels: Éditions de l'Université de Bruxelles, 1976), pp. 171–82.

non plante, comme animant . . . né à paix, non à guerre, animant
né à jouissance mirificque de tous fruictz et plantes végétables,
animant né à domination pacificque sus toutes bestes.

(TL.VIII.355)

Once again the madman has become a polemic instrument, this
time in the ongoing debate between art and nature. In casting off their
modern clothing, and with it the "progress" of civilization, Panurge
and Orlando act to counterbalance the books' main encomiastic theme.
In an intrasocial perspective, one may view the fools' regression and
nudity or near-nudity as the ultimate degradation, a return to that
bestiality whence man's ingenuity has elevated him. After all, do not
the elaborate gowns and coats of mail, the statues and paintings, the
castles and ordered gardens mark the level of their acquired stature?

By force of contrast with the fools' ascetic existence, however, Renaissance culture takes on an air of materialistic decadence, an air of
stultifying falsity which is symptomatic of a less lucid dementia than
that of the natural fool. While the civilized fool masks senselessness
and absurdity with pleasant delusions, his alienated twin lives the
human condition as a continuous and unadulterated life style. The
postbreakdown Orlando does not attempt to navigate but puts himself at the mercy of nature, confusing bread with acorns and failing
to recognize Angelica; nor can he communicate but reverts, like Panurge or Triboullet, to wild babbling and childlike gibberish.

Within an irrational universe, however, blindness doubles as illumination, lunatic ravings as truth, and temporal regression as transcendence. Thus, when Pantagruel tells Panurge "qu'un fol enseigne
bien un saige," he is not completely in jest:

> Par l'advis, conseil et prædiction des folz, vous sçavez quants
> princes, rois et républicques ont esté conservéz, quantes batailles
> guaingnées, quantes perplexitéz dissolues . . . Vous acquiescerez
> en ceste raison, car, comme celluy qui de près regarde à ses affaires
> privéz et domesticques, qui est vigilant et attentif au gouverne-
> ment de sa maison, duquel l'esprit n'est poinct esguaré, qui ne
> pert occasion quelconques de acquérir et amasser biens et richesses,
> qui cautement, sçayt obvier ès inconvéniens de paoüreté, vous ap-
> pellez saige mondain, quoyque fat soit-il en l'estimation des Intel-
> ligences cœlestes; aussi faut-il, pour davant icelles saige estre, je
> dis sage et præsage par aspiration divine et apte à recepvoir béné-

fice de divination, se oublier soy-mesmes, issir hors de soy-mesmes, vuider ses sens de toute terrienne affection, purger son esprit
de toute humaine sollicitude et mettre tout en nonchaloir. Ce que
vulgairement est impute à folie.   (TL.XXXVII.461–62)

This concept of the fool as sage seer is not new to Rabelais and Ariosto
but harks back to both Christian and more generally occult tradition.
Within this superstitious framework the madman's exclusion from
society suggests that he is integrated into a higher order. This theory
is given further impetus by the infantile syndrome in madness, that
reversion to childhood which accompanies psychosis, but which also
represents a potential return to the primitive sources of truth.[36]

There is, however, a major difference between the sublime fool's
verity and that of Orlando and Panurge. Whereas the idiot-mage deals
in absolute verities, messages from heaven and hell, the Ariostan and
Rabelaisian madman's revelations hypothesize relativism and folly as
the universal form of existence. His blindness, his dependence upon
fortune, and his mutterings are all metaphorical of our own. The only
difference is that he has seen himself clearly and crossed over into
that mirror of truth, the acquatic reflections of his own muddled mind.[37]
It is, after all, not the illusion itself but its collapse which provokes
the breakdown: Panurge's realization, in the *Quart Livre* calamities,
that "les hommes meurent," and Orlando's discovery, within the forest, that "ils ne sont pas heureux."[38] Reactions to this revelation are,
first of all, a state of hysteria, a literal enactment of the chaos they have
intuited. The net result of this trauma is total reversal of the nervous
system and the creation of a looking-glass second self which in many

36. From this standpoint man's socialization constitutes an alienation from
both God and the self. According to Christian doctrine, those pretensions acquired
with adulthood must be cast aside before man can rejoin his creator: "Unless you
turn round and become like children, you will never enter the kingdom of
Heaven" (Matt. xviii.4). To follow the letter of these teachings is to become
the fool in Christ. See Walter Kaiser, *Praisers of Folly* (Cambridge, Mass.: Harvard
University Press, 1963), pp. 84–90. For the surrealists and a number of modern
psychologists, the "truth" uncovered by this regression is merely a realm of dream,
fantasy, and subjective reality, which grown men have been taught to repress.

37. Cf. Gregory Bateson, ed., *Perceval's Narrative: A Patient's Account of His
Psychosis* (Stanford, Calif.: Stanford University Press, 1961), pp. xiii–xiv: "He [the
patient] is, as it were, embarked upon a voyage of discovery which is only com-
pleted by his return to the normal world, to which he comes back with insights
different from those of the inhabitants who never embarked on such a voyage.
Once begun, a schizophrenic episode would appear to have as definite a course as
an initiation ceremony—a death and rebirth."

38. Albert Camus, *Caligula* (Paris: Gallimard, 1958), p. 12.

ways parodies its double. Ariosto, particularly, exploits this mirror technique, accentuating the difference between sane and mad Orlando ("che per amor venne in furore e matto, / d'uom che sí saggio era stimato prima" [I.2]), yet linking them with ironic parallels. Heroic "rabbia," the "sane" warrior's slaughter of his foes, differs little from the lunatics' assault upon farmers and peasants ("Fece morir diece personne e diece" [XXIV.10]). Similarly, Panurge's inane babbling during the storm (QL.XIX) is at once a degradation and a realization of the sophist's original dementia (P.IX).

It is on a linguistic level that Rabelais and Ariosto unfold much of their dialectic between folly and reason, incorporating the myth of Babel into their thematic development.[39] Panurge's multilingualism and subsequent lapses into "tongues" remind readers that human presumption—the desire to reach the sky or know everything—is punished by fragmentation of the Word. Reread in this light, the beginning of Orlando's epistemological quest may be seen as an anticipation of the "gran follia," since this climactical scene both echoes the initial multilingualism and explodes into "gridi" and "urli" (XXIII. 124). Not necessarily metaphysical in import, these episodes also use foreign language as a simultaneous figure of alienation from one's senses and symbol of nature's deformation through art: "A ceste heure parle-tu naturellement" (P.VI.193), says Pantagruel, advising a pretentious schoolboy to speak his native Limousin. Ironically, however, the works' most natural expressions are those uttered by the natural fool—Triboullet's gibberish, Panurge's "bebebe bous bous" (QL.XIX. 594–95), and Orlando's visceral screams and yells.

Indeed, language itself, no matter how simple, is one of those maze-like social structures which deform both subjective and objective reality and thus correspond to our definition of folly.[40] To speak is al-

39. See Valesio for a discussion of the linguistic manifestations of madness in the Renaissance. He notes that silence is characteristic of medieval literary dementia while the use of popular language distinguishes mad Renaissance protagonists from their predecessors.

40. On a seemingly contradictory note Derrida affirms that language is inextricably united to reason and hence irrevocably opposed to folly: "Tout notre langage européen, le langage de tout ce qui a participé, de près ou de loin, à l'aventure de la raison occidentale, est l'immense délégation du project que Foucault définit sous l'espèce de la capture ou de l'objectivation de la folie" (p. 58). In another sense, however, language may be classified as folly precisely because it excludes and neutralizes madness. As if in recognition of this fact, Rabelais—and, to a lesser extent, Ariosto—confront this dilemma by introducing nonsense, ambiguities, and paradox into their discourse. See Marcel de Grève, "Le Discours rabelaisien: la raison en folie," in *Folie et déraison à la Renaissance*, pp. 149–57.

ready to falsify reality, to mold internal thought patterns to external forms, until, totally demented, one ceases to think and comes to believe that the rhetorical façade is real. Common Renaissance catchphrases such as "light" and "thirst" preexist and form the Utopians' wild aspirations, while an acquired stock of Petrarchan imagery aggravates Orlando's lovesickness. As an externally directed process, oriented toward the "other" ("donner parolles estoit acte des amoureux" [QL. LVI.693]), verbalization indeed approximates the derangement produced by love itself, as described by Ariosto: "E quale è di pazzia segno piú espresso / che, per altri voler, perder sé stesso?" (XXIV.1).

Language, like many institutional structures, tends to give man a false sense of security, suggesting that reality can be verbally—and thus mentally—comprehended. Instead, words not only dissipate the speakers' cognitive ego and deform subjective reality but may also, on a communicative as well as expressive level, act to delude the listener. Incapable of distinguishing between falsehood and truth, the fool projects his own dementia into the message. Paranoia throws a pall over good tidings, and self-love sugarcoats even tragedy. Blinded by his own love, Sacripante reads willingness into Angelica's treacherous wiles, while Panurge—even though both suspicious and desirous of auspicious prophecies—defensively refuses to believe in bad ones and is prepared to accept only those words which reconcile happiness and truth. In the following warning to Panurge, Pantagruel explicitly relates this selective and subjective listening to deception, insisting that "philautie et amour de soy vous déçoit" (TL.XXIX.434). Transformation of the associative preposition *de* into the dissociative prefix *dé* further suggests that this deceptive love of self is not a consolidation of but rather an alienation from the truly conscious ego; for the negative *déçoit* reflects on the positive *de soy* to generate an alternate meaning of *dé-soy* or *unself*.

Since language is associated with madness, it would stand to reason that wisdom belongs to the contemplative self, to that narcissistic figure who communicates with silence. Certainly, reticence is a prime characteristic of the wise, stoic hero. Pantagruel's meditative retreats counterbalance Panurge's verbal inebriation, while Orlando's uncharacteristic and sporadic loquacity parallels the uneven festering of his folly. In fact, the upside-down bottle with its slow-dripping water, which captures the dialectics of Orlando's breakdown, may be viewed as the microcosm of a long-term experience, in which each drop is a verbal exteriorization of the malady:

L'impetuosa doglia entro rimase,
che volea tutta uscir con troppa fretta.
Cosí veggiàn restar l'acqua nel vase,
che largo il ventre e la bocca abbia stretta;
che nel voltar che si fa in su la base,
l'umor che vorria uscir, tanto s'affretta,
e ne l'angusta via tanto s'intrica,
ch'a goccia a goccia fuore esce a fatica.   (XXIII.113)

When the bottle finally is empty, the sage's silence is replaced by that of the fool, by a void which doubles as fullness and tantalizes readers with the lure of transcendent wisdom. It is Silenzio which San Michele sends as a potential antidote to the mad hubbub of earthly life, and in which Rabelaisian heroes—during the Thaumaste and Triboullet episodes—seek answers to their epistemological quest. Throughout, of course, the ineffable wisdom of silence is synonymous with stark, raving lunacy and ambiguously wavers between revelation and oblivion, sage introspection and senseless annihilation of the self.

A CONVERGENCE OF MEANING AND MADNESS

When manifested in characters, folly is not absolute but polemic in value, used largely to question the sanity of society's comfortable institutions, those inessential edifices which lull man into unconsciousness. Ostensibly, the narrators will turn their furor to more positive ends, incorporating into their text the theory of divine inspiration. Further perusal of the works, however, reveals that this transcendent dementia is only one equivocal facet of the creator's madness and that he has used it as a base from which to develop the dialectics of wisdom and folly.

According to Neoplatonic theory, the inspired artist is a mere receptacle for transmission of the Word. Yet in Rabelais and Ariosto this tradition serves a divisive rather than integrative function. As he cites Apollo (III.1), Ariosto appears to espouse that wise and prophetic illumination so often alluded to by Rabelais. The Gallic monk, speaking in lofty terms of allegory, promises the answers to abstruse mysteries and advises the readers to "know thyself"—the motto of Apollo's temple. This introspective, meditative principle quite naturally engenders its opposite, however, since the implied narcissism, even pathologically speaking, is inextricably linked to schizophrenia. The doubling of Apollo with Bacchus is made clear in Rabelais's ebullient references to wine, as well as in his shifts between high and low narrative styles.[41] Similarly, an antithetical inspiration renders comic Ariosto's very reference to Apollo, as the author admits that his usual furor is less elevated: "Molto maggior di quel furor che suole / ben or mi convien che mi riscaldi il petto" (III.1).

This division of the creative self is at once an exploitation of Platonic inspiration's multiplicity, its division into four furors, and a half-playful, half-serious espousal of the clinical fool's disordered viewpoint. It is possible to see in Ariosto's avowed lovesickness ("Non men son fuor di me, che fosse Orlando" [XXX.4]), for example, an allusion to Plato's fourth kind of delirium.[42] As a functioning part of the whole, however, this additional deviation is used less as an elevating device than as a means for the author to insert himself within the madman's camp.

A look at the narrator's aberrations, indeed, reveals that he is much madder than the figures he generates. These fictitious fools are themselves the figments of his own split personality, of a schizophrenia which manifests itself in myriad fashions throughout the work and, most particularly, in the narrator's rapidly changing stances. His shifts between silence and loquacity, arrogance and humility, insight and ignorance constitute an alternating exaltation and degradation of the ego which is characteristic of many psychoses. If Orlando and Panurge confuse fact with fantasy, their creators do so on a much grander scale,

41. For a further discussion of this ambiguity, see Alice F. Berry, "Apollo versus Bacchus: The Dynamics of Inspiration," *PMLA* 90 (1975): 88–95.

42. While the four furors are expounded by Plato in his *Ion*, they were diffused in the Renaissance primarily by Marsilio Ficino: "Quapropter sicut per quattuor discendit gradus, per quattuor ascendat necesse est. Furor autem divinus est, qui ad supera tollit, ut in eius definitione consistit. Quattuor ergo divini furoris sunt species. Primus quidem poeticus furor; alter mysterialis; tertius vaticinium; amatorius affectus est quartus" (VII.14). *Marsilio Ficino's Commentary on Plato's Symposium*, ed. and trans. Sears Reynolds Jayne, University of Missouri Studies, vol. 19, no. 1 (Columbia: University of Missouri Press, 1944), p. 115. Like Plato, however, Ficino opposes divine madness and love to "amore ferino, qui insanie species est" (VII. 3, p. 107).

intertwining history with their own hallucinations and insisting upon the veracity of blatant myth. The narrative's overall discontinuity, finally—Ariosto's abrupt shifts of subject matter and Rabelais's ever-modulating language—mirrors the mental vagaries of Panurge and the various paladins, the rapid associations and fluctuating thoughts which underlie their volatile energy. These dramatic deviations from normality have, of course, been consciously assumed and together form an integral thematic and technical part of the artist's design. Indeed, Foucault's description of psychotic behavior might equally well apply, in its general outlines, to the Rabelaisian and Ariostan creative process:

> Il s'agit d'éléments dissociés qui se libèrent dans un style d'incohérence absolue. A la synthèse complexe du dialogue s'est substitué le monologue fragmentaire; la syntaxe à travers laquelle se constitue un sens est brisée, et il ne subsiste plus que des éléments verbaux d'où s'échappent des sens ambigus, polymorphes et labiles; la cohérence spatio-temporelle qui s'ordonne à l'ici et au maintenant s'est effondrée, et il ne subsiste plus qu'un chaos d'ici successifs et d'instants insulaires.[43]

Far from being the naive expression of a troubled psyche, the disorder is obviously contrived, a fact corroborated by successive reworkings of the manuscript and, more importantly, by that truth beyond reason which issues from the most apparently senseless scenes. An inventory of the narrator's idiosyncrasies clarifies this same intentionality. "L'incapacité à se repérer dans le temps et l'espace" produces a sense of temporal relativism; "les ruptures de continuité dans sa conduite" represent a conscious rejection of systems and rational order; and "la perte de la fonction du réel" interrogates the basic ontological and epistemological premises of Western culture.[44]

If folly works in the service of wisdom, however, the converse is equally true. Quite frequently, the narrator's grandiose epistemological pretensions make him appear more foolish. In fact, the schizophrenic's fragmented viewpoint derives, in these works, from a "lucid" attempt at synthesis, evident in the rudimentary allegory and would-be apocalyptic structure of both epic romances. Like their heroes, the narrators experience madness as a function of presumption, proof that "qui veut

---

43. *Maladie mentale et psychologie*, pp. 20–21.
44. Ibid., pp. 4–18.

faire l'ange fait la bête."[45] This looking-glass reversal occurs not only on a macrocosmic level, evident from an overview of the work, but at various points within the discourse, when the narrative takes on an intellectual or transcendental twist. Throughout both works learned borrowings and allusions are seldom fully integrated into a unified discourse but are rather ostentatiously superimposed as garish digressions upon the narrative mainstream; as such, they resemble the fool's motley garb.

While the "wise" narrator inflates his ego with reminders of Dante, Petrarchan concetti, mythological tableaux, and Socratic aspirations, his "demented" double allows us an objective view of these pretensions by counterbalancing them with his own contradictory perspective. Ariosto's invocation of Apollo and subsequent highflown panegyrics are, for example, made equivocal by an incongruous juxtaposition of the lofty and the lowly. The unbridgeable gap between his encomiastic hyperbole ("non vedi . . . / piú gloriosa stirpe . . . fin che d'intorno al polo il ciel s'aggiri" [III.2]) and learned reference to "Febo" on the one hand, and his familiar, skeptical asides on the other ("s'in me non erra / quel profetico lume che m'inspiri" [III.2]), splinters the discourse's purported sense into nonsense. Although Ariosto's self-depreciating interjections are narrative commonplaces, ostensibly designed to elevate his material, they at the same time cast a new light upon the surrounding encomium. The "if" in "s'in me non erra" first of all renders the entire passage hypothetical. By way of contrast with this low narrative voice, secondly, the wise fool's elevation—erudite allusions, flowery language, and divine frenzy—seems extravagant, the mad "other" of "quel furor che suole."

More dramatically in Rabelais, paradox infects "rational" discourse on both the stylistic and semantic levels, destroying its logic and mocking man's epistemological pretensions. The Gallic monk enthusiastically incorporates scholarly sources into his text only to ridicule many of them, expressing both his indifference to them ("ce m'est tout un" [P.II. 179]) and his doubt of their veracity ("si ne le croiez, non foys-je, fistelle" [P.I.177]). In such instances the fool shows its face through the wise man's mask and proclaims the latter mad. Yet at the same time the reverse also holds true: "Rabelais conteste son époque en tournant

45. Pascal, no. 358, p. 164. Cf. also Montaigne II.xii: "La présomption est nostre maladie naturelle et orginelle. La plus calamiteuse et fraile de toutes créatures, c'est l'homme, et quant et quant la plus orgueilleuse" (1: 496).

en déraison la manie des citations, mais dans le même temps, il tourne la déraison même en dérision en citant correctement et en veillant qu'on le sache."[46] Even as these examples from Rabelais and Ariosto parody past literary convention and its horde of wise fools, they also illustrate the duplicity of narrative folly: it has two opposite aspects, the one elevated and the other base, each of which finds the other mad.

Thus manipulating his narrator, the behind-the-scenes artist never allows one to forget that the intellectual furor, no less than its Dionysian counterpart, is pure madness, which, within the context of the Renaissance, is not merely the opposite of "reason" but the universal, integral form of existence. In his vacillation between wise and foolish folly, the Ariostan and Rabelaisian narrator reminds one of Erasmus's Stultitia, who—even as she philosophizes and flaunts her *savior faire*—asserts that all of life is mad. Within this cognitive structure the One does not replace, but rather *is*, the Many, a paradox symbolically illustrated by the Silenus principle:

> For first of all, the fact is that all human affairs, like the Sileni of Alcibiades, have two aspects, each quite different from the other; even to the point that what at first blush (as the phrase goes) seems to be death may prove, if you look further into it, to be life. What at first sight is beautiful may really be ugly; the apparently wealthy may be the poorest of all; the disgraceful, glorious; the learned, ignorant; the robust, feeble, the noble, base; the joyous, sad; the favorable, adverse; what is friendly, an enemy; and what is wholesome, poisonous. In brief, you will find all things suddenly reversed, when you open the Silenus.   (36)[47]

In this Erasmian example, it is true, Stultitia seems to promise an absolute truth, an essence beyond that appearance which "sane" men perceive; and following in her footsteps, Ariosto and Rabelais pattern their entire fiction after the box, directing both the narrator's and characters' epistemological quest outside the "city walls," and mirroring

---

46. De Grève, p. 153.

47. "Principio constat res omneis humanas, velut Alcibiadis Silenos, binas habere facies nimium inter sese dissimiles. Adeo ut quod prima, ut ajunt, fronte mors est, si interius inspicias, vita set: contra quod vita, mors: quod formosum, deforme: quod opulentum, id pauperrimum: quod infame, gloriosum: quod doctum, indoctum: quod robustum, inbecille: quod generosum, ignobile: quod laetum, triste: quod prosperum, adversum: quod amicum, inimicum: quod salutare, noxium: breviter omnia repente versa reperies, si Silenum aperueris" (47–48).

back from this thematic and stylistic netherworld the other side of rationality. Underneath the book's grotesque facade—its anti-Aristotelian structure and hallucinatory images—Rabelais seems to promise, there lies a hermetic wisdom:

> Silènes estoient jadis petites boites, telle que voyons de présent ès bouticques des apothecaires, pinctes au-dessus de figures joyeuses et frivoles, comme de harpies, satyres, oysons bridéz, lièvres cornuz, canes bastées, boucqs volans, cerfz limonniers et aultres telles pinctures contrefaictes à plaisir pour exciter le monde à rire (quel fut Silène, maistre du bon Bacchus); mais au dedans l'on réservoit les fines drogues comme baulme, ambre gris, amomon, musc, zivette, pierreries et aultres choses précieuses. (G.prol.3)

Subsequent negations and reaffirmations, however, constitute a dialectic rather than a preferential progression, reestablishing the Silenus symbolism as ambiguity instead of hermeticism. Similarly, the Ariostan lunarworld may also be likened to the Silenus box, in both its initial promise (one of magical otherness) and its ambivalent realization. Folly is not replacing the old Word with a new one but merely questioning the absolutism of cultural definitions by developing the opposite point of view.[48]

What is seen in these reversals derives, in part, from that popular, polemic tradition which produced the feast of fools.[49] During this period idiots were made kings and magistrates mocked, in a satiric masquerade. It is in concurrence with carnival practice, then, that Rabelais deposes princes and crowns paupers, giving Diogenes Alexander's robe and sceptre (P.XXX.300). In Ariosto a similar process occurs when the once-wise Orlando is "resensed" by the once-mad Astolfo (XXXIX.57), or when sense is transferred to the moon and lunacy left on earth: "sol la pazzia non v'è poca né assai; / che sta qua giú, né se ne parte mai" (XXXIV.81).

Rather than asserting the superiority of one value over another, this stultification process demonstrates the relativity of wisdom and folly. Instead of seeing the madman through "sane" eyes, as is his custom, the reader is introduced to the fool's point of view and is forced to

48. See Mikhaël Bakhtine, *L'Œuvre de François Rabelais et la culture populaire au Moyen Age et sous la Renaissance*, trans. André Robel (Paris: Gallimard, 1970), for an exhaustive study of Rabelais in this context.

49. See David Quint, "Astolfo's Voyage to the Moon," *Yale Italian Studies* 1 (1977): 398–408.

judge wise men and heroes insane. This reversal of optics takes on broader significance in relationship to the Wheel of Fortune. In both authors' upside-down netherworlds one finds "ció che si perde o per nostro difetto / o per colpa di tempo o di Fortuna" (XXXIV.73). Men's fame and social values change with time, just as they vary through space, and what one eye considers wise may be considered mad by another.

The shifting perspectives which establish folly's relativity may also be considered reflective, a classically schizophrenic alienation from and objectification of the self, which results in a kind of lucidity. Spatially detached from the islands they visit and temporally removed from the netherworlds, characters confront their own madness in picaresque fashion while the fragmented narrative structure ensures that each figure will, at some time, be viewed as the "other." In Ariosto this detachment functions frequently between narrator and characters. Substantives such as *rabbia, furore,* and *pazzia,* along with their adjectival derivatives, recur throughout the *Furioso,* as referents to a wide range of characters.[50] It is figures themselves, in Rabelais, who objectify their comrades' behavior and label each other fools. Pantagruel, for example, asserts that the Dipsodes behave "follement" (P. XXVIII.284), refers to both "sotz sophistes" (P.XVIII.249) and the uneducated "folz" (P.X.216); and if he himself is called "fol" by Panurge (P.XXIX.293), the latter is termed "meschant fol" (P.XXI.260) by the lady of Paris and "fol enragé" (TL.XLVI.489) by the madman himself, Triboullet.

More important than the relativity of folly, in Rabelais and Ariosto, is its universality ("tout est fol," says Panurge [TL.XLVI.490]), a con-

---

50. Less frequently, this same process occurs among characters. A good example is found in the exchange between Ferraú, who has lost his helmet, and Orlando, who will soon go mad:

—Deh, — disse Orlando al re di Circassia
—in mio servigio a costui l'elmo presta,
tanto ch'io gli abbia tratta la pazzia;
ch'altra non vidi mai simile a questa.—
Rispose il re: —Chi piú pazzo saria?
Ma se ti par pur la domanda onesta,
Prestagli il tuo; ch'io non sarò men atto,
che tu sia forse, a castigare un matto.—

Suggiunse Ferraú: —Sciocchi voi, quasi
che, se mi fosse il portar elmo a grado,
voi senza non ne fosse già rimase:
che tolti i vostri avrei, vostro mal grado.   (XII.41–42)

cept which emerges, stylistically, from the prismatic interplay of mad-
men and sages; and philosophically, from an intuition of man's condition. If, within society, madness is a function of vacillating values, it
is determined, on a metaphysical level, by unvarying mortality, that
great equalizer which renders all terrestrial action futile. Superficially,
it is true, death and destruction seem mere steppingstones to rebirth.
Gargantua's tears for his dead wife are swiftly followed by laughter at
his son's birth; fallen paladins quickly pick themselves up and ride
off indestructibly; lineage and continuity are more important than
mortality. Increasingly, however, *il penseroso* supplants *l'allegro*, as
stultifying illusions such as Alcina are destroyed. The *Quart Livre*
storm, Panurge's fear, the loss of Brandimarte, and those debacles that
darken Ariosto's climactic chapters—all this brings us to a contemplation of death and a redefinition of folly.

Stultification represents, in one sense, a negation of terrestrial values—reduction of life into pure game, annihilation of man-the-hero
and substitution of man-the-player. On an esthetic level this operation
is fully realized by a dialectical process and through polyvalent exploitation of laughter. This latter element is at once a prototypic
symptom of hysterical lunacy and one of "sane" man's instinctive reactions to aberrant behavior. As comic artists Rabelais and Ariosto
effect a deliberate distortion of verbal and behavioral models, using
incongruous culinary language in battle situations (IX.68;QL.XL), injecting puppets into heroic frames, and themselves deviating from the
narrative norm. When, however, from his rational pedestal the reader
senses the absurdity of Panurge's erudition, sees through the paladins'
lovesick illusions, and derisively chuckles at the author's ineptitude,
that same behind-the-scenes artist who provoked this reaction turns
the tables again, forcing one to see in the folly one laughs *at* a mirror
with which one must laugh. Not only the heroes but readers as well
have become puppets of the gods, the Olympian narrator's unwitting
fools.

By detaching himself in effect from humanity, the backstage artist
creates a metaphysical metaphor; conversely, it is by playing the fool
and infecting readers with his folly that he provokes in them an awakening of the consciousness. Deliberately he has engaged in an act of
madness, choosing fiction over philosophy or science and laying himself open to the same criticism which Montesquieu will elicit some two
hundred years later in his *Lettres persanes*: "Si l'on savait qui je suis on

dirait: 'Son livre jure avec son caractère; il devrait employer son temps à quelque chose de mieux: cela n'est pas digne d'un homme grave.' "[51] In the case of Rabelais and Ariosto, however, the levity not only serves as a facade for more serious matters but also questions the very existence of "quelque chose de mieux," of a better way to pass the time. Given the assumption that all is folly in face of death and eternity, the most monumental acts are reduced to pastime ("l'ozio lungo d'uomini ignoranti" [XXXIV.75]), while, conversely, consciously assumed madness constitutes a kind of perverse sagacity; for "to be a fool is to act the play of life."[52] It is this wisdom which the artist would communicate to the audience, when—addressing himself to the leisured classes and creating a work of pure diversion—he merely implies that we are all "foulz de séjour" (G.prol.3).

If the Renaissance's parade of fools were totally negative in its implications, there would be little to distinguish it from the earlier Dance Macabre. But the entire work of Rabelais and Ariosto seems a negation of this morbidity, a hymn to life rather than death. Granted, their subject matter—war, tempests, degraded heroes, broken dreams— is the stuff of which tragedy is made, risible for the wise man only in an absurdist sense. But then Ariosto and Rabelais have not solicited an audience of sages, who would reject as insane "whatever life has to offer."[53] Instead, they direct their appeal to fools like themselves, who—in full cognizance of life's futility—prefer it to the alternative, realizing that nothingness is all, and terrestrial illusion their only reality.

It is from within this paradoxical conceptual structure that Rabelais and Ariosto derive the esthetic and epistemological unity of their work, reestablishing life in all its diversity and reconciling contradictions on the other side of despair. Far from launching an irresponsible cry of *carpe diem* or chanting a morose *vanitas vanitatum*, the artists have composed an encomium of folly, in which tragedy is transformed, made an integral part of the human comedy, and the monstrous universe made equal to mad-made monuments in its awful fascination. By constantly doubling the various follies, moreover—social, cosmic, and

---

51. Charles-Louis de Secondat, baron de la Brède et de Montesquieu, *Lettres persanes,* ed. Jacques Roger (Paris: Garnier-Flammarion, 1964), p. 23.

52. Kaiser, p. 4. Cf. also Pascal: "Les hommes sont si nécessairement fous que ce serait être fou par un autre tour de folie de n'être pas fou" (no. 414, p. 173).

53. " . . . qui quiquid in omni vita geritur, velut insanum damnet rideatque" (52).

psychological—they open the doors to relativism of values and establish a more authentic *modus vivendi*. Born as it is of negation and nothingness, and thus necessarily creative in nature, their tribute to folly constitutes a thoroughly modern brand of humanism; and their art, as the near-perfect expression of this intuition, becomes the ultimate humanistic act.

CONCLUSION

As Rabelais and Ariosto found, it is more in keeping with their antithetical world view to leave the book unfinished, or at least to leave readers suspended on an ambiguous note, than to tie up all the loose ends. Why, then, should the critic attempt to improve upon art? To offer the countervoyage as a global interpretation of either the works or their period seems unauthentic, a contradiction in terms; for the essence of its structure in multiplicity, a self-differentiating diversity which places even so consolidative a form as comparison on shaky conceptual ground.

Yet to consider the countervoyage as an end in itself is no less fallacious. It is a change of perspective that enables one to judge more authentically; and it is the critic's duty to judge. The countervoyage into madness, after all, requires a return to reason. In psychotherapy supervised reversions into infancy are only one-half of a corrective journey, the goal of which is reconstruction of a healthier and happier adulthood. Likewise in art Rimbaud cannot sustain his drunken odyssey indefinitely but comes to regret "l'Europe aux anciens parapets." The return enables him to collect his thoughts and communicate them to the reader in a linguistic act which is necessarily rational. The journey's "end" is thus always a new beginning. Their odysseys into unreason leave both Orlando and Astolfo, upon their return, much wiser than before. The latter "lungo tempo saggio visse" (XXXIV.86), while the former's intellect is "più che mai lucido e netto" (XXXIX.57). Often, moreover, the return involves a recapitulation. At the end of the *Fifth Book*, the Utopians doubtless return home to recount their story *da capo*. Therefore, it is only appropriate that one recapitulate the countervoyage itself, using its own dialectical methods to place it in critical perspective; for this, after all, is what the reversible structure is all about—judging from different distances and points of view.

The countervoyage of Rabelais and Ariosto is, at its most basic level, a stylistic and structural phenomenon, easily recognizable in the authors' bipolar, ambiguous discourse. To speak of ambiguity in art is, granted, somewhat problematical; for all literature, by virtue of the defective nature of language and the reader-writer gap, is ultimately double, a question without the response. Yet the work of Rabelais and Ariosto is more than merely ambivalent. If in most books multiple interpretations are mere by-products of the literary process, they are the essence itself—form and content—of the *Orlando furioso* and Pantagrueline tales. Not only allowing the reader to exercise his eternal prerogative of contestation, the two authors actively solicit interrogation of their word. The Ariostan storyteller delights in binary structures such as "o . . . / o . . .," while Alcofribas tells us that "si ne le croiez, non foys-je, fist-elle" (P.I.177). In brief, the narrators contradict themselves right and left, alternate between high and low styles, give voice to their own doubts, and generate "symbols" with multiple senses that also double as a possible "non-sense."

At first glance, it may seem superfluous to label mere ambivalence a "countervoyage." The term has been essential to this study not only because of its bipolar structure, which mirrors that of the text, however, but also because of its semantic value. By referring to stylistic ambiguities as a "countervoyage," one transfers them by metaphorical association from the domain of meaningless form to a specific conceptual context—that of the traditional and topical voyage. On an intratextual level, the figure provides both structural continuity and thematic unity to the *Orlando furioso* and Pantagrueline tales. The various expeditions to Alcina's realm, the moon, and the *Quart Livre* islands not only advance the plot chronologically but are also conceptually united as figures of man's ongoing epistemological quest. The extratextual associations of the voyage are moreover particularly important within the Renaissance context. During this time of New World discoveries and Old World advances, it doubles as the figure itself of man-conquering and man-progressing.

The themes and forms chosen for analysis in this study may be interpreted positively as a function of this heroic odyssey; for by virtue of their potentially transcendent, epistemological value, they constitute the outline for a possible humanistic voyage of conquest. Ideally, *mythology* is a structure of knowledge containing hermetic truths, which the inspired *narrator*, often speaking from a state of divine *madness*, affirms and communicates to his public. *Time* ("père de vérité" [TL.XL.473]) can moreover be an instrument of this revelation, which is at once captured and eternalized in *art*. Clearly, however, each of these figures is potentially double. Myth can also be falsity; the narrator, a liar; time, destructive; art, deceitful; and folly, sin. Ariosto and Rabelais exploit this virtuality to its fullest in a critical countervoyage, neutralizing each positive symbolism with its negative double to destroy both the medieval and Renaissance spirit of synthesis.

While both authors appear filled with admiration for contemporary explorers, first of all, textual analysis reveals subversive countercurrents that undercut this positive attitude toward the voyage. The injection of low, earthy details into situationally or stylistically elevated passages turns praise into mockery. Rabelais, for example, mentions recent exploration ("comment il naviga par la mer Athlanticque" [P.XXXIV.311]) in the same sentence as Pantagruel's visit to hell and breaking of Lucifer's "corne au cul" (312), while Ariosto makes the airborne Astolfo satisfy his natural needs ("a natura il duca aventuroso / satisfece di quel che se le debbe" [XXXIV.61]) before touring the Earthly Paradise. Such physical and stylistic descents support Panurge's suspicion, in the *Quart Livre*, that "l'homme nasquit pour labourer et travailler, comme l'oyseau pour voler" (QL.XXIV.608), and illustrate a similar contention on the part of Ariosto:

> perché, salendo lo intelletto in suso
> per veder Dio, non de' parerci strano
> se talor cade giú cieco e confuso.   (*Satira* VI.46–48)

This conflict between man's ambition and his limitations is complemented by further tensions in the voyage structure, which provide meaningful insights into the authors' world view: in the vacillation between utopia and arcadia one sees an ambiguous attitude toward humanistic civilization; in the unresolved allegorical sequences, an inability to resolve multiplicity in oneness; and in the gap between signified and signifier, a reflection of the dislocated relationship between noumena and phenomena in the Renaissance.

The myth and fantasy which appear, secondly, to express the hyperbolic nature of humanistic aspirations and potentials also serve, in Rabelais and Ariosto, to undermine both the stature of the hero and man's basic ontological precepts. Encomiastic comparisons of the Renaissance hero to classical gods and demigods, for example, are neutralized by animal and insect analogies, which interrogate rather than affirm man's rank in the Great Chain of Being. Traditional quest forms, such as the encounter with monsters and netherworld descents, are likewise diffused in diversional, mercenary, circular, and even comic directions, to reflect the problematic nature of initiation in such a complex and fragmented culture. The fluctuating boundary between reality and fantasy in the voyage landscape is no less meaningful, serving both to poeticize the experience of discovery and to express the weightless, disoriented vertigo that accompanies radical change; for in a world where fantasies are being realized, and old truths being disputed, man's ontological equilibrium is severely upset.

A potential source of stability within this vertiginous fiction, thirdly, is the narrator, whose visibility has escalated with the rise of Renaissance individualism, in a profusion of *je*'s and *io*'s. While the poet does frequently assume an omniscient, authoritarian stance, however, he just as often plays the fool, feigning ignorance, mocking his own pretensions, and mystifying readers with his unreliability. This fragmented narrative structure serves, first of all, to reflect a very real cognitive crisis on the part of the Renaissance writer: if his omniscient stance stems from the humanists' *soif d'absolu*, so does its negative antipode signal the poet's feeling of inadequacy before this ideal and the difficulty of knowing in a world of rapidly changing values and realities. At the same time this fragmentation of the narrative voice develops as an essay in self-knowledge, which reflects the contradictions of both human nature in general and the poet's own fractured ego. Transferal of this conceptual dichotomy to the narrative structure works, finally, to communicate the writer's own critical spirit to the public, for whom the text is no longer an absolute to be accepted passively, but rather a kinetic mechanism which depends upon reader participation for completion.

The generational rupture precipitating this fragmented narrative structure, of course, is frequently vaunted by humanists as a positive phenomenon. Both Rabelais and Ariosto, however, combine this depiction of progressive, melioristic time with a sustained critique of the present, expressions of nostalgia for the past, and references to nonprogressive historical theories such as the circular Wheel of Fortune and the retrogressive Golden Age myth. For Rabelais and Ariosto, then, the Renaissance discovery of time is double. Just as Janus looks backward and forward, passage is shown to be flux as well as progress; a source of trauma as well as joy; exile as well as liberation from eternity. A potential means of bridging this gap—of uniting the real and the ideal, time and timelessness, mortality and immortality—is art, a theme which also undergoes bipolar development. For both this transcendent art and the eternity of fame that it promises prove, upon closer scrutiny, to be temporal: the one "a nostra etade è estinta" (XXXIII.5), relegated to the oracular past of prelapsarian poetry, while the other is dependent upon man's short memory, his fickle tastes, and the impermanence of paper itself.

For a reconciliation of the countervoyage's contradictions, one must look not to some mythical apocalyptic art but rather to the definitional alterity of folly. Linguistic and thematic analysis indeed reveals just what Panurge tells us, that "tout est fol": not only the new world, with its monsters and phenomenological chaos, but the old world as well, with its stultified institutions and irrational values; not only the sage and hero, with their delusions of grandeur and maniacal *raisons d'être*, but also the fool, whose madness doubles as illumination; not only the ignorant narrator, who recognizes the futility of feigning wisdom, but also his wise twin, whose wisdom becomes foolish in a world where all is folly. The text functions, indeed, as a mirror of fools, in which the would-be sage points out his mad other, only to find the accusing finger reversed and turned toward him. Thus viewed in perspective, the entire countervoyage emerges as an odyssey into mad otherness, which, for all its negativity, carries with it an apocalypse all its own: a negation of outmoded synthetic systems in favor of critical methods; a recognition that truth is not absolute but relative; and a revaluation of life in all its diversity as one great feast of fools.

The countervoyage movement is not only stylistic and thematic, of course, but generic as well. The hybrid mock epic genre chosen by each author at once helps impose and reinforces the texts' bipolar structure. On one level the works are romances, unfolding in a fantasy world and consecrated to an impossible, unworldly ideal: to heroism, gallantry, the quest for beauty and truth. While the genre, in its particulars, is anachronistic, it expresses a very real structure of thought in the Renaissance. Not only is there a good measure of nostalgia for chivalry, and even an effort to preserve or resurrect its traditions in the fifteenth and sixteenth centuries, but so are, in a different way, certain ambitions of the humanists equally idealistic. Since the romance heritage of both France and Ferrara coincides, structurally at least, with this High Renaissance idealism, it is not surprising to see a merger of the old and the new transcendence in the *Orlando furioso* and Pantagrueline tales.

Yet from another standpoint the works are epics as well, rooted in the empiric reality of their times. The voyages of discovery, material and spiritual advances, seem to promise a realization of the ideal, a reunion of noumena and phenomena similar to that of Homer's immanent universe. From the outset, however, romance idealism and epic historicity do not converge but rather thwart each other's progress; and the inherently positive thrust of each genre is further undermined by burlesque and Menippean negativity. What results is a highly charged tension between the real and the ideal, the vulgar and the sublime, which parallels extratextual conflicts between speculative reason and empiric fact.

That the countervoyage should permeate all levels of the Rabelaisian and Ariostan discourse—style, themes, and genre—is certainly a mark of the works' extraordinary structural coherence. To study the intertextuality of this dialectic, without posing the question of influence and imitation, is moreover to imply its extratextuality as well, by raising it to the level of cultural significance. This hypothesis finds support in the unusually rich topical content of the countervoyage's themes and forms, to be sure, which yield an abundance of ideas on subjects of contemporary interest: a love of learning but an intuition of its vanity; a feeling that the voyage is exciting but vertiginous; speculation that firearms are useful but barbaric. But even more importantly the countervoyage's abstract form—its negativity, antitheses, and multiplicity —can be related to extratextual structures.

As a descending movement, first of all, bent on exploring negative otherness, the countervoyage of Rabelais and Ariosto is not an isolated phenomenon. On one level, its heaven-earth dialectic outlines the transition from a theocentric world to one which wills itself anthropocentric: the descent thus represents a toppling of the medieval system's transcendent hierarchy of laws, values, and institutions. At the same time this negative polemic is clearly directed against the lofty pretensions of classical humanism as well. Far from being atypical of the period, this negativity exists coevally with its opposites throughout the Renaissance. Folengo also demystifies the hero; Scève and Petrarch combine self-aggrandizement with self-denigration; and even Pico—in his manifesto of humanism, *De hominis dignitate*—explores man's bestiality as well as his divinity. Obviously, then, this negative movement is itself double, deriving in part from humanistic curiosity, which explores even the negative other; in part from a retrogressive notion concerning man's fallen nature; and in part from a progressive empiricism that confronts and destroys ideals with fact.

In Rabelais and Ariosto, secondly, countervoyage descents from the sublime to the vulgar may be interpreted as just such a confrontation between ideals and reality. Not just a literary structure, moreover, this conceptual descent from noumena to phenomena characterizes much Renaissance historical, scientific, and political theory. Of such a tenor are the nontranscendent, pragmatic, and unheroic politics of Machiavelli, Guicciardini, and Bodin; the naturalistic science of Agrippa; and the particularistic, phenomenological self-study of Montaigne. The decentralization of these works, thirdly, is another effect of both the intratextual and extratextual countervoyage, which tends to fragment traditional oneness into multiplicity. The most striking examples of this phenomenon are found in geography, religion, and astronomy, as one hemisphere gives way to a second; one catholic church, to many sects; and the earth's old centrality in the cosmos, to a multiplicity of concentric planets.

Such negativity, obviously, is not without its positive other, and vice versa. On a structural level, idealism, oneness, and positivity are ever present in the *Orlando furioso* and the Pantagrueline tales, just as they are in Renaissance culture as a whole. It is this ascendant pole, indeed, which lends the works their perfect ambiguity, thereby enabling them to express the divided consciousness of an entire era. This antithetical structure may be explained, in historical and theoretical terms, as a natural by-product of the Renaissance voyage of discovery. It is a universal rule, after all, that one learns and progresses only through a dialectical balancing of opposites, in which antithesis precedes synthesis: both the allegorical progressions and sophistic dialectics of the Middle Ages, for example, were based upon the resolution of contradictions within a closed system.

Vacillating between the medieval synthesis and the humanistic hypothesis, the Renaissance voyage has even more reason to progress "à tâtons." Logic requires that any new hypothesis be repeatedly tested before acceptance as a structure of knowledge: the positive must be negated; the ideal subjected to the test of reality; and the new measured up against the old. This dialectic is intensified by the era's transitional status. Situated like Janus on the threshold of modernity, the Renaissance is caught up in a tension between tradition and invention, order and adventure, which both rejects and regrets the old system. This is not to say, however, that the countervoyage does not lead to a new synthesis of its own: for Cusanus, it is *docta ignorantia*; for Montaigne, nescience; and for Rabelais and Ariosto, the oneness-in-multiplicity of folly.

In such an age of diversity, multiplicity, and otherness, however, consideration of the sameness and oneness of these two works takes on a certain irony. While it is a simple task for the "omniscient" critic, like the manipulative Ariostan or Rabelaisian narrator, to bring together these two separate manifestations of Renaissance culture for a brief comparison, their union is necessarily contrived. Like the unreliable storyteller, the critic as well must finally descend from Olympia and restore to each work its difference. To suggest that there are no temporal, cultural, or esthetic dissimilarities between these two writers would, after all, be grossly misleading. In many ways "ils ne sont comparables." The popular or folk element is much more pronounced in the Pantagrueline tales: the language is earthier, the characters more buffoonish, the humor more visceral. In this respect the French monk bears closer kinship with Pulci and Folengo than with his courtly Ferrarese counterpart. Certainly the one's lusty *rire*, appropriate for "buveurs" and "véroléz," is scarcely mistakable for the other's restrained *sorriso*, directed toward noble lords and gentle ladies. Also absent from the *Furioso* is the shadow of the Sorbonne, whose censorious scholastic tradition provides the topical springboard for much of Rabelais's satire and lends it a particularly Gallic flavor. Equally foreign to Ariosto are the evangelical overtones which color the Rabelaisian opus and which distinguish the northern Renaissance from its southern relative.

The differences between Rabelais and Ariosto are not only geographical but temporal as well. Although both publish in 1532, the artists ride opposite sides of the Wheel of Fortune. When Ariosto dies in 1533, Rabelais is just beginning his literary career; and as the Italian Renaissance fades, its French counterpart is bursting into bloom. Explicable in this light is that implacable sophistication and sporadic world-weariness which distinguish the Ariostan narrator, imperceptibly, from the ebullient Alcofribas, and which appear symptomatic of a period in its decadence. For the Ferrarese poet, all the shouting is over. Between him and the glorious rebirth of letters there lies not just a lifetime of critical distance but Italy's century and a half of humanistic rule as well. In Rabelais, on the contrary, we experience the transition from Middle Ages to Renaissance, from the dawn of France's golden age to the eve of her civil wars, in all its immediacy, its violent emotions and contrasts, its expectations and deceptions. Just as Ariosto never equals the elevated heights of the Pantagruel's opening scenes, neither does he ever descend to the cataclysmic depths of the *Quart Livre*. Rabelais, unlike his Ferrarese counterpart, has chosen not to mute the rupture's rough edges. Thanks to the southern experience, however, which it assimilates and builds upon, the Rabelaisian brand of humanism is born into the world an old man, an infant giant which is wise beyond its years.

The very differences between Rabelais and Ariosto serve, finally, to render their profound similarities all the more intriguing. Given these considerable disparities, one might well ask why the *Orlando furioso* and Pantagrueline tales nonetheless remain closer in affinity to each other than to works of the artists' own countrymen or contemporaries. The key to this similarity lies, ironically, in their difference itself. As pivotal figures between northern and southern, early and late Renaissance, Rabelais and Ariosto unite almost all the diverse tendencies—or differences—of the period within their works. Satire and lyricism, piety and heresy, poetry and prose, the grotesque and the sublime all find their way into these conglomerate masterpieces, which by virtue of their very heterogeneity, are perhaps the most representative monuments of a contradictory age which resists definition. Thus while the various components that make up the two mock epics are often commonplace or similar to themes and forms in other works, the ensemble is unique and different. And it is because, paradoxically, each work is "sans parragon" that the two are ultimately comparable: each is the kind of authentic, truly representative art form that a single culture seldom produces twice.

BIBLIOGRAPHY

I. PRIMARY SOURCES

Agrippa, Cornelius. *De incertitude & inanitate scientarum* [Cologne? 1539?].
Ariosto, Ludovico. *Opere*. Edited by Giuliano Innamorati. Bologna: Zanichelli, 1968.
————. *Orlando furioso*. Edited by Mario Apollonio and Pio Fontana. 2d ed. Brescia: La Scuola, 1971.
Aubigné, Theodore Agrippa d'. *Les Tragiques*. In *Œuvres*, edited by Henri Weber. Paris: Bibliothèque de la Pléiade, 1969. Pp. 3–243.
Bade, Josse. *La Nef des folles des cinq sens de la nature*. Translated by Jean Drouyn. Paris: Marnef, n.d.
Baudelaire, Charles. *Les Fleurs du mal*. In *Œuvres complètes*, edited by Y.-G. Le Dantec. Paris: Bibliothèque de la Pléiade, 1961. Pp. 5–127.
Beckett, Samuel. *Fin de partie*. Paris: Minuit, 1957.
————. *Oh les beaux jours!* Paris: Minuit, 1957.
Blake, William. *Milton*. In *Poetry and Prose of William Blake*, edited by David Erdman. New York: Doubleday, 1965. Pp. 94–143.
Boiardo, Matteo. *Orlando innamorato*. Edited by Pio Rajna. 2 vols. Milan: Istituto Editoriale Italiano, n.d.
Camus, Albert. *Caligula*. Paris: Gallimard, 1958.
Cartas de relación de la conquista de America. Edited by Julio le Riverend. Mexico: Nueva España, [1945?].
Castiglione, Baldessar. *Il libro del cortegiano*. Edited by Michele Scherillo. Milan: Hoepli, 1928.
Céline, Ferdinand. *Voyage au bout de la nuit*. In *Romans*. 2 vols. Paris: Bibliothèque de la Pléiade, 1962.
Corpus hermeticum. Edited by A. D. Nock; translated by A.-J. Festugière. Paris: Société d'Édition "Les Belles Lettres," 1945.
Dante Alighieri. *Opere*. Edited by Fredi Chiappelli. Milan: Mursia, 1965.
Erasmus, Desiderius, *The Praise of Folly*. Translated by Hoyt Hopewell Hudson. Princeton, N.J.: Princeton University Press, 1941.
————. *Stultitiae laus*. The Hague: M. Nijhoff, 1898.

Ficino, Marsilio. *Marsilio Ficino's Commentary on Plato's Symposium*. Edited and translated by Sears Reynolds Jayne. University of Missouri Studies, 19, no. 1. Columbia: University of Missouri Press, 1944.

Folengo, Teofilo. *Il Baldo*. Edited by Giampaolo Dossena; translated by Giuseppe Tonna. 2 vols. Milan: Feltrinelli, 1958.

Les Grands et inestimables chronicques du grant et énorme géant Gargantua. Appendix in *The Tale of Gargantua and King Arthur*, by Frances Girault. Edited by Huntington Brown. Cambridge, Mass.: Harvard University Press, 1932. Pp. 103–28.

Hugo, Victor, *Cromwell*. Paris: Flammarion, 1932.

Malraux, André. *La Condition humaine*. In *Romans*. Paris: Bibliothèque de la Pléiade, 1947. Pp. 181–432.

Montaigne, Michel de. *Essais*. Edited by Maurice Rat. 2 vols. Paris: Garnier, 1962.

Montesquieu, Charles-Louis de Secondat, baron de la Brède et de. *Lettres persanes*. Edited by Jacques Roger. Paris: Garnier-Flammarion, 1964.

Pascal, Blaise. *Pensées*. Edited by Léon Brunschvicg. Paris: Garnier, 1948.

Petrarca, Francesco. *Rime, Trionfi e poesie latine*. Edited by F. Neri and others. Milan: Ricciardi, 1951.

Pico della Mirandola. *Oratio de hominis dignitate*. Edited by Eugenio Garin; translated by Elizabeth Livermore. Lexington, Ky.: Anvil Press, 1953.

Rabelais, François. *Œuvres complètes*. Edited by Jacques Boulenger. Paris: Bibliothèque de la Pléiade, 1955.

Rimbaud, Arthur. *Œuvres complètes*. Paris: Bibliothèque de la Pléiade, 1972.

Sartre, Jean-Paul. *La Nausée*. Paris: Gallimard, 1938.

———. *Qu'est-ce que la littérature?* Collection Idées. 1948; rpt. Paris: Gallimard, 1969.

Sidney, Sir Philip. *Defence of Poesy*. London: Macmillan, 1919.

Valéry, Paul. *Œuvres*. Edited by Jean Hytier. 2 vols. Paris: Bibliothèque de la Pléiade, 1960.

II. SECONDARY SOURCES

Atkinson, Geoffrey. *Les Nouveaux horizons de la Renaissance française*. Paris: E. Droz, 1935.

Bakhtine, Mikhaël. *L'Œuvre de François Rabelais et la culture populaire au Moyen Age et sous la Renaissance*. Translated by André Robel. Paris: Gallimard, 1970.

Baldini, Massimo. *Il linguaggio delle utopie. Utopie e ideologia: una rilettura epistemologica*. Rome: Edizione Studium, 1974.

Barthes, Roland. *Essais critiques*. Paris: Seuil, 1964.

Bateson, Gregory, ed. *Perceval's Narrative: A Patient's Account of His Psychosis*. Stanford, Calif.: Stanford University Press, 1961.

Battaglia, Salvatore. "La nave dei folli." In *Mitografia del personnaggio*. Milan: Rizzoli, 1968. Pp. 141–59.

Beaujour, Michel. *Le Jeu de Rabelais.* Paris: l'Herne, 1969.

Benveniste, Émile. *Problèmes de linguistique générale.* Paris: Gallimard, 1966.

Berry, Alice F. "Apollo versus Bacchus: The Dynamics of Inspiration." *PMLA* 90 (1975): 88–95.

Bertoni, Giulio. *La biblioteca estense.* Torino: Loescher, 1903.

————. *Il duecento.* 3d ed. Storia letteraria d'Italia, 2. 1939; rpt. Milan: Vallardi, 1964.

Bigeard, Martine. *La Folie et les fous littéraires en Espagne 1500–1650.* Paris: Centre de recherches hispaniques, 1972.

Binni, Walter. *Ludovico Ariosto.* Torino: Radiotelevisione Italiana, 1968.

Biondolillo, Francesco. *Poeti e critici.* Palermo: A. Trimarchi, 1910.

Blunt, Anthony. *Artistic Theory in Italy 1450–1600.* 1940; rpt. Oxford: Oxford University Press, 1973.

Bolza, Giovanni Battista, *Manuale ariostesco.* Venice, 1866.

Bonnet, Jacques. *Les Symboles traditionnels de la sagesse.* Roanne: Horvath, 1971.

Bonomo, Dario. *L'Orlando furioso nelle sue fonti.* Rocca San Casciano: Cappelli, 1953.

Booth, Wayne. *The Rhetoric of Fiction.* Chicago: University of Chicago Press, 1961.

Branca, Daniela D. *L'Orlando furioso e il romanzo cavalleresco medievale.* Florence: Olschki, 1973.

Brunel, Pierre. *Le Mythe de la métamorphose.* Paris: A. Colin, 1974.

Burckhart, Jacob. *The Civilization of the Renaissance in Italy.* Edited by Irene Gordon; translated from 2d ed., 1865, by S. G. C. Middlemore. New York: Mentor, 1960.

Busson, Henri. *Le Rationalisme dans la littérature française de la Renaissance.* Paris: J. Vrin, 1957.

Campbell, Joseph. *The Hero with a Thousand Faces.* New York: Pantheon Books, 1949.

————. *The Masks of God.* New York: Viking Press, 1959.

Cantimori, Delio. *Eretici italiani del Cinquecento.* 1939; rpt. Florence: Sansoni, 1967.

Cappellani, Nino. *La sintassi narrativa dell'Ariosto.* Florence: Nuova Italia, 1952.

Cassirer, Ernst. *The Individual and the Cosmos in Renaissance Philosophy.* Translated by Mario Domandi. Oxford: Blackwell, 1963.

————. *Language and Myth.* Translated by Susanne K. Langer. 1946; rpt. New York: Dover, 1953.

————, and others. *The Renaissance Philosophy of Man.* Chicago: University of Chicago Press, 1948.

Chastel, André, and Klein, Robert. *L'Age de l'humanisme.* Paris: Éditions des Deux-Mondes, 1963.

Chinard, Gilbert. *L'Exotisme américain dans la littérature française du XVIe siècle.* Paris: Hachette, 1911.

Cioranescu, Alexandre. *L'Arioste en France des origines à la fin du XVIIIe siècle.* 2 vols. Paris: Éditions des Presses Modernes, 1939.

Coleman, Dorothy Gabe. *Rabelais: A Critical Study in Prose Fiction.* Cambridge: University Press, 1971.

Coutaud, Albert. *La Pédagogie de Rabelais.* Edited by Gabriel Compayre. 1899; rpt. Geneva: Slatkine Reprints, 1970.

Croce, Benedetto. *Ariosto, Shakespeare e Corneille.* Bari: Laterza, 1920.

Curtius, Ernst. *European Literature and the Latin Middle Ages.* Translated by Willard R. Trask, 1948. Bollingen Series, 36. Princeton, N.J.: Princeton University Press, 1953.

De Blasi, G. "L'Ariosto e le passioni." *Giornale storico della letteratura italiana,* 129–30 (1952–53): 318–62, 178–203.

Defaux, Gérard. *Pantagruel et les sophistes: Contribution à l'histoire de l'humanisme chrétien au XVIe siècle.* The Hague: M. Nijhoff, 1973.

———. "Rabelais et son masque comique." *Études rabelaisiennes* 11 (1974): 89–135.

De Grève, Marcel. "Le Discours rabelaisien ou la raison en folie." In *Folie et déraison à la Renaissance.* Brussels: Éditions de l'Université de Bruxelles, 1976. Pp. 149–57.

Del Fiume, Cordelia. *De l'influence de quelques auteurs italiens sur Rabelais.* Florence: Ramella, 1918.

Delumeau, J. *La Civilisation de la Renaissance.* Paris: Arthaud, 1967.

Demerson, Guy. *La Mythologie dans l'œuvre lyrique de la Pléiade.* Travaux d'Humanisme et Renaissance, 119. Geneva: Droz, 1972.

Denoix, L. "Les Connaissances nautiques de Rabelais." *Études rabelaisiennes* 7 (1953): 171–90.

Dermenghem, Émile. *Thomas Morus et les utopistes à la Renaissance.* Paris: Plon, 1927.

Derrida, Jacques. "Cogito et histoire de la folie." *Revue de métaphysique et de morale,* nos. 3–4 (1964). Rpt. in *L'Écriture et la différence.* Paris: Seuil, 1967. Pp. 51–97.

Doutrepont, Georges. *Les Mises en prose des épopées et des romans chevaleresques du XIVe au XVIe siècle.* Liège: Thone, n.d.

Dubois, Claude-Gilbert. *Les Problèmes de l'utopie.* Paris: Archives des Lettres Modernes, 1968.

Durand, Gilbert. *L'Imagination symbolique.* Paris: Presses Universitaires de France, 1964.

———. *Les Structures anthropologiques de l'imaginaire.* 2d ed. Paris: Presses Universitaires de France, 1963.

Durling, Robert. *The Figure of the Poet in Renaissance Epic.* Cambridge, Mass.: Harvard University Press, 1965.

Durmenghem, Émile. *Thomas Morus et les utopistes à la Renaissance.* Paris: Plon, 1927.

Eckhert, Charles W. "Initiatory Motifs in the Story of Telemachus." *Classical Journal,* 59 (1963). Reprinted in *Myth and Literature,* edited by John Vickery. Lincoln: University of Nebraska Press, 1966. Pp. 161–69.

Ehrmann, Jacques. "La Temporalité dans l'œuvre de Rabelais." *French Review* 37 (1963): 188–99.

Éliade, Mircea. "Le Symbolisme des ténèbres dans les religions archaïques." In *Polarité du symbole. Études carmélitaines.* Bruges: Desclée de Brouwer, 1960. Pp. 15–28.

Febvre, Lucien. *Le Problème de l'incroyance au XVIe siècle: La Religion de Rabelais.* 1942; rpt. Paris: Albin Michel, 1968.

Ferroni, Giulio. "L'Ariosto e la concezione umanistica della follia." In *Atti dei convegni lincei.* Rome: Accademia Nazionale dei Lincei, 1975. Pp. 73–92.

Foucault, Michel. *Histoire de la folie à l'âge classique.* 1961; rpt. Paris: Gallimard, 1972.

———. *Maladie mentale et psychologie.* Paris: Presses Universitaires de France, 1972.

Gardner, Edmund G. *Dukes and Poets in Ferrara.* 1904; rpt. New York: Haskell House, 1968.

Genette, Gérard. *Figures III.* Paris: Seuil, 1972.

Giamatti, A. Bartlett. *The Earthly Paradise and the Renaissance Epic.* Princeton, N.J.: Princeton University Press, 1966.

Glauser, Alfred. *Rabelais créateur.* Paris: Nizet, 1966.

Goldmann, Lucien. *Le Dieu caché.* Paris: Gallimard, 1959.

Graf, Arturo. *Miti, leggende e superstizioni del Medioevo.* Torino: Loescher, 1893.

Grasso, Ernesto. "La mania ingegnosa." In *L'Umanesimo e la follia,* by Enrico Castelli and others. Rome: Abete, 1971. Pp. 107–26.

Gray, Floyd. *Rabelais et l'écriture.* Paris: Nizet, 1974.

Greene, Thomas. *The Descent from Heaven.* New Haven, Conn.: Yale University Press, 1963.

Griffin, Robert. *Ludovico Ariosto.* New York: Twayne, 1974.

Grout, Donald Jay. *A History of Western Music.* New York: Norton, 1960.

Gundersheimer, Werner L. *Ferrara: The Style of a Renaissance Despotism.* Princeton, N.J: Princeton University Press, 1973.

Hagiwara, Michio Peter. *French Epic Poetry in the Sixteenth Century.* The Hague: Mouton, 1972.

Hay, Denys. *The Italian Renaissance in Its Historical Background.* Cambridge: University Press, 1966.

Haydn, Hiram. *The Counter-Renaissance.* New York: Harcourt, Brace and World, 1950.

Hornik, Henry. "Time and Periodization in French Renaissance Literature: Rabelais and Montaigne." *Studi francesi* 13 (1969): 477–81.

Huguet, Edmond E. *Dictionnaire de la langue française du seizième siècle.* Vols. 4 and 5. Paris: Didier, 1950 and 1961.

———. *Étude sur la syntaxe de Rabelais, comparée à celle des autres prosateurs de 1450 à 1550.* Paris: Hachette, 1894.

Huizinga, Johan. *Homo Ludens: A Study of the Play-Element in Culture.* Translated by R. F. C. Hull. London: Routledge and Kegan Paul, 1949.

————. *The Waning of the Middle Ages.* Translated by F. Hopman, 1924; rpt. New York: Doubleday Anchor Books, 1954.

Joukovsky, Françoise. *Montaigne et le problème du temps.* Paris: Nizet, 1972.

Jung, Marc-René. *Hercule dans la littérature française du XVIe siècle.* Travaux d'Humanisme et Renaissance, 79. Geneva: Droz, 1966.

Kaiser, Walter. *Praisers of Folly: Erasmus, Rabelais, and Shakespeare.* Cambridge, Mass.: Harvard University Press, 1963.

Keller, Abraham. *The Telling of Tales in Rabelais: Aspects of His Narrative Art.* Frankfurt am Main: V. Klostermann, 1963.

Kennedy, William J. "Ariosto's Ironic Allegory." *Modern Language Notes* 88 (1973): 44–67.

Klein, Robert. "Le Theme du fou et l'ironie humaniste." *Umanesimo e ermeneutica, Archivo di Filosofia,* no. 3 (1963). Rpt. in *La Forme et l'intelligible.* Bibliothèque des Sciences Humaines. Paris: Gallimard, 1970. Pp. 433–50.

Laing, Ronald D. *The Politics of Experience.* 1967; rpt. New York: Ballantine Books, 1974.

Lattimore, Richmond. Introduction to *The Iliad of Homer.* Chicago: University of Chicago Press, 1951.

Lefebvre, Joel. *Les Fols et la folie: Étude sur les genres du comique et la création littéraire en Allemagne pendant la Renaissance.* Paris: Leclerc, Klincksieck, 1968.

Lefranc, Abel. *Les Navigations de Pantagruel.* Paris: Leclerc, 1905.

Levin, Harry. *The Myth of the Golden Age in the Renaissance.* Bloomington: University of Indiana Press, 1969.

————. "Some Meanings of Myth." *Daedalus* 88, no. 2 (Spring 1959): 223–31. Rpt. in *Myth and Mythmaking,* edited by Henry R. Murray. Boston: Beacon Press, 1968. Pp. 103–14.

Lévi-Strauss, Claude. "The Structural Study of Myth." In "Myth, a Symposium," *Journal of American Folklore* 78 (Oct.-Dec. 1955): 428–44. Rpt. in *Structural Anthropology,* translated by Claire Jacobson and Brooke Grundfest Schoepf. New York: Basic Books, 1963. Pp. 206–31.

Lovejoy, Arthur O. *The Great Chain of Being.* Cambridge, Mass.: Harvard University Press, 1936.

Lukács, György. *La Théorie du roman.* Translated by Jean Clairevoye. Geneva: Gonthier, 1963.

Mabille, Pierre. *Le Miroir du merveilleux.* Paris: Minuit, 1962.

Martin, Alfred von. *Sociology of the Renaissance.* New York: Oxford University Press, 1944.

Maskell, David. *The Historical Epic in France 1500–1700.* Oxford: Oxford University Press, 1973.

Masters, Mallary. *Rabelaisian Dialectic and the Platonic Hermetic Tradition.* Albany: State University of New York, 1969.

Momigliano, Attilio. *Saggio sull'Orlando furioso.* Bari: Laterza, 1928.

Montano, Rocco. *Follia e saggezza nel Furioso e nell'Elogio di Erasmo.* Naples: Humanitas, 1942.

Moorman, Charles. "Myth and Medieval Literature: *Sir Gawain and the Green Knight.*" *Medieval Studies* 18 (1956): 158–72. Rpt. in *Myth and Literature,* edited by John Vickery. Lincoln: University of Nebraska Press, 1966. Pp. 171–86.

Natali, Giulio. *Ludovico Ariosto.* Florence: Nuova Italia, 1964.

Nencioni, Enrico. "Le tre pazzie: Orlando, King Lear, Don Chisciotte." In *Saggi critici di letteratura italiana.* Florence: Le Monnier, 1898. Pp. 143–75.

Olschki, Leo. *Storia letteraria delle scoperte geografiche.* Florence: Olschki, 1937.

Ossola, Carlo. "Métaphore et inventaire de la folie." In *Folie et déraison à la Renaissance.* Brussels: Éditions de l'Université de Bruxelles, 1976. Pp. 171–95.

Pampaloni, Leonzio. "Per una analisi narrativa del Furioso." *Belfagor* 26 (1972): 133–50.

Panofsky, Erwin. *Studies in Iconology.* 1939; rpt. New York: Harper Torchbooks, 1962.

Paris, Jean. *Rabelais au futur.* Paris: Seuil, 1970.

Pettinato, Concetto. "Rabelais e l'Italia." *Illustrazione italiana* 55 (Feb. 1933): 400–401.

Pool, Franco. *Interpretazione dell'Orlando furioso.* Florence: Nuova Italia, 1968.

Poulet, Georges. *Études sur le temps humain.* Paris: Plon, 1949.

Quinones, Ricardo. *The Renaissance Discovery of Time.* Cambridge, Mass.: Harvard University Press, 1972.

Quint, David. "Astolfo's Voyage to the Moon." *Yale Italian Studies* 1 (1977): 398–408.

Rahv, Philip. "Myth and the Powerhouse." *Partisan Review* 20 (1953), 635–48. Rpt. in *Myth and Literature,* edited by John B. Vickery. Lincoln: University of Nebraska Press, 1966. Pp. 109–18.

Rajna, Pio. *Le fonti dell'Orlando furioso.* 2d ed. Florence: Sansoni, 1900.

Ramat, Rafaello. *Per la storia dello stile renascimentale.* Messina: G. d'Anna, 1953.

Renaudet, Augustin. *Érasme et l'Italie.* Travaux d'Humanisme et Renaissance, 15. Geneva: Droz, 1954.

Rigolot, François. "Cratylisme et Pantagruelisme: Rabelais et le statut du signe." *Études rabelaisiennes* 13 (1976): 115–32.

———. *Les Langages de Rabelais.* Études rabelaisiennes, 10. Geneva: Droz, 1972.

Rosario, Romeo. *Le scoperte americane nella coscienza italiana nel cinquecento.* Milan: Ricciardi, 1971.

Rossi, Vittorio. *Il quattrocento.* 3d ed. Storia letteraria d'Italia, 5. 1933; rpt. Milan: Vallardi, 1964.

Royce, Josiah. *Lectures on Modern Idealism.* New Haven, Conn.: Yale University Press, 1919.

Sainéan, Lazare. "Les Sources modernes du roman de Rabelais." *Revue des études rabelaisiennes* 10 (1912): 375–420.

———. "Les Termes nautiques chez Rabelais." *Revue des études rabelaisiennes* 8 (1910): 1–56.

Salza, Abd-el-Kader. "Imprese e divise d'arme e d'amore nel *Furioso*." *Giornale storico della letteratura italiana* 38 (1901): 310–63.

Saulnier, Verdun Louis. *Le Dessein de Rabelais*. Paris: Société d'enseignement supérieur, 1957.

Scott, John C. "De Sanctis, Ariosto, and *La poesia cavalleresca*." *Italica* 45 (1968): 428–61.

Screech, Michael A. *L'Évangélisme de Rabelais: Aspects de la satire religieuse au XVIᵉ siècle*. Études rabelaisiennes, 2. Geneva: Droz, 1959.

———. *The Rabelaisian Marriage: Aspects of Rabelais's Religion, Ethics, and Comic Philosophy*. London: Arnold, 1958.

Segre, Cesare. *Esperienze ariostesche*. Pisa: Nistro Lischi, 1967.

Servier, Jean. *Histoire de l'utopie*. Collection Idées. Paris: Gallimard, 1967.

Seznec, Jean. *The Survival of the Pagan Gods*. Translated by Barbara F. Sessions from 1940 ed. Bollingen Series, 38. Princeton, N.J.: Princeton University Press, 1953.

Simone, Franco. *La coscienza della rinascita negli umanisti*. Rome: Storia e Letteratura, 1949.

Soyer, Jacques. "A propos de quelques termes nautiques chez Rabelais." *Revue des études rabelaisiennes*, 9 (1911): 109–24.

Stanford, W. B. *The Ulysses Theme: A Study of the Adaptability of a Traditional Hero*. 2d ed. Oxford: Blackwell, 1968.

Starobinski, Jean. *Portrait de l'artiste en saltimbanque*. Geneva: Skira, 1970.

Stegmann, André. "Richness and Ambivalence of the Symbol in the Renaissance." *Yale French Studies* 47 (1972): 5–19.

Swain, Barbara. *Fools and Folly during the Middle Ages and Renaissance*. New York: Columbia University Press, 1932.

Tetel, Marcel. *Étude sur le comique de Rabelais*. Florence: Olschki, 1964.

———. *Rabelais*. New York: Twayne, 1967.

Thuasne, Louis. "Rabelais et Érasme." *Études sur Rabelais*. 1904; rpt. Paris: H. Champion, 1969. Pp. 27–157.

Toldo, Pietro. "L'Arte italiana nell'opera di Francesco Rabelais." *Archiv für das Studium der neuern Sprachen* 100 (1898): 103–48.

Turchi, Marcello. *Ariosto o della liberazione fantastica*. Ravenna: Longo, 1969.

Utopisti italiani del cinquecento. Edited by Carlo Curcio. Milan: Colombo, 1944.

Valesio, Paolo. "The Language of Madness in the Renaissance." *The Yearbook of Italian Studies* 1 (1971): 199–234.

Vernero, Michele. *La geografia nell'Orlando furioso*. Torino: Bonio e Rossi, 1913.

Waille, Victor. "Les Voyages de Rabelais à Rome et l'influence que l'art italien de la Renaissance a pu exercer sur lui." *Atti del congresso internazionale di scienze storiche* 7 (1904): 327–33.

Weinberg, Florence. *The Wine and the Will*. Detroit, Mich.: Wayne State University Press, 1972.

Weinrich, Harald. *Tempus*. Stuttgart: Kolhammer, 1964.

Wind, Edgar. *Pagan Mysteries of the Renaissance*. New York: Norton, 1968.

Zumbini, Bonaventura. "La Badia di Thélème del Rabelais." In *Studi di letteratura straniera*, 2d ed. Florence: Le Monnier, 1907. Pp. 331–71.

———. "La follia di Orlando." In *Studi di letteratura italiana*, 2d ed. Florence: Le Monnier, 1906. Pp. 303–58.